THE PRINCETON REVIEW

Cracking the
MILLER ANALOGIES
TEST

THE PRINCETON REVIEW

Cracking the
MILLER ANALOGIES
TEST

MARCIA LERNER

2ND EDITION

RANDOM HOUSE, INC.
NEW YORK 1997
http://www.randomhouse.com

Princeton Review Publishing, L.L.C.
2315 Broadway
New York, NY 10024
e-mail: info@review.com

ISBN: 0-679-77866-7

Editor: Amy E. Zavatto
Production Editor: Bruno Blumenfeld
Proofreader: Maria Russo
Designer: Illeny Maaza
Production Supervisor: Chee Pae
Illustrations by: The Production Department of The Princeton Review

Manufactured in the United States of America on partially recycled paper.

9 8 7 6 5 4 3 2 1

2nd Edition

ACKNOWLEDGMENTS

I would like to thank Liz Buffa, Michael Freedman, Nell Goddin, Geoff Martz, and Laurice Pearson for their help both practical and spiritual. Many thanks also to Amy Zavatto, Chris Kensler, Bronwyn Collie, Bruno Blumenfeld, Meher Khambata, Illeny Maaza, Greta Englert, Peter Jung, Adam Hurwitz, John Bergdahl, John Pak, Jeff Nichols, Lisa Ruyter, and Sara Kane for their invaluable technical assistance.

CONTENTS

PART I

Overview

1

What is the Miller Analogies Test?

The Miller Analogies Test—from now on referred to as the MAT—is a fifty-minute test of one hundred analogies devised as a "high-level mental ability test," according to its literature. There is only one section, and the words that the analogies use cover areas as diverse as art history, mathematics, science, anagrams, and literature.

WHERE DOES THE MAT COME FROM?

The bowels of the earth—no, wait, that's not quite true. The MAT is published by the creepily named Psychological Corporation, a subdivision of Harcourt, Brace, and Company. You'll hear more about this insidious bunch in the next chapter.

HOW IS THE MAT SCORED?

Two to three weeks after you take the MAT you will receive a smudgily printed envelope from the Psychological Corporation containing your raw score, your percentile within your intended major, and your percentile within the total group of test takers. Your raw score is the number of questions you have gotten right, which can range from 0 to 100. There are no points taken off your raw score for incorrect answers. The percentile represents your score's rank within the scores of everyone taking the test.

PERCENTILES—HUH?

A percentile shows your position within a group. If you are in the seventy-second percentile of test takers within your major, it means you've scored higher than 72 percent of the people in that group.

HOW IMPORTANT IS THE MAT?

That entirely depends on the program to which you are applying. Some schools rely heavily on this sort of information, others don't even require that you take the test. Call the admissions office of whichever program you want to know about and *ask*.

WHAT IS THE PRINCETON REVIEW?

The Princeton Review is a coaching school based in New York City. It has branches in over fifty cities across the country and several branches abroad. The Princeton Review's techniques are unique and powerful. They work because they are based on the same principles used in writing the tests.

The Princeton Review's techniques for beating the MAT will help you improve your scores by teaching you to:

1. Think like the test writers.

2. Take full advantage of the limited time allowed.

3. Find the answers to questions you don't understand by using our unique process-of-elimination techniques.

4. Avoid the traps that have been set for you (and use those traps to your advantage).

A WARNING

Many of our techniques for beating the MAT are counterintuitive. Some of them seem to violate "common sense." To get the full benefit of our techniques, you must trust them. The only way to develop this trust is to practice the techniques and convince yourself that they work. By practicing our techniques, you will be able to prove to yourself that the techniques work and increase your confidence when you actually take the test.

WHEN AND WHERE

To sign up for the MAT you need to call or write the Psychological Corporation. There are no set test dates for the MAT; it is given according to the needs and demands of each test center. The address is:

Miller Analogies Test
The Psychological Corporation
555 Academic Court
San Antonio, Texas 78204-3956
Telephone: (210) 921-8802 Fax: (210) 921-8861
Monday to Friday, 8:30 AM to 5:00 PM Central Time
(800) 622-3231

Call the corporation (using the toll-free 800 number, of course) and get them to send you a Miller Analogies Test Candidate Information Booklet. This booklet will tell you where the nearest test center is, and provide you with the test center's phone number; you will then communicate directly with the test center. Your test fee goes directly to the test center. You must also let the test center know if you have ever taken the MAT before; this is very important. If you don't let them know ahead of time you will probably not be allowed to take the test when you show up as they will have discovered your duplicity via computer. Don't set yourself up—let them know of any previous MAT test center activity!

If you are something of a hermit and live over 100 miles away from any of their testing centers, the Psychological Corporation will provide you with an alternative testing site. This is only for people who live over 100 miles from an existing site, and the number for these people to call is: (800) 622-3231. For the rest of you, sorry, no special treatment for you. You must go the sites already designated; just think of it, you may meet each other.

> Communicate directly with your test center.

> Let the test center know if you have ever taken the MAT before.

How to Think About the MAT

Are You a Genius or an Idiot?

If you're like most people, you tend to take test scores rather seriously. You see them as some kind of gauge of your intelligence, your aptitude, your mental acuity. This is exactly what the Psychological Corporation wants you to think. But this vision is wrong.

The MAT Is Not a Test of Intelligence

The MAT isn't a test of intelligence, and it isn't a test of reasoning. After all, we're going to improve your performance on this test in a few short weeks, and that sure doesn't mean we're going to make you more intelligent; it just means that the MAT relies on a bunch of tricks. Once you learn the tricks, you will discover that tests like this can't tell a thing about your personal abilities. We're going to demystify the whole process for you, get you past this uncomfortable obstacle, and help you to score well.

You Must Learn to Think Like the People in The Psychological Corporation

To answer questions the way the makers of the MAT want you to, you will need to understand how they think. This isn't as hard as it sounds. As weird as this test seems, it is actually very predictable. There are a limited number of analogies the test-makers use, and the more familiar you become with the types, the easier it will be to anticipate them.

What is The Psychological Corporation?

The Psychological Corporation is the oldest test publisher in the country (established 1921). This means that they are the ones who made standardized tests the unavoidable constant annoyance they are today. Don't you love them already? They create tests for all types of fields, most particularly education and social sciences, as well as tests that classify leadership skills, clerical speed, mechanical comprehension, and a person's ability to name colors. No kidding. The Psychological Corporation is located in San Antonio, Texas, and makes gobs of money by selling tests like the MAT.

Who Writes the MAT?

The same people who write all those color, typing, and personality tests. People who have studied education and are now locked up in a little room somewhere figuring out rhyming words and wrong answer pairs especially formulated to distract you from the right answer.

How to Crack the System

Over the next several chapters we're going to teach you how to crack the MAT. Read each chapter carefully. Some of our techniques might seem a little odd or unusual, but you are taking an unusual test. It is necessary, sometimes, to fight fire with fire. True, these techniques won't help you when you get to graduate school or nursing school, or when you're on-the-job at your social worker position, or when you need to figure out something *really* important, but then they're not supposed to. These techniques are designed with the sole purpose of getting you a better score on the MAT.

3

Taking the MAT

ON THE DAY OF THE REAL TEST

Get up early, make sure you eat breakfast, and do a few analogies to get your juices flowing. Mercifully, the test is short, so as long as you eat and take care of any bathroom needs beforehand, you won't be distracted during the exam itself. Afterwards and beforehand, resist the temptation to chat with others around you who seem intent on working themselves into a frenzy of terror. You will know what you're doing by the time you're done with this book—no need to absorb tension from others.

On the day of the test, remain as relaxed as you can.

AT THE TEST SITE YOU WILL NEED:

◆ your admissions ticket;

◆ two forms of identification, one with a picture (a driver's license or passport will do);

◆ four sharpened number 2 pencils with erasers;

◆ a reliable watch without a beeping mechanism.

You may NOT bring a calculator, but don't worry—there are only a few math questions per test, they don't require much calculation, and if you hate and fear them, you can skip them.

Before the test starts, make sure your seat is comfortable and you have adequate light. If there is any problem, politely request a new seat from the proctor.

You may be given what the Psychological Corporation calls "a tryout test." This is essentially a scam: You have paid money to take the test; they respond by using you as a guinea pig in their research. They will use your responses to torture the next set of unlucky test takers.

Though they expressly state that you may not disqualify yourself from this section, and must answer all the questions, don't let this little exercise rattle you. Just put down all Cs, or Ds, or whichever your favorite letter happens to be. Use the rest of the time to rest and relax while you await the questions that count.

One thing to beware of is that you may receive a used test booklet. The Psychological Corporation appears to be a very cheap company. One of the reasons they prohibit you from writing in your test booklet is that they want to reuse it. However, as you yourself will find, it's very hard to have a booklet and not write in it. Everything should have been erased but it usually isn't, and the answers in your test book may have been circled. If this is the case, IGNORE THE CIRCLED ANSWERS. Of course they will make you a little nervous, especially if you choose different answers. Don't worry about it: There is no guarantee that the test taker who had the book before you knew anything. Just try to do the questions without even *seeing* those little markings.

AT THE END OF THE TEST

Once you've finished, the proctors will give you the opportunity to fill in a circle that cancels your score. We highly recommend that you do not do this, unless you have fallen asleep during the test and haven't answered any questions. Most people feel nervous and unsure following a test; don't let that force you into taking the test again.

ONE FINAL THOUGHT BEFORE YOU BEGIN

No matter how high or low you score on this test, and no matter how much you improve your performance with this book, you should never accept the score you receive as an assessment of your abilities.

The temptation to see a high score as evidence that you're a genius, or a low score as evidence that you're an idiot, can be very powerful.

When you've read this book and used our techniques on real MAT questions, you'll be able to judge for yourself whether the MAT actually measures much besides how well you do on the MAT.

Think of this as a kind of game—a game you can get good at.

No matter how high or low you score on this test, and no matter how much you improve your performance with this book, you should never accept the score you receive as an assessment of your abilities.

4

Cracking the System:
Basic Principles

HOW TO IMPROVE YOUR SCORE

The most important consideration when taking the MAT, or any other standardized test, is the test's structure. This is a timed, multiple-choice test, so what does that mean for you?

DON'T ANSWER ALL THE QUESTIONS

Most people like to take the MAT as if it were a race with points awarded for completing the course. You will hear people around you on test day who self-importantly rustle their paper every time they turn the page as if to say, "Look! I'm on to the next page already, a full three minutes before anyone else. I'm going to WIN!" These people are making life worse for themselves, and they should be ignored. For them, answering every single question hastily is more important than answering most of the questions carefully. Nothing could be further from the truth.

While it will never make sense to leave the answer sheet completely blank, as you will see in the upcoming section, it may be completely reasonable not to look at some of the questions; the way to use your time on the MAT is to concentrate on tackling the questions you know you can get right.

YOU MAY THINK YOU ALREADY SKIP QUESTIONS

Most students think they skip questions as it is. Of course, they're not really skipping questions. They look at a question, spend five minutes trying to puzzle it out, and then end up guessing, or worse, leaving it blank after wasting all that time attempting to answer it (somethings you will never again do after reading this chapter). This method means wasting time agonizing over the question, and not getting the benefits of guessing and moving on.

PROCESS OF ELIMINATION

Your score on the MAT will immediately improve if you can remember this: On most questions you should not try to find the right answer; you should try to eliminate the wrong answers.

> What is the capital of Uganda?

On most questions you should not try to find the right answer; you should try to eliminate the wrong answers.

Now, most people would have a tough time answering that question as is, and you won't see this question in exactly this format on the MAT. We're using this one to make a point, and the point is that the MAT *does* use a multiple-choice format. Is the question any easier when you have the wrong answers there with it?

> What is the capital of Uganda?
> (a) Paris
> (b) London
> (c) Kampala
> (d) Madrid

Pretty amazing, no? A lot of the time, wrong answers are easier to spot than right answers, and will allow you to select right answers you might not have recognized otherwise.

No Blanks!

No matter if you get every single guess wrong, you still haven't lost a single point, because nothing is subtracted for a wrong answer. If you haven't finished your test, take the last two minutes of the test time to fill in all the blanks. Use the same letter for all of them to ease the stress of choosing, and just fill them in. Don't worry about how wrong your answer will be; no schools will ever know what you guessed, they'll just see your increased raw score for those questions that you are lucky to hit.

If you haven't finished your test by the last two minutes, take the time to fill in the answers for the ones you've left blank.

Guessing

Sometimes you'll look at a question and have no idea of what the answer might be. What should you do? Guess, always guess. Guessing will dramatically increase your score—without even looking, you have a one out of four chance of getting it right. Let's say you were playing one of those state-sponsored lottery games; if you can cancel even one of those answer choices, you're practically a millionaire.

Which Leads Us to the Three-Pass System

What is the difference between guessing and not leaving any blanks? The difference is the three-pass system. The MAT is arranged in order of difficulty, but the order of difficulty they give you is never precisely *your* order of difficulty. So, to combat this problem, you are going to go through the test and create your own order of difficulty.

First Pass: On your first pass, you will go through and do every question you can do easily.

Second Pass: Go through and try to nab all the questions you sort of know by using the process of elimination.

Third Pass: When there are two minutes left on your watch, fill in all the remaining questions until you haven't left a single one blank.

An important note about the three pass system: Be careful when filling in the answers! Skipping questions temporarily is helpful, but only if you are meticulous with your answer sheet. Look carefully at the number of the question and the number on your answer sheet, and make sure the two correspond.

Be careful when filling in the answers! Skipping questions temporarily is helpful, but only if you are meticulous with your answer sheet.

Use That Scratch Paper

Use that scratch paper!

Unfortunately, you are prohibited from writing in the MAT test booklets. You may find yourself writing in them anyway, which is fine. When the proctor tells you to stop, do so. It's an unconscious reaction to trying to work out problems. However, you have the right to demand scratch paper from your test center. Place the top of the scratch paper directly under the problem you are working on, and draw the letters of the choices, and physically cross out the answer choices you eliminate.

Keep folding over the top of the paper so you have a clear place to write down the next set of answer choices. Use the paper to work out math problems, and use the scratch paper to draw arrows between related words (you'll find out more about this in the next chapter). Use that scratch paper!

SUMMARY

1. Don't be afraid to guess, even if you aren't sure of the answer.

2. If you don't know the right answer to a question, try to identify and cancel the wrong answers.

3. Never leave a question blank.

4. Be aggressive about requesting and using your scratch paper.

5

Cracking the System: Advanced Principles

CRACKING THE MAT

In the preceding chapter you learned some basic techniques to use on the MAT. You learned that it is possible to

- ◆ find correct answers by using POE—the process of elimination—to get rid of incorrect ones

- ◆ guess rather than leave any question blank

- ◆ use the three-pass system

But, you may be asking yourself, how do you decide which answers to eliminate? In this chapter you will begin to learn how to

1. use the order in which the questions are asked to improve your score

2. use your time more efficiently by getting the easy points first

3. find the traps the Psychological Corporation has laid for you

4. turn those traps into points

To use all these tools well, you first need to understand a bit more about the MAT's order of difficulty.

ORDER OF DIFFICULTY

Spend your time making sure you answer the questions you can get right.

On the MAT, as on all standardized tests, the questions are arranged in order of difficulty. The first thirty-three questions are easy, the second thirty-three or so are medium, and the last thirty-three or thirty-four are difficult, though you should bear in mind the instructions regarding your own order of difficulty and the three-pass system on page 17.

HOW DOES THIS AFFECT YOU?

Well, if someone offered to pay you either $10 to carry one textbook, or $10 to carry forty textbooks, which would you do? The one textbook, of course. You want to reap the most benefit for the least work, and on the MAT that means using your time efficiently. Spend your time making sure you answer the questions you can get right. It is better to work carefully through the easy and medium questions, keeping in mind your own order of difficulty, than it is to rush through these making a number of careless mistakes, and waste the bulk of your time being frustrated by difficult questions.

WHY THEY'RE DIFFICULT

How do they make these difficult questions difficult? Not just by using hard words or concepts, but by using the format of the test itself; by taking advantage of the fact that it's a multiple-choice test.

DISTRACTOR ANSWERS

In the previous chapter we discussed POE (Process of Elimination) and guessing techniques. When test takers like you are stumped, one of the first things they do is look at the answer choices. Now, this is a wonderful technique, but you will need to vary the way in which you assess these answer choices on the more difficult problems. Why, you ask? Because one of the ways the Psychological Corporation tries to make sure that people don't inadvertently get the difficult questions right is by dressing up the wrong answers to make them look attractive to the untrained eye. For instance, they will have a question with the word "green" on it, and one of the answer choices will have the word "beret," or they'll have a question with the word "beauty" in it and one of the answers will be the word "pageant." Now, these could easily be right on an easy or medium question, but on a difficult question, the obvious answer is almost always wrong. You'll see why in a minute, when you read about the "tryout tests." But whatever the reason, you need to be aware of these kinds of traps. These dressed-up, too-good-to-be-true answers are distractors, made to lure you away from the right answer, and on the last thirty or so questions of the test these distractors are almost always wrong. That means you can cancel them, and are that much more likely to guess the right answer.

> Dressed-up, too-good-to-be-true answers are distractors, made to lure you away from the right answer.

THE DIAGNOSTIC TESTS

At the back of this book you will find seven diagnostic tests. Wait until you've read the rest of the book, then try one of the tests. We know it is tempting to practice as much and as immediately as possible, but make sure you don't start on these practice tests until you have a firm foundation in the techniques. After you've done the test, review it, looking at the answer key and explanations we have provided, so you can analyze your weaknesses and your strengths, and improve your strategy as much as possible.

> We know it is tempting to practice as much and as immediately as possible, but make sure you don't start on these practice tests until you have a firm foundation in the techniques.

SUMMARY

1. Use order of difficulty to decide where to spend your time.

2. Use order of difficulty to find distractor answers and eliminate them.

3. Practice and refine your strategy, using the diagnostic tests in this book.

PART ◆ II

How to Crack the MAT

6

The Analogies

The people who write the MAT want you to think about their analogies as though the subject matter were the most important thing. There are analogies that use history, math, geography, vocabulary, linguistics, science, and mythology. But you could study every one of these subjects exhaustively and still not do well on the MAT. Why? Because the MAT doesn't test what you know; it tests how well you can imitate the way its writers think.

The MAT doesn't test what you know; it tests how well you can imitate the way its writers think.

How Do They Think?

The way the people who write the MAT think is not by analogy subject but by analogy *relationship*. That means you need to learn to think that way too.

Forget "Is To"

You were probably taught that whenever you see the construction "X:Y::W:Z" you should say, "X is to Y as W is to Z." For the purposes of the MAT, wipe that construction out of your mind; it isn't useful. Since you want to imitate the way the makers of the MAT think, you need to figure the way the words in an analogy relate, rather than whether they sound good with an "is to" between them. So, the way we want you to look at the analogies is by relationship.

Relationship?

The way we want you to look at the analogies is by relationship.

To view analogies by relationship, we first need to clarify what an analogy is.

> An analogy is a pair of words that constitutes a specific relationship.

For instance, APPLE : FRUIT is an analogy, and the relationship is: An apple is a type of fruit. Making a sentence like this—an apple is a type of fruit—is the way to make the relationship between pairs of words clear.

Good Sentences

A sentence that makes the relationship between the two words clear is a good sentence.

A sentence that makes the relationship between the two words clear is a good sentence. It is usually helpful if the sentence is short and to the point.

APPLE : FRUIT	An apple is a type of fruit.
SHEET : BED	A sheet covers a bed.
HAT : HEAD	A hat is used to cover the head.
MOUSE : WHALE	A mouse and a whale are both mammals.

Bad Sentences

"My mother likes all kinds of fruit, except for apples, actually, because apples give her all kinds of digestive problems. . . ." This is an example of a narrative sentence—a sentence that tells a story. A sentence that is narrative or meandering won't help you find the answer to an analogy. The point of constructing a sentence is to find the right answer. You can do this by seeing if the answer choice fits into the sentence well. Since it will be extremely difficult to find any word that will fit into a sentence about your mother, that type of sentence isn't going to help you. That makes it a bad sentence.

MORE BAD SENTENCES

Sentences that are too short are not helpful either. "An apple is fruit," or "Fruit is an apple." These are so unspecific as to be useless in describing the exact relationship between the two words.

Sentences that are too short are not helpful.

TERMINOLOGY

To discuss the analogies clearly, we will need to have distinct terminology. We are going to call the words that are written outside the parentheses **stem words**. There are three stem words or phrases in every MAT analogy.

APPLE : FRUIT :: LOLLIPOP : (*a*. candy, *b*. chocolate, *c*. vegetable,
   d. sugar)

   ↖   ↑   ↗

        Stem words

SHEET : MASK :: BED : (*a*. ear, *b*. ghost, *c*. costume, *d*. hair)

   ↖   ↑   ↗

      Stem words

HAT : HEAD :: HAND : (*a*. glove, *b*. finger, *c*. scarf, *d*. winter)

   ↖   ↑   ↗

      Stem words

MOUSE : GRASSHOPPER :: WHALE : (*a*. ant, *b*. worm, *c*. slug, *d*. frog)

   ↖   ↑   ↗

        Stem words

In answering a MAT analogy question, your first task is to find which two of the three stem words form an analogy pair.

FINDING THE ANALOGY PAIR

The irritating thing about MAT analogies is that at first you can't be sure which stem words are the ones that form the proper relationship. But it isn't an impossible task. There are only two types of MAT analogies: 1:2 analogies and 1:3 analogies.

A 1:2 analogy is one in which the first two words are related.

A 1:2 analogy is one in which the first two words are related. That means the other matching relationship will be between words three and four.

APPLE : FRUIT :: LOLLIPOP : (*a*. candy, *b*. chocolate, *c*. vegetable, *d*. dessert)

The first two words in the above analogy go together easily with the sentence we used earlier, "An apple is a type of fruit." If you had any doubt, you would look to see if this question fits the only other type of analogy there is, the 1:3 analogy. To do this, ask yourself if the 1 and 3 words are possibly related. Can you easily make a sentence with the words "apple" and "lollipop"? Not really, so it is a 1:2 analogy.

A 1:3 analogy is one in which the first and third words are related. That means the other matching relationship will be between words three and four.

SHEET : MASK :: BED : (*a*. ear, *b*. ghost, *c*. costume, *d*. hair)

Again, first look at words one and two; can you easily make a sentence with "sheet" and "mask"? Not really. Then look to see whether you can make a sentence with the first and the third words. Can you easily make a sentence with "sheet" and "bed"? Probably. A good sentence might be, "A sheet is used to cover a bed." That's a 1:3 analogy.

OTHER DIFFICULTIES

Sometimes analogies will have answer choices instead of a stem word in the one, two or three word place.

Sometimes analogies will have answer choices instead of a stem word in the one, two, or three word place. Not to worry, you can still determine if it is a 1:2 or 1:3 analogy.

HAT : (*a*. glove, *b*. finger, *c*. scarf, *d*. winter) :: HEAD : HAND

This time it will be easier if you look first to see if it is a 1:3 analogy. Do the first and third stem words easily form a sentence? Yes. "A hat is worn on the head," is a good sentence. Good enough, you have a 1:3 analogy here. But you are probably worried—what if you hadn't been able to make a sentence between the first and the third words? Simple enough, just look at stem words three and four. If they have a good relationship, then you have a 1:2 relationship.

WHAT ABOUT WHEN THERE IS NO FIRST WORD?

(*a*. ant, *b*. worm, *c*. slug, *d*. frog) : MOUSE :: GRASSHOPPER :
WHALE

Well, since you can't really tell if it's 1:2 or 1:3, look and see if you can spot the other end we talked about, 2:4 (which is really the same as 1:3), or 3:4 (which is really the same as 1:2). You look at words two and four, mouse and whale. They form a sentence, "A mouse and a whale are both the same type of animal," or "a mouse and a whale are both mammals." Sounds OK. Now, to be safe, check words three and four. A grasshopper and a whale—they don't have much in common, do they? So stick with the two and four word sentence, and you have a 1:3 analogy.

DON'T FORGET THE OTHER SIDE

Since the parentheses containing the answer choices can appear first, second, third, or fourth, you may need to match up the existing pairs with some flexibility. But remember: the only types of pairs are 1:2 (which is also 3:4) and 1:3 (which is also 2:4).

> "The only possible analogy pairs are 1:2 and 1:3"

AREN'T THERE ANY OTHER WAYS TO COMBINE THEM?

No, there aren't any other ways to combine them. Only the 1:2 and the 1:3 types of analogies are used on the MAT. If you find yourself trying to work out a relationship between the far ends of an analogy, you're heading in the wrong direction.

If you find yourself trying to work out a relationship between the far ends of an analogy, you're heading in the wrong direction.

WHAT TO DO ONCE YOU'VE IDENTIFIED THE PAIR WITH THE RELATIONSHIP

On your sheet of scratch paper, draw an arrow connecting this pair and indicating what direction your sentence goes in.

APPLE : FRUIT :: LOLLIPOP : (*a.* candy, *b.* chocolate, *c.* vegetable, *d.* sugar)

Next, we will show you how to select the answer choice that fills out the matching pair. But first, try some practice in identifying analogy pairs.

EXERCISE ONE

With the next few groups, identify the related pair with an arrow, and write a clear sentence identifying the relationship in the space provided. Use a piece of scratch paper for all of your work, as it is best to get used to the conditions that you will be faced with in the real MAT. Remember, good sentences clearly identify the relationship between the words.

Good sentences identify the relationship between two words.

1. EXTEND : LENGTH :: INFLATE : (   )
2. (   ) : SYMPHONY :: CHAPTER : MOVEMENT
3. MAMMAL : MOLLUSK :: (   ) : CLAM
4. PICASSO : (   ) :: YEATS : POETRY
5. PINE : CONIFEROUS :: OAK : (   )

6. TRIANGLE : CIRCLE :: (   ) : SPHERE

7. INCH : (   ) :: TABLESPOONS : CUP

8. 15 : 45 :: 2 : (   )

9. NAPOLEON : (   ) :: FRANCE : ITALY

10. (   ) : TYCOON :: DANCE : BUSINESS

You can check your answers against the answer key at the back of the chapter on page 38.

WHAT IF YOU CAN'T MAKE A SENTENCE?

If you can't make a sentence, this might be one of the questions to skip on your first pass of the three-pass system (page 17). There are other ways to get the correct answers on these, and we'll show you these methods in a later section.

WHAT TO DO WITH YOUR SENTENCE

Once you have determined whether it is a 1:2 or a 1:3 analogy and devised a sentence that clearly describes the relationship, you are ready to look at the answer choices.

Let's look at the APPLE : FRUIT example one more time. The sentence we used was "An apple is a type of fruit." Here is where you can see that both the clarity and the word order of a sentence matter. Let's say the analogy looks like this:

APPLE : FRUIT :: LOLLIPOP : (*a.* candy, *b.* chocolate, *c.* vegetable, *d.* sugar)

What you are going to do is try the words in the answer choice to see which one forms an identical pair with the unmatched stem word.

An <u>APPLE</u> is a type of <u>FRUIT</u>.

We will call <u>APPLE</u> word 1, and <u>FRUIT</u> word 2. Then, we can use LOLLIPOP as the first word of its pair, and use it in the sentence to see which of the answers works.

A <u>LOLLIPOP</u> is a type of _____.

Always match the word order; for instance, if you had made the sentence to read "One type of fruit is the apple," you would have to make sure that the sentence for the lollipop was also reversed. The MAT writers mix up their pairs a lot, and you don't want to let it rattle you.

Now, try the answer choices in your open pair.

A <u>LOLLIPOP</u> is a type of <u>CANDY</u>? Yes, but try the other answer choices just to make sure.

A <u>LOLLIPOP</u> is a type of <u>CHOCOLATE</u>? No. Cross out choice (*b*) on your scratch paper.

A LOLLIPOP is a type of VEGETABLE? No. Cross out choice (c) on your scratch paper.

A LOLLIPOP is a type of SUGAR? No. Cross out choice (d) on your scratch paper.

The correct answer here is (a).

ISN'T THIS TAKING A LITTLE LONG?

You might be asking yourself, "Isn't this taking a little long? I could have gotten that question right in two seconds!" What you have to remember is that we are here to improve your score on the MAT *as a whole*, not to get any one particular question right. Once you learn to use these techniques on every single question, you will become more adept at using them. Besides, as we mentioned in chapter 2, you don't need to complete *all* the questions to do well. It makes sense to spend the time on the ones you can get right, and just guess on the really impossible ones.

> You don't need to complete all the questions to do well.

CRACKING MORE ANALOGIES

Try another.

> 2. WEIGHT : LENGTH :: GRAM : (*a.* cup, *b.* volume, *c.* distance, *d.* meter)

First, decide whether it is a 1:2 or a 1:3 analogy, then make a sentence for the related pair. This analogy is a 1:3 analogy; "weight" and "gram" are more clearly related than "weight" and "length."

> 2. WEIGHT : LENGTH :: GRAM : (*a.* cup, *b.* volume, *c.* distance, *d.* meter)

A good sentence might be, "A GRAM is a measure of WEIGHT." Notice that we've reversed the order of the words here. This means we need to reverse the order when we plug the answer choices in as well.

A CUP is a measure of LENGTH? No. Cross out choice (a) on your scratch paper.

A VOLUME is a measure of LENGTH? No. Cross out choice (b) on your scratch paper.

A DISTANCE is a measure of LENGTH? No. Cross out choice (c) on your scratch paper.

A METER is a measure of LENGTH? Yes!

You've got it; the correct answer is (d).

What if You Didn't Make That Sentence, or Choose That Related Pair?

There is only one way for a MAT analogy to work, so if you've chosen a pair that isn't yielding an answer, take another look at your sentence and make sure there isn't another related pair to choose.

Your choices don't have to jibe exactly with ours, as long as you are using the techniques so you can become proficient with them over time and are getting the questions right. There is only one way for an MAT analogy to work, so if you've chosen a pair that isn't yielding an answer, take another look at your sentence and make sure there isn't another related pair to choose.

Summary

1. Identify whether the analogy is a 1:2 analogy or a 1:3 analogy.

2. Make a clear sentence showing the relationship of the stem words in the pair.

3. Go through the answer choices by plugging each one into that sentence with the remaining stem word, canceling wrong answers on your scratch paper until you find one that fits.

Try a Few

Do these ten analogies. Work slowly and carefully, and use the sentence techniques you have learned so far.

Exercise Two

1. COCKROACH : (*a.* arachnid, *b.* insect, *c.* fish, *d.* ant) :: WHALE : MAMMAL

2. (*a.* diploma, *b.* deed, *c.* exam, *d.* registration) : CERTIFICATE :: GRADUATE : TEACHER

3. STUPIDITY : (*a.* brute, *b.* dolt, *c.* idiocy, *d.* bully) :: GRACE : DANCER

4. IRAN : PERSIA :: TOKYO : (*a.* Edo, *b.* Rome, *c.* Chad, *d.* Turkey)

5. (*a.* 0, *b.* 32, *c.* 100, *d.* 763) : 0 :: FAHRENHEIT : CELSIUS

6. CALCULATOR : ABACUS :: (*a.* wagon, *b.* cart, *c.* computer, *d.* vehicle) : CHARIOT

7. SALT : PEPPER :: (*a.* spice, *b.* mineral, *c.* seasoning, *d.* herb) : PLANT

8. ANTHROPOLOGY: HAGIOGRAPHY:: MAN : (*a.* history, *b.* civilization, *c.* saints, *d.* linguistics)

9. SPECIES : GENUS :: (*a.* homo sapiens, *b.* order, *c.* primates, *d.* family) : HOMO

10. WATER : ELECTRICITY :: (*a.* ocean, *b.* blender, *c.* faucet, *d.* lake) : SOCKET

You can check your answers against the answer key in the back of this chapter on page 39.

UNKNOWN WORDS

You probably noticed that for a few of the analogies you just worked on, you may not have known the correct answer right off, but you knew the wrong answers. Don't be afraid to select answer choices whose meanings you don't know. This is one of the ways the Psychological Corporation tries to scare you off the right answer. Don't let them. If you've found three wrong answers, you've found the right answer, too.

Don't be afraid to select answer choices whose meaning you don't know.

SOME ADVANCED TIPS ON MAKING SENTENCES

Sometimes you'll look at the three stem words and you won't know how anyone could have imagined a relationship between two of them. What can you use to help you?

PARTS OF SPEECH

Sometimes a word can have another meaning, and can be used in various parts of speech.

For instance:

DOG : BAY :: (*a.* cow, *b.* sheep, *c.* fish, *d.* bark) : BLEAT

Be on your guard for words that have different meanings when they are used as different parts of speech.

It looks like there isn't any relationship among these words, but if you take a moment to look at "bay" as a verb instead of a noun, things may get better.

A dog makes a sound by baying.

Have you heard of dogs baying at the moon? Or the baying of the hounds? Well, here it is.

Which kind of analogy is it now? A 1:2 analogy. Can you make a sentence? Sure, we just did.

A dog makes a sound by baying. Notice, we've changed the form of "bay" a little bit; that means you have to change the form of the words in the answer choices that way too.

A sheep makes a sound by bleating.

WORKING WITH THE ANSWER CHOICES

All this is well and good if you can determine the relationship among the stem words. What if you can't?

As we've already said, perhaps the most important aspect of the MAT is that it's a multiple-choice test. That means the correct answer is already there! All you have to do is figure out which answers are the wrong ones.

The most important aspect of the MAT is that it's a multiple choice test. That means that the correct answer is already there! All you have to do if figure out which answers are the wrong ones.

IDENTIFYING DISTRACTORS

The way to determine which answers are wrong is to think about how the test is written. The three wrong answers didn't get there out of nowhere; they were carefully selected by the test writer based on how attractive they would be to test-takers like you.

Watch out for distractor answers.

AHA!

This is why they have the experimental section; it doesn't just calculate how many people get the question right or wrong, it indicates which wrong answers were chosen. That way they can tell if they have a really tempting choice—one that can trap people. They use these tempting traps to make their difficult questions—numbers 66 to 100—more difficult, so on these questions you can ...

USE THEIR TRAP TACTICS TO TRAP *THEM*

Now that you know some answers are there to lead you down the wrong path, you can eliminate answers that look tempting, even without knowing the correct relationship you're trying to find. Look at this analogy. We've blacked out the related stem pair so you can see that it's possible to get the right answer without knowing which of the stem words are related or how they are related.

> 71. XXXX : XXXX :: ELITE : (*a.* special, *b.* typing, *c.* superiority,
> *d.* achievement)

HERE'S HOW TO CRACK IT

> 71. XXXX : XXXX :: ELITE : (*a.* special, *b.* typing, *c.* superiority,
> *d.* achievement)

Which answer choices in this problem look tempting? Since you are trying to match up the word "elite" with one of them, the most obvious associations are "special" and "superiority." And, since it's question number 71 out of 100 questions, and they go in order of difficulty, that means those answer choices are probably wrong. Cross them out and take a guess—you've got a fifty-fifty shot. Elite is a measure of typing, besides being an adjective meaning special or chosen. Of course, you won't always be able to cancel all the answers, but any answer you can cancel means you're that much more likely to get the question right and improve your score.

OTHER TACTICS FOR TOUGH QUESTIONS

WORKING BACKWARDS

Don't waste more time on a question if there are other questions you might be able to answer more easily.

You can sometimes find an answer by working backwards.

There will be times when you can cancel some answer choices, but even when you have done so you are still confused about the question. There are two things to remember about this situation. One is that you shouldn't waste time on a question when there are other questions you might be able to answer more easily, and two is that you can sometimes find the answer by **working backwards**.

Take a look at the following analogy.

> 87. JADE : (*a.* gem, *b.* tired, *c.* animal, *d.* mineral) :: COW : INTIMI-
> DATED

You may not even know where to begin with a question like this. As always, resort to the techniques. Is it a 1:2 or a 1:3 analogy? Since the second word is missing, it is easiest to look at words one and three. "Jade" and "cow" do not appear to be related, so you reluctantly decide it is a 1:2 analogy. Then you try to make a sentence. Since it is a 1:2 analogy, the sentence must be with words three and four. If you're like most people, you can't make a sentence between "cow" and "intimidated." Rather than changing your first decision, here is where you can try working backwards. Instead of hammering away at COW and INTIMIDATED, try to make a sentence with the words in the answer choices and the remaining stem word.

Try it with (*a*). How about the sentence, "Jade is a gem." Yes, maybe. Now the working backwards part; see if the pair could work with your other stem words.

Cow is an intimidated. It doesn't make any sense for something to be "an intimidated," cancel (*a*).

Try it with (*b*). If you know the word "jade" as a verb, you can make the sentence "To jade means to make tired." Now try working backwards by putting the other stem words in the sentence.

To cow is to make intimidated. It could make sense to make someone intimidated. Leave (*b*). And what if you didn't know the verb "to jade?" Then you wouldn't have been able to tell whether the sentence could have made sense, so you would have just left that choice and made a guess when you had gone through the others.

Try it with (*c*). Can you make any sentence with "jade" and "animal?" No, so leave this answer choice as you did (*b*).

Try it with (*d*). How about the sentence, "Jade is a mineral." Yes, maybe. Now the working backwards part; see if the pair could work with your other stem words.

Cow is an intimidated. Just as in (*a*), it doesn't make any sense for something to be "an intimidated," so cancel (*d*).

You now have the choice between (*b*) and (*c*), but remember, this is question number 87, so it is difficult. Which of these two is a tempting distractor answer? Well, "animal" looks a whole lot like "cow," and that's probably what a lot of other MAT takers thought. Choose (*b*)—the road less traveled makes all the difference on difficult questions—and get the right answer. Jade means to exhaust or make tired, cow means to make afraid or intimidated.

Do I *HAVE* to?

These techniques, POE and working backwards, are difficult to work with at first. But they can help you throughout the test, so it's best to learn to use them, and then you can really rely on them always.

Another Example

Try this question:

53. GOAT : (*a*. sift, *b*. sheep, *c*. rift, *d*. shoat) :: GLOAT : SHIFT

First, is it a 1:2 analogy or a 1:3 analogy? Maybe you know. If so, terrific. Make a sentence as usual and go on to the next one. But what if you don't know?

Your first step is always to check whether you have a 1:2 or a 1:3 analogy.

HERE'S HOW TO CRACK IT

Gloat means take malicious satisfaction. Study that vocabulary!

Try it as a 1:3 analogy first, because the second word is the answer choice. Are goat and gloat related? Maybe you don't know what the words mean. You can try it as a 1:2 analogy, which means that gloat and shift are related, but you may not know what their relationship is either. So what do you do? Take a guess as to which kind of analogy it is; which words seem more related, goat and gloat or goat and shift? Probably goat and gloat (more on this type of relationship in the next chapter), so if you can't make a sentence, try working backwards again.

(a) Sift and shift. Can you think of any crazy sentence? How about, "Shift is sift with one extra letter in it." Could that work with goat and gloat? It sure could. Leave (a).

(b) Sheep and shift. Try it out, is there any way to make a working sentence out of these two words? Not really. Since this may mean you don't know them, leave (b).

(c) Rift and shift. Okay, a shift causes a rift. Now try working backward, does a gloat cause a goat? No. Can anything "cause" a goat? No. Cancel (c).

(d) Shoat and shift. You probably can't make a sentence. If it's because you don't know the words, leave it in, if it's because you do know the words and they can't be related, cancel (d).

The last step is to assess the difficulty of the analogy by looking at the question number. Since this is question 53, there is no need to go overboard in canceling tempting answers. Which of the answer choices worked best when working backwards? Answer choice (a), so that is the one to choose, and, happily enough, this time it's correct. If you guessed (b) that's fine too; getting these questions is gravy, but learning to guess aggressively and eliminate answers will help you overall even if you guess wrong some of the time. By the way, gloat means to express malicious satisfaction, and a shoat is a young pig.

WILL WORKING BACKWARDS WORK EVERY TIME?

Nothing works every single time, but this technique and others will work the majority of the time. Since many of the techniques are used with more difficult questions you may not have gotten right anyway, using them will increase your chances of getting more answers correct—already a vast improvement.

Let's Try It Again

Try another problem:

47. NAPOLEON : WAGON :: (*a.* coin, *b.* pastry, *c.* war, *d.* strategy) : DRAY

Now if you're like a lot of people, you don't know the word DRAY and you can't for the life of you figure out the relationship between NAPOLEON and WAGON. You think to yourself, if Napoleon's parents had given him the wagon he wanted as a child, he wouldn't have been so power-hungry? A bit of a stretch. Therefore, it's probably a 1:3 analogy.

HERE'S HOW TO CRACK IT

Again, you want to try to find a relationship between Napoleon and one of the answer choices. So, try those answer choices.

(a) Napoleon coin. Can you make a sentence? Not really. Possibly, Napoleon was on a coin. Wagon was on a dray? Could a wagon be on something? Unlikely. Cancel (a).

(b) Napoleon pastry. Hmm. Here's where our previous techniques can help. Did Napoleon like pastries? Maybe, but maybe not, it seems like a weak relationship, but hold on a second—is there another meaning of the word? Yes. A Napoleon is a type of pastry.
Could a wagon be a type of dray? Who knows? Keep the answer choice, but always try all the possibilities before selecting one.

(c) Napoleon war. "Terrific!" you think to yourself. "What a great relationship!" But be careful. Don't move so fast. You have to see if the relationship works with the other choice. First, what is the sentence? Napoleon was involved in war. Sounds good. Now, let's see if the other pair fits in. Wagon was involved in dray. Have you ever heard of WAGON the person? No. So you know this can't quite work. Cancel (c) and try the last choice.

(d) Napoleon strategy. A sentence might be, Napoleon used a strategy. OK. Now try it with the other pair. Wagon used a dray.

Again, wagon would need to be a person here, or something capable of using something else. Since to your knowledge it isn't, you can cancel (d).

The correct answer is (b) pastry. A wagon is a type of dray, or cart. And you can get the question right without even knowing that.

SUMMARY OF STEPS WHEN YOU KNOW ALL THE WORDS

1. Determine whether the analogy is 1:2 or 1:3.

2. Make a sentence describing the pair's relationship.

3. Match up the sentence with the answer choices.

SUMMARY OF STEPS WHEN YOU DON'T KNOW THE WORDS

1. Try to determine whether an analogy is 1:2 or 1:3.
2. Consider a word's alternate meanings.
3. Work backwards.
4. Use POE.
5. Guess!

1. Try to determine if it is a 1:2 or a 1:3 analogy.

2. Make sure you consider an alternative meaning of the words, and pay attention to parts of speech.

3. Work backwards to see which answer choices work.

4. Use POE (process of elimination) to eliminate distractor answers.

5. Guess!

EXERCISE THREE

Try the following ten analogy pairs, using everything you know.

1. WALK : WRITE :: (*a.* crawl, *b.* scramble, *c.* shamble, *d.* gamble) : SCRAWL

2. CONSECRATE : SULLY :: HOLY : (*a.* sad, *b.* pure, *c.* filth, *d.* dirty)

3. HUCK FINN : TWAIN :: (*a.* cupid, *b.* Sawyer, *c.* Achilles, *d.* Euripides) : HOMER

4. C : (*a.* X, *b.* I, *c.* D, *d.* M) :: D : L

5. PRUSSIA : GERMANY :: (*a.* Gold Coast, *b.* Ivory Coast, *c.* Zimbabwe, *d.* Guyana) : GHANA

Try to think flexibly when you're working on difficult questions.

6. ARID : UNCTUOUS :: DRY : (*a.* wet, *b.* chapped, *c.* chafed, *d.* oily)

7. (*a.* etc., *b.* ibid., *c.* qed, *d.* i.f.) : ET. AL. :: IN THE PLACE OF : AND OTHERS

8. DONNE : HEMINGWAY :: (*a.* painter, *b.* composer, *c.* philosopher, *d.* poet) : NOVELIST

9. 3^2 : 3^3 :: (*a.* 1, *b.* 9, *c.* 3, *d.* 6) : 3

10. CRANIUM : CRANIA :: MOUSE : (*a.* cat, *b.* rat, *c.* mice, *d.* rodent)

ANSWER KEY TO EXERCISE ONE

1. This is a 1:2 analogy, and a good sentence is: To extend means to increase in length.

2. This is a 1:3 analogy (in this case, a 2:4 sentence): A movement is a section of a symphony.

3. This is a 1:3 analogy (in this case, a 2:4 sentence): A clam is a type of mollusk.

4. This is a 1:2 analogy (in this case, a 3:4 sentence): Yeats created poetry.

5. This is a 1:2 analogy. A pine is a coniferous tree.

6. This is a 1:2 analogy: A triangle and a circle are both two-dimensional shapes.

7. This is a 1:2 analogy, but with a 3:4 sentence. A cup is made up of tablespoons.

8. This is a 1:2 analogy: 45 is three times 15.

9. This is a 1:3 analogy: Napoleon was a general of France.

10. This is a 1:3 analogy (in this case a 2:4 sentence): A tycoon is a person who is powerful in business.

ANSWER KEY TO EXERCISE TWO

1. (b) A whale is a type of mammal, and a cockroach is a type of insect.

2. (a) To become a teacher one must earn a certificate, and to become a graduate one must earn a diploma.

3. (b) A dancer is characterized by grace, and a dolt is characterized by stupidity.

4. (a) Iran was formerly called Persia, and Tokyo was formerly called Edo. You could have used POE on this question.

5. (b) The freezing point of water is 0 degrees Celsius, and 32 degrees Fahrenheit.

6. (d) An abacus is a primitive calculator, and a chariot is a primitive vehicle.

7. (c) Salt is a type of seasoning, and pepper is a type of plant.

8. (c) Anthropology is the study of man, and hagiography is the study of saints.

9. (a) Homo is the human genus, and homo sapiens is the human species.

10. (c) A socket is the man-made source of electricity, and a faucet is the man-made source of water.

ANSWER KEY TO EXERCISE THREE

1. (c) To scrawl is to write in a messy or awkward manner, to shamble is to walk in a messy or awkward manner.

2. (d) To consecrate is to make holy, to sully is to make dirty. Filth is the wrong part of speech.

3. (*c*) Huck Finn is the main character in a work by Twain, and Achilles is the main character in a work by Homer.

4. (*a*) The ratio of C to D is 100 to 500 or 1 to 5, (C and D are Roman numerals and will be discussed at greater length on page 73), and the ratio is the same between 10 and 50, or X and L.

5. (*a*) Germany was formerly called Prussia, and Ghana was formerly called the Gold Coast.

6. (*d*) Arid means the condition of being dry, and unctuous means the condition of being oily.

7. (*b*) Et. al. is the abbreviation of a Latin expression meaning "and others," and ibid. is the abbreviation of a Latin expression meaning "in the place of."

8. (*d*) Donne was a poet, and Hemingway was a novelist.

9. (*a*) The ratio of three squared to three cubed is 9 to 27, or 1 to 3.

10. (*c*) Crania is the plural form of cranium, and mice is the plural form of mouse.

The Types of Analogies

7

TYPES OF RELATIONSHIPS

As you saw in the preceding chapters, you can answer questions even when you don't know the words or the relationships. Practice these techniques as much as you can—it's the best way to improve your score on the MAT.

But a familiarity with the types of relationships on the test will help, too. Knowing what types of relationships to expect makes it easier to recognize the type of relationship you are dealing with, so you can make a sentence and get through the test more quickly and easily.

What follow are some of the major types of relationships you will see on the MAT. Of course, they don't cover every eventuality, but they account for almost all of the analogies that appeared on the most recent version.

MEASURING UP

TEMPERATURE : DEGREE

CARAT : WEIGHT

KNOT : MACRAME

LETTERS : ALPHABET

These pairs are all variations on a theme, the theme being "a unit or measurement of."

A DEGREE is a unit to measure TEMPERATURE.

A CARAT is a unit to measure WEIGHT. (as in diamonds).

A KNOT is a unit of MACRAME.

Sometimes the sentences can describe how the units function.

LETTERS are units of the ALPHABET, or

LETTERS make up the ALPHABET.

WORD GAMES

PEELS : SLEEP

BOAT : BLOAT

HIE : HIGHER

LIVES : VEILS

Some of the analogies on the MAT don't have anything to do with the meanings of the words, they have to do with the letters of the word, or the letter order.

Maybe you've always hated the jumble on the comics page; maybe you think people who do those word search puzzles need to try doing something *really* important, like reading Ann Landers. If so, you might want to wake up and smell the coffee, at least for the time remaining before your MAT exam. Some of the analogies on the MAT don't have anything to do with the relationships between the *meanings* of the words involved; they have to do with the *letters* of the words involved, or the pronunciation, or the letter order. The best way to deal with these types of analogies is first to recognize them, and then to play around with the words until you can see their relationship.

For instance:

PEELS is SLEEP, spelled backwards.

BLOAT is BOAT with an extra letter put in the second place.

HIGHER sounds like HIE with an "er" sound added to the end.

VEILS is a word using the same letters as LIVES in a different order—these are also called anagrams.

Crazy stuff, but the more familiar you get with them, the easier these kinds of questions will be. And start practicing that jumble.

The more familiar you get with the different types of questions, the easier these questions will be.

CHARACTERIZATIONS

> PUGILIST : AGGRESSION
>
> GRACE : DANCER
>
> MAZE : CONFUSION
>
> MYSTERIOUS : ENIGMA

All the above pairs are members of the same group—the characterized-by group. These analogies start out as the most dangerous group for unwary test takers, but can easily be tamed with a little preparation. Why are they dangerous? Because most test takers will look at the words PUGILIST (a pugilist is a fighter or a boxer, by the way) and AGGRESSION and think that the relationship is "A pugilist has aggression." Unfortunately for these vulnerable test takers, this sentence can work for almost any pair of words, "Napoleon has a wagon," for instance. Thus, all the answer choices fit and the miserable MAT victim is left back where she started. The best sentences for these types of pairs are:

A pugilist is a fighter. An enigma is a difficult or puzzling question. Study that vocabulary!

A PUGILIST is characterized by AGGRESSION.

With this type of relationship, reversal is always possible:

GRACE characterizes a DANCER, or, GRACE is a characteristic of a DANCER.

The purpose of a MAZE is to produce CONFUSION. (This is only one of many variations you may come up with.)

An ENIGMA is characterized by MYSTERY.

Would you get trapped into choosing, "Napoleon is characterized by a wagon"? Not likely.

ALSO KNOWN AS . . .

For reasons probably tied to their own deep and hidden shame regarding their motives, the test writers of the MAT tend to focus lots of questions around false or former names, as well as aliases.

SRI LANKA : CEYLON

MUNRO : SAKI

A working sentence for these might be,

SRI LANKA is the country formerly known as CEYLON.

SAKI was the pseudonym for H. H. MUNRO.

Don't let not knowing a word intimidate you!

What can make these problems difficult is not recognizing the names or words in the pairs, but don't let not knowing intimidate you. An awareness of the existence of this kind of relationship makes working backwards and eliminating wrong answers much easier.

DEGREE RELATIONSHIPS

Relationships in which one word is an extreme version of the other are degree relationships.

DISLIKE : HATRED

DOWNPOUR : DRIZZLE

RIPPLE : TSUNAMI

BOULDER : PEBBLE

These pairs all form degree relationships, relationships in which one word is the extreme version of the other. A good sentence for this type of relationship is:

DOWNPOUR is an extreme form of a DRIZZLE , or a
DOWNPOUR is a lot of DRIZZLE.
Of course, sometimes it is necessary to reverse the words.

HATRED is an extreme form of DISLIKE.

Sometimes you will need to use size words to indicate the degree.

A BOULDER is an extremely large PEBBLE.

Or, a TSUNAMI is an extremely large RIPPLE. A TSUNAMI
is a tidal wave, by the way.

WORK, WORK, WORK

SURGEON : SCALPEL

SMELTING PLANT : ORE

ACTUARY : PROBABILITIES

SCORE : COMPOSER

As you can see from the above pairs, the exact definition of a working tool can be a bit hazy. For the first pair,

A SCALPEL is the work tool of a SURGEON, is a good, clear sentence. Avoid sentences such as: A SURGEON uses a SCALPEL. Although this sentence may seem fine, it's really too vague and can lead to confusion among the answer choices. The problem is that a surgeon uses tools other than a scalpel, and you could have choices such as "needle," "scissors," and "thimble." You need to be very clear about just how the tool is used to get the right answer to some questions.

Similar relationships can be recognized among the places where work is produced. A good sentence here might be,

A SMELTING PLANT processes ORE.

This clearly shows the relationship between the two words.
What about the last two?
These are also relationships between workers and what they work with. There are some subtle variations, so you have to keep alert.

An ACTUARY works with PROBABILITIES. This, or some version of this, expresses the relationship.

Another common variation is when the work or product itself is given.

A COMPOSER creates a SCORE.

All these worker-type analogies are easy to recognize once you know what you're looking for.

> Avoid vague sentences; they make questions much more difficult.

GO AHEAD, JUDGE A BOOK BY ITS COVER

WHITE FLAG : SURRENDER

RANK : CHEVRON

32 : FREEZING

WIMPLE : NUN

The folks who write the MAT are big on external indications. What's good about this is that these types of pairs lend themselves to terrific sentences, making your job a whole lot easier. Words like "indicates" or "represents" are useful in these sentences.

> The folks who write the MAT are big on analogies that rely on external indications.

A WHITE FLAG represents SURRENDER.

Rank is indicated by CHEVRONS. (Chevrons are the V-shaped bars on military uniforms.)

32 indicates the FREEZING point of water.

A WIMPLE is clothing worn by a NUN.

HERE WE SEE THE RARE AUSTRALIAN LEMUR, A FINE EXAMPLE OF THE DISAPPEARING . . .

KANGAROO : MARSUPIAL

CURRENCY : DINAR

PEA : LEGUME

ICE BOX : REFRIGERATOR

All the above pairs are variations on that wonderful first sentence "An apple is a type of fruit." For some of them, though, the word "example" can be easier to use than "type"; try them and see which you find more comfortable.

A KANGAROO is an example of a MARSUPIAL.

A DINAR is a type of CURRENCY.

A PEA is a type of LEGUME.

A marsupial is a type of mammal found in Australia. A legume is a type of plant whose seed splits in two. Study that vocabulary!

The last example has a particular shade to it; it is an older or more primitive type of thing, just as a sundial is a primitive type of watch.

An ICE BOX is a primitive type of REFRIGERATOR.

There are other modifications to the type, and you will notice these as you come across them. Be sure to make clear, specific sentences with these, and everything will go smoothly.

STUDY OF . . .

ANTHROPOLOGY : HUMANKIND

COINS : NUMISMATICS

SEISMOLOGY : TREMORS

TISSUE : HISTOLOGY

Even if you don't know all of the words in the pairs listed above, their subgroup of relationships is extremely helpful. For one thing, the suffix "ology" generally means "study of," so you can work backwards with the answer choices and generally eliminate one or two, making a correct guess that much more likely. Also, you can look at the prefixes and actually figure out the relationship that way. Often, you may somehow be familiar with a word—even if you don't exactly know the definition of it. (More on suffixes, roots, and prefixes in chapter 14.)

You may be somewhat familiar with a word even if you don't know its exact definition; this familiarity can help you.

ANTHROPOLOGY is the study of HUMANKIND.

NUMISMATICS is the study of COINS.

SEISMOLOGY is the study of TREMORS.

HISTOLOGY is the study of TISSUE.

AND THE REST

Other relationships don't occur with enough regularity for us to classify them, but not to worry. The relationships given here represent most of the questions on the MAT—getting these questions and NONE of the others would place you in the seventy-fifth percentile of all majors. Besides, the other types of relationships aren't necessarily more difficult—just try to determine which pair is related and go on to make a great, clear sentence.

EXERCISE FOUR

Now that you're more familiar with the major types of relationships, hone your sentence-making skills by identifying the relationships and making sentences for the following

1. DIPLOMA : GRADUATION

2. POD : WHALE

3. THIN : EMACIATED

4. PLANE : CARPENTER

5. INFECTION : BOIL

6. MAIZE : CORN

7. NAIF : UNWORLDLINESS

8. BIRDS : ORNITHOLOGY

9. SCULPTOR : CHISEL

10. COLUMN : DORIC

Practice making sentences for related pairs of words whenever you get the chance; it will get your mind in shape.

Answer Key to Exercise Four

1. A DIPLOMA is received upon GRADUATION. A variation of the *indicates* relationship.

2. A POD is a group of WHALES. A variation on the *unit of* relationship.

3. EMACIATED is extremely THIN. A *degree* relationship.

4. A PLANE is the tool of a CARPENTER. A *working tool* relationship.

5. A BOIL is a type of INFECTION. A *type of* relationship, though it could also be true that the word boil is being used as a verb here, but you would have to see the other words to know.

6. MAIZE is another name for CORN. An *alternative name* relationship.

7. A NAIF is characterized by UNWORLDLINESS. A *characterized-by* relationship.

8. ORNITHOLOGY is the study of BIRDS. A *study of* relationship.

9. A CHISEL is the tool of a SCULPTOR. A *working tool* relationship.

10. DORIC is a type of COLUMN. A *type of* relationship.

Remember, if you didn't have these exact sentences, that's OK; just keep your sentences this simple and you should be fine.

PART III

Vocabulary

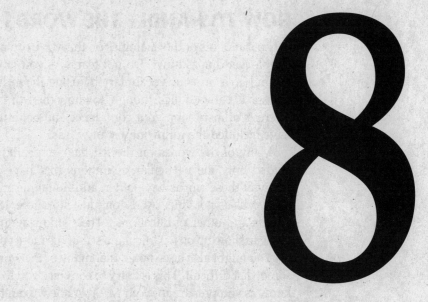

8

Vocabulary

HOW TO HANDLE THE WORDS

Lots and lots of the analogies on the MAT contain words that lots and lots of people just don't know. Do not fear! As you have already seen, you can get around holes in your vocabulary by using the techniques and process of elimination. It's always nice, though, to know the words you come across, and in the interests of increasing your confidence and bettering your score even more, we have included the following list of words.

Many of the words on the list have appeared on recent MATs. We've included only the particular definitions that have been used on specific tests. Many of these words have other, additional meanings. Try to learn as many of the words as possible. And don't just stop here; learn words by reading newspapers and other publications. There's no way to tell exactly which words are going to show up on a particular test, but the more you know, the better off you are.

You might also have noted that many of the words in the text of this book are somewhat difficult. This is to try to convince you to look up any words you don't know as you prepare for your MAT. While we can't possibly hope to cover every word that will appear on the MAT, you never know which of those words that you look up and write in your MAT preparation notebook will miraculously appear on your test and nudge you up to the next percentile. It would also behoove you to study all of the words—both the stem words and the answer choices—that appear in the MAT Candidate Information Booklet that you will receive after calling The Psychological Corporation about selecting a test site. So look everything up, and study those words.

When you get to the sample tests, take some time (after you've taken them, of course) to look up those words you don't know. And remember, secondary definitions and the ways in which the words are related are your number one concerns. So read on, and good luck.

> **Behoove:** To be appropriate for. Study that vocabulary!

aberration: something not typical; a deviation from the standard

abstemious: sparing or moderate, especially in eating and drinking

abstinent: abstaining; voluntarily not doing something

abstract: theoretical; lacking substance (the opposite of concrete)

abstruse: hard to understand or grasp

acclaim: praise; applause; admiration

accolade: an award or honor; high praise

accrete: to increase by growth or addition

acquiesce: to give in; to agree

acute: sharp; shrewd

advocate: to speak in favor of; to support

aesthetic: having to do with artistic beauty; artistic

alacrity: cheerful readiness; liveliness or eagerness

alleviate: to lessen; to relieve, usually temporarily or incompletely; to make bearable

allocate: to distribute; assign; allot

allusion: an indirect reference to something else, especially something in literature; a hint

amass: to accumulate

ambiguous: unclear in meaning; confusing; capable of being interpreted in at least two similarly plausible ways

ambivalent: undecided; blowing hot and cold

ambulatory: able to walk; walking

ameliorate: to make better or more tolerable

amiable: friendly

amity: friendship

anarchy: absence of government or control; lawlessness; disorder

anecdote: a brief, entertaining story

animated: alive; moving

animosity: resentment; hostility; ill will

anomaly: an aberration; an irregularity; a deviation

antipathy: firm dislike; dislike; hatred

antiseptic: free from germs; exceptionally clean

apathy: lack of emotion or interest

apocryphal: of doubtful origin; false

appease: to soothe; to pacify by giving in to

apprehensive: worried; anxious

arbiter: one who decides; a judge

arid: extremely dry; unimaginative; dull

arrogant: feeling superior to others; snooty

articulate: speaking clearly and well

ascetic: hermitlike; practicing self-denial

assiduous: hardworking; busy; diligent

assuage: to soothe; to pacify; to ease the pain of; to relieve

astute: perceptive; intelligent

atrophy: to waste away from lack of use

audacity: boldness; reckless daring; impertinence

augment: to add to; to increase; to make bigger

auspicious: favorable; promising; pointing to a good result

austere: unadorned; stern; forbidding; without much money

authentic: real

authoritarian: like a dictator

axiom: a self-evident rule or truth; a widely accepted saying

baleful: menacing; harmful

banal: unoriginal; ordinary

bastion: stronghold; fortress; fortified place

beget: to cause or produce; to engender

belittle: to make to seem little

belligerent: combative; quarrelsome; waging war

benefactor: a generous donor

beneficent: doing good

benevolent: kind; good-hearted; generous

benign: gentle; not harmful; kind; mild

bereave: to deprive or leave desolate, especially through death

bias: prejudice; tendency; tilt

blasphemy: irreverence; an insult to something held sacred; profanity

blithe: carefree; cheerful

brawn: bulk; muscles

brevity: briefness

brook: to bear or tolerate; to put up with something

cacophony: a harsh-sounding mixture of words, voices, or sounds

cajole: to deceptively persuade someone to do something he or she doesn't want to do

candid: honest; frank

capricious: unpredictable; likely to change at any moment

caustic: like acid; corrosive

censure: to condemn severely for doing something bad

chronology: an order of events from earliest to latest

circumlocution: an indirect expression; use of wordy or evasive language

coalesce: to come together as one; to fuse; to unite

coda: a passage concluding a composition (in music)

cognizant: perceptive; observant

complacent: smug; self-satisfied; pleased with oneself; contented to a fault

compliant: yielding; submissive

comprehensive: covering or including everything

conciliatory: making peace; attempting to resolve a dispute through goodwill

concise: brief and to the point; succinct

condescend: to stoop to someone else's level, usually in an offensive way; to patronize

condone: to overlook; to permit to happen

congenial: agreeably suitable; pleasant

conjoin: to join or act together

conjure: to summon or bring into being as if by magic

connoisseur: an expert, particularly in matters of art or taste

consensus: unanimity or near unanimity

conspicuous: standing out; obvious

contempt: reproachful disdain

contentious: argumentative; quarrelsome

contrite: deeply apologetic; remorseful

contumacious: stubbornly rebellious or disobedient

conundrum: a puzzle; a riddle

conventional: common; customary; unexceptional

correlate: to find or show the relationship of two things

corroborate: to confirm; to back up with evidence

credulous: believing; gullible

cryptic: mysterious; mystifying

cynic: one who deeply distrusts human nature; one who believes people are motivated only by selfishness

dearth: a lack of; scarcity

debacle: violent breakdown; sudden overthrow

debauchery: corruption by sensuality; intemperance; wild living

decorous: in good taste; orderly

deference: submission to another's will; respect; courtesy

deleterious: harmful

denounce: to speak out against; to condemn

deplete: to use up; to reduce; to lessen

depravity: moral corruption

deride: to ridicule; to laugh at contemptuously

desecrate: to profane a holy place (the opposite is consecrate)

desiccate: to dry out

deter: to prevent; to stop; to keep from doing something

didactic: instructive; intended to instruct

diffident: timid; lacking in self-confidence

digress: to go off the subject

diligent: hardworking

disavow: to deny

discernment: insight; ability to see things clearly

discomfit: to confuse, deject, frustrate, deceive

discord: disagreement (the opposite of concord)

discourse: to converse; to formally discuss a subject

discriminate: to differentiate; to make a clear distinction; to see the difference

disdain: arrogant scorn; contempt

disinterested: unbiased

disparage: to belittle; to say uncomplimentary things about, usually in a somewhat indirect way

disparate: different; incompatible

dispassionate: without passion; objective; neutral

disseminate: to scatter or spread widely

dissent: disagreement

dissonant: inharmonious; in disagreement

divergent: differing in opinion; deviating

diverse: varied

divert: to change the direction of; to alter the course of; to amuse

doggerel: comic, loose verse

dogmatic: arrogantly assertive of unproven ideas; arrogantly claiming that something (often a system of beliefs) is beyond dispute

drone: to talk on and on in a dull way

dubious: doubtful; uncertain

eccentric: not conventional; a little kooky; irregular

eclectic: choosing the best from many sources; drawn from many sources

economical: frugal; thrifty

efface: to erase; to rub away the features of

effluvium: a disagreeable or noxious vapor; an escaping gas

elaborate: detailed; careful; thorough

elusive: hard to pin down; evasive

emulate: to strive to equal or excel, usually through imitation

engender: to create; to produce

enhance: to make better; to augment

enigma: mystery

enthrall: to thrill

ephemeral: short-lived; fleeting; not lasting

equivocal: ambiguous; intentionally confusing; capable of being interpreted in more than one way

erratic: unpredictable or wandering

erudite: scholarly; deeply learned

esoteric: hard to understand; understood by only a select few; peculiar

euphony: pleasant sound (the opposite is cacophony)

evanescent: vanishing or fading; scarcely perceptible

exemplary: outstanding; setting a great example

exemplify: to serve as an example of

exhaustive: thorough; complete

exigent: demanding prompt action; urgent

exonerate: to free completely from blame

exorbitance: an exceedingly large amount

expedient: providing an immediate advantage; serving one's immediate self-interest

expedite: to make faster or easier

exposition: expounding or explaining; explanatory treatise

extol: to praise

extraneous: irrelevant; extra; unnecessary; unimportant

exuberant: extremely joyful or vigorous; profuse in growth

facetious: humorous; not serious; clumsily humorous

facilitate: to make easier

fallacious: false

fanatic: one who is extremely devoted to a cause or idea

fastidious: meticulous; demanding

feasible: able to be done

fecund: fertile; productive

fervor: passion

fickle: capricious; whimsical; unpredictable

flag: to weaken; to slow down

flagrant: shocking; outstandingly bad

flaunt: to show off; to display ostentatiously

flippant: frivolously shallow and disrespectful

forbear: to refrain from; to abstain

fortuitous: accidental; occurring by chance

foster: to promote the growth or development of

frenetic: frantic; frenzied

frivolous: not serious; not solemn; with levity

frugal: economical; penny-pinching

fulsome: excessive, insincere and disgusting

furtive: secretive

futile: hopeless; without effect

gainsay: to deny; to speak or act against

garner: to gather and store; to earn

garrulous: extremely chatty or talkative; wordy or diffuse

genial: cheerful and pleasant; friendly; helpful

genre: an artistic class or category

gerrymander: to divide a state or county into election districts to gain political advantage

goad: to urge forcefully; to taunt someone into doing something

gravity: seriousness (secondary meaning)

guile: cunning; duplicity

gullible: overly trusting; willing to believe anything

hackneyed: banal; overused; trite (a cliché is a hackneyed expression)

hedonistic: pleasure-seeking; indulgent

heed: to listen to

heresy: an opinion violently opposed to established beliefs

hermetic: impervious to external influence; airtight

hindrance: an obstruction; an annoying interference or delay

homeostasis: the tendency of an organic system to maintain internal stability

hone: to sharpen

hypothetical: uncertain; unproven

idiom: a peculiar expression

idyllic: charming in a rustic way; naturally peaceful

immutable: unchangeable; permanent

impartial: unbiased; neutral

impede: to hinder; to obstruct; to slow something down

impervious: not allowing anything to pass through; impenetrable

implement: to carry out

implicit: implied rather than expressly stated

impromptu: without preparation; on the spur of the moment

improvident: lacking prudent foresight; careless

impudent: bold; impertinent

impugn: to attack, especially to attack the truth or integrity of something

inadvertent: lax; careless; without intention

incessant: unceasing; never-ending

inchoate: just beginning; not organized or orderly

incisive: cutting right to the heart of the matter

incoherent: jumbled; chaotic; impossible to understand

incongruous: not harmonious; not consistent; not appropriate

incursion: a hostile invasion

indifferent: not caring one way or the other; mediocre; lacking a preference; neutral

indignant: angry, especially as a result of something unjust or unworthy

indolence: laziness

indulgent: lenient; yielding to desire

ineluctable: inescapable; unavoidable

inept: clumsy; incompetent

inert: inactive; sluggish; not reacting chemically

inevitable: unavoidable; bound to happen

infamous: shamefully wicked; having an extremely bad reputation; disgraceful

infer: to conclude; to deduce

ingenuous: unwarily simple; candid; naive

inherent: part of the essential nature of something; intrinsic

innate: existing since birth; inborn; inherent

innocuous: harmless

innovate: to be creative; to introduce something new

innumerable: too many to number or count; many

insipid: dull; banal

insolvent: unable to pay one's bills

instigate: to provoke; to stir up

intransigent: uncompromising; stubborn

invective: insulting or abusive speech

irascible: irritable

ironic: satiric; unexpected

jeopardy: danger

judicious: exercising sound judgment

kinship: natural or family relationship

laconic: using few words, especially to the point of being rude

lament: to mourn

languish: to become weak, listless, or depressed

laudable: worthy of praise

lax: careless; not diligent; relaxed

lethargy: sluggishness; laziness; drowsiness; indifference

levee: an embankment designed to prevent the flooding of a river

levity: lightness; frivolity; unseriousness

ligneous: woodlike

litigate: to try in court; to engage in legal proceedings

lucid: clear; easy to understand

luminous: giving off light; glowing; bright

malleable: easy to shape or bend

mandatory: authoritatively ordered or commanded; necessary

manifest: visible; evident

marred: damaged; bruised

maverick: a nonconformist; a rebel

meander: to wander slowly, like a winding river

mellifluous: sweetly flowing

merger: a joining or marriage

mitigate: to lessen the severity of something

motility: spontaneous movement

munificent: very generous; lavish

negligence: carelessness

neophyte: a beginner

neutral: unbiased; not taking sides; objective

nostalgia: a sentimental longing for the past; homesickness

novel: new; original

nullify: to make unimportant

obdurate: stubborn; inflexible

objective: without bias (as opposed to subjective)

obscure: unclear; clouded; partially hidden; hard to understand

orthodox: conventional; adhering to established principles or doctrines, especially in religion; by the book

oscillate: to swing back and forth; to fluctuate

ossify: to convert into bone; to become rigid

ostentatious: excessively conspicuous; showing off

palliate: to hide the seriousness of something with excuses or apologies

panegyric: lofty praise

paradox: a true statement or phenomenon that nonetheless seems to contradict itself; an untrue statement or phenomenon that nonetheless seems logical

parallel: a comparison made between two things

parsimony: stinginess

partisan: one who supports a particular person, cause, or idea

pathology: the science of diseases; any deviation from a healthy, normal condition

paucity: scarcity

pedagogue: a teacher

pedestrian: common; ordinary; banal (secondary meaning)

penchant: strong taste or liking

peripheral: unimportant

permeate: to spread or seep through; to penetrate

pervade: to spread throughout

petulant: rude; cranky; ill tempered

philanthropy: love of mankind; donating to charity

pious: reverent or devout; outwardly (and sometimes falsely) reverent or devout

piquant: pungent

pivotal: crucial

placate: to pacify; to appease; to soothe

placid: pleasantly calm; peaceful

plumb: to measure the depth of something

polemic: a powerful argument made in refutation of something

pragmatic: practical; down-to-earth; based on experience rather than theory

precipitate: to cause to happen abruptly

preclude: to prevent; to make impossible; to shut out

predecessor: someone or something that came before another

pretentious: pompous; self-important

pristine: original; unspoiled; pure

probity: integrity; uprightness; honesty

problematic: doubtful or questionable

prodigal: extravagant; wasteful

prodigious: extraordinary; enormous

prodigy: an extremely talented child; an extraordinary accomplishment or occurrence

profound: deep; insightful (the opposite of superficial)

profuse: flowing; extravagant

propinquity: nearness

propriety: properness; good manners

prosaic: dull; unimaginative

proselytize: to convert someone from one religion or doctrine to another; to recruit converts to a religion or doctrine

provincial: limited in outlook to one's own small corner of the world; narrow

provocative: exciting; attracting attention

prudent: careful; having foresight

pundit: a learned person; an expert in a particular field

pungent: forceful; sharp or biting to the taste or smell

qualify: to modify or restrict

rampart: a fortification; a bulwark or defense

recalcitrant: stubbornly defiant of authority or control

reciprocal: mutual; shared; interchangeable

recondite: hard to understand; over one's head

redundant: repetitive; unnecessary; excessively wordy

refute: to disprove; to prove to be false

rejuvenate: to make young and strong again

relegate: to banish; to send away

relevant: important; pertinent

remorse: sadness; regret

renaissance/renascence: a rebirth or revival

reprehensible: worthy of blame or censure

repress: to hold down

reproach: to scold

reprobate: a wicked, sinful, depraved person

repudiate: to reject; to deny

repugnant: distasteful or offensive

rescind: to repeal; to take back formally

resignation: reluctant acceptance of a bad situation (secondary meaning)

resolute: determined; firm; unwavering

respite: a rest; a period of relief

reticent: restrained; uncommunicative

retract: to take back; to withdraw; to pull back

revere: to worship; to honor (think of a reverend)

ribald: vulgar or indecent speech or language, as in a ribald joke

rigorous: strict; harsh; severe

rivet: to fix one's attention on

saccharine: sweet; excessively or disgustingly sweet

sagacious: wise; possessing wisdom derived from experience or learning

sage: wise; possessing wisdom derived from experience or learning; a wise person

salubrious: promoting health

sanction: authorize or approve; ratify or confirm

satiric: using sarcasm or irony

saturnine: a sluggish, gloomy temperament

savor: to linger on the taste or smell of something

scanty: inadequate; minimal

scrupulous: strict; careful; hesitant for ethical reasons

scrutinize: to examine closely

servile: submissive and subservient; like a servant

sinuous: having many curves

skeptical: doubting (opposite of gullible)

slander: to defame; to speak maliciously of someone

solemn: serious; grave

solicit: to ask for; to seek

spendthrift: extravagant or wasteful, especially with money

spurious: doubtful; bogus; false

squalid: filthy; repulsive; wretched; degraded

squander: to waste

stagnation: motionlessness; inactivity

stanza: a section of a poem; verse

static: stationary; not changing or moving (not radio fuzz)

sterile: unimaginative; unfruitful; infertile

stoic: indifferent (at least outwardly) to pleasure or pain, to joy or grief, to fortune or misfortune

stringent: strict; restrictive

subjugate: to subdue and dominate; to enslave

substantive: having substance; real; essential; solid; substantial

subtle: not obvious; able to make fine distinctions; ingenious; crafty

sullen: gloomy or dismal

supercilious: haughty; patronizing

superficial: on the surface only; shallow; not thorough

superfluous: extra; unnecessary

surreptitious: sneaky; secret

sycophant: one who sucks up to others

synthesis: the combining of parts to form a whole

tacit: implied; not spoken

taciturn: untalkative by nature

tangible: touchable; palpable

taut: tightly drawn, as a rope; emotionally tense

tedious: boring

temerity: boldness; recklessness; audacity

temperament: one's disposition or character

temperate: moderate; restrained

tenacious: tough; hard to defeat

tentative: experimental; temporary; uncertain

timbre: the quality of a sound independent of pitch and loudness

torpor: sluggishness; inactivity; apathy

tractable: easily managed or controlled; obedient

transitory: not staying for a long time; temporary

trepidation: fear; apprehension; nervous trembling

truculent: savagely brutal; aggressively hostile

turpitude: shameful wickedness or depravity

uniform: consistent; unchanging; the same for everyone

unprecedented: happening for the first time; novel; never seen before

untoward: unfavorable or unfortunate; improper

vacillate: to be indecisive; to waver back and forth

vacuous: lacking ideas or intelligence

vehement: urgent; passionate

venerate: to revere; to treat as something holy, especially because of great age

veracity: truthfulness

verbose: wordy; overly talkative

vex: to annoy; to pester; to confuse

vilify: to say vile things about; to defame

vindicate: to clear from all blame or suspicion

virtuoso: masterful musician; a masterful practitioner in some other field

virulent: extremely poisonous; malignant; full of hate

viscous: thick and sticky

visionary: a dreamer; someone with impractical goals or ideas about the future

volatile: quick to evaporate; highly unstable; explosive

volition: will; conscious choice

voluminous: very large; spacious (this word has nothing to do with sound)

voluntary: willing; unforced

welter: a confused mass; a commotion or turmoil

willful: deliberate; obstinate; insistent on having one's way

zealous: fervent; enthusiastically devoted to something

PART ◆ IV

Knowledge and Culture, MAT Style

9

Culture

KNOWLEDGE, BUT WHOSE CULTURE?

As you have already seen, the best way to improve your score on the MAT is to become adept at using the techniques, which will help you on almost every single analogy. However, in the words of one MAT taker who went on to place in the ninety-ninth percentile on the MAT and to glory in the Boston University School of Social Work, "The Miller Analogies Test is the most culturally biased test I've ever seen in my life."

NOT MY CULTURE

What does this cultural bias mean to you? Basically, it means that there is a lot of information on the test that is there because someone at the Psychological Corporation thinks it's important. The kick is, only a particular segment of the population will have this information, and if you've been raised outside that segment, you won't have that information. Now, lacking the information *doesn't* mean you're less intelligent than someone with that information—after all, how much smarter are you if you know that a Napoleon is a pastry? Not much. And that example just goes to show you how narrow this culture is. In France, where this pastry was invented, people don't even call it a Napoleon; they call it a "mille feuille" or "a thousand layers." So much for knowing the "right name."

The culture tested includes elements of religion, art history, and even nursery rhymes. For instance, on a recent MAT it helped to know, "Mary Mary quite contrary," and "Jack be nimble, Jack be quick." But if you weren't brought up saying these particular nursery rhymes, it doesn't say a thing about your intelligence. So don't feel bad about not knowing this information, because not knowing doesn't mean you're stupid. The trouble is, they still put this kind of junk on the MAT.

SO WHAT DO I DO?

Become familiar with the information in this section. The subjects tested on the MAT are, thankfully, limited, and the next few pages cover much of what the last few tests have covered. Of course, we can't cover every eventuality, but learning this, and mastering the techniques, will help you raise your score as much as possible.

HOW TO USE THIS SECTION

There are seven divisions of knowledge here, and we've arranged them in the order in which they are most likely to appear on the MAT. You should probably take a look through the different sections, try to identify which areas of knowledge you are weakest in, and start there. When you are comfortable with the information and the techniques, you can begin to use the practice tests in the second half of the book.

The best way to improve your score on the MAT is to become adept at using the techniques.

The Miller Analogies Test is the most culturally biased test.

10
Artistic Culture

LITERATURE

For reasons known only to themselves, the MAT test writers are fond of quizzing students on major figures in literature, along with the fictional subjects they create. What if you are taking the MAT to gain entrance to a program in, say, nursing, and don't need to be tested on who wrote *Little Dorrit*? Apparently, they couldn't care less. But don't lose heart—they are only checking for a surface knowledge of the great works of Western literature, which can easily be acquired by becoming familiar with the following list.

Now, these lists may appear daunting, but remember: You are only interested in this information to the extent that it is useful on the MAT. This means you can confine your knowledge to the fact that Rodin was a sculptor and James Joyce was an Irish novelist. All you need to do is make one, small sentence, and this chapter gives you the type of information you need to make that sentence. Of course, these people deserve far more attention than we give them here, but the MAT is not where they're going to get it. Study what you need to for this test, and go on to expand your cultural education apart from your test preparation. But for now, look at these lists and try to absorb only the surface information we present you with; you'll have time after your MAT to learn things that are really important. And by the way, Charles Dickens wrote *Little Dorrit*.

Aesop: A Greek writer of fables or "fabulist." Fables are stories with moral messages.

Jane Austen: An English novelist who wrote comedies of manners, among them *Pride and Prejudice* and *Emma*.

Honoré de Balzac: A French author who wrote novels set mostly in Paris.

Lord Byron: (Also known as George Gordon Byron.) English poet of the romantic era, who wrote in the early nineteenth century, along with other romantic poets John Keats and Percy Shelley. One of his most famous works was *Don Juan*.

Albert Camus: French existentialist novelist of the twentieth century who wrote *The Stranger*.

Lewis Carroll: An English writer who wrote the famous children's books *Alice in Wonderland* and *Through the Looking Glass*, which take place in the fictional place Wonderland. His real name was Charles Dodgson.

Giacomo Casanova: An Italian author and adventurer, he was particularly famous for his memoirs of his sexual conquests.

Miguel de Cervantes: The Spanish author of the literary classic *Don Quixote*, which featured the prevailing symbol of windmills.

Geoffrey Chaucer: Medieval English poet whose most influential work was *The Canterbury Tales*.

Anton Chekhov: Russian fiction writer and playwright of the late nineteenth and early twentieth centuries, known for writing the plays *The Cherry Orchard*, and *Three Sisters*, among numerous others.

Sidonie-Gabrielle Colette: French female novelist of the late-nineteenth and early-twentieth centuries.

The culture tested includes elements of religion, art history, and even nursery rhymes.

When you are comfortable with the information and the techniques, you can begin to use the practice tests.

Honore De Balzac

Lewis Carroll

Dante Alighieri: Italian poet and author of *The Divine Comedy*, which contains the famous sections Inferno, Purgatorio, and Paradiso, which are often referred to independently (e.g., Dante's *Inferno*).

Charles Dickens: English novelist of the nineteenth century, author of such works as *Hard Times*, *Oliver Twist*, *David Copperfield*, *Great Expectations*, *A Christmas Carol*; most of his work is set in London.

Emily Dickinson: American poet of the nineteenth century.

Fyodor Dostoevsky: Russian novelist whose most famous works were *The Brothers Karamazov* and *Crime and Punishment*, the latter of which featured the protagonist Raskalnikov.

George Eliot: the pen name of the nineteenth-century English novelist Mary Ann Evans; she wrote *Middlemarch* and *Adam Bede*.

T. S. Eliot: American-born British poet of the early twentieth century, he was enormously influential and wrote *The Wasteland* and *Four Quartets*, as well as "The Love Song of J. Alfred Prufrock."

Ralph Waldo Emerson: American essayist and poet.

Euripides: Greek playwright of the fifth century B.C., He wrote *Medea*, among other plays.

William Faulkner: American novelist of the twentieth century, widely praised for his works *Absalom! Absalom!* and *As I Lay Dying*. He created the fictional town of Jefferson, in the equally fictional Yoknapatawpha county, both located in the real state of Mississippi.

Gustave Flaubert: French nineteenth-century novelist who wrote *Madame Bovary*, featuring the protagonist Emma Bovary.

Johann Wolfgang Goethe: German author of the late eighteenth and early nineteenth centuries, most well-known for his depiction of a man, Faust (which is also the title of the work), who sells his soul to the devil, Mephistopheles.

Homer: Greek epic poet, credited with having written *The Iliad* and *The Odyssey*, which feature the main characters Achilles and Odysseus, respectively.

Victor Hugo: French nineteenth-century author, who set his works in Paris and wrote *The Hunchback of Notre Dame*, among other works.

James Joyce: Irish twentieth-century author who wrote *Ulysses*, *Dubliners*, and *Finnegan's Wake*, among other works.

John Keats: English lyric poet from the early 1800s most well-known for his odes, which include "Ode to a Grecian Urn," and "Ode to a Nightingale."

Herman Melville: American nineteenth-century author who wrote *Moby-Dick*, which concerns the one-legged, mad Captain Ahab, who searches for a white whale named Moby Dick.

John Milton: English poet of the seventeenth century who wrote *Paradise Lost*.

Vladimir Nabokov: Russian-born American novelist, whose most well-known work is *Lolita*, featuring the main characters Lolita and Humbert Humbert.

Charles Dickens

Emily Dickinson

Keats

George Orwell: English author of the twentieth century who wrote the ominous *1984* and *Animal Farm*.

Ovid: Roman poet, author of the "Metamorphoses."

Pindar: Greek lyric poet of the fourth century B.C.

Luigi Pirandello: Italian author who wrote the play *Six Characters in Search of an Author*.

Plautus: Roman playwright of the second century B.C.

Plutarch: Greek biographer and philosopher.

Edgar Allan Poe: American poet and short story writer who specialized in tales of the macabre. Some of his more famous poems and stories include "The Raven" and "The Fall of the House of Usher."

Marcel Proust: French novelist of the late nineteenth and early twentieth centuries, most famous for his multi-volume novel *A la Recherche des Temps Perdu* or *Remembrance of Things Past*.

Sappho: Greek poet of the seventh century B.C.; a woman who primarily wrote lesbian love poems.

William Shakespeare: Remember him? Most of what you need to know is the titles of some of his works: *Romeo and Juliet, Macbeth, Hamlet, King Lear, Merchant of Venice, A Midsummer Night's Dream, The Tempest*—though it would be helpful to know the characters in some of them too.

Sophocles: Greek playwright of the fifth century B.C.

Edmund Spenser: English poet of the sixteenth and seventeenth centuries, most well-known for having written *The Faerie Queen*.

Jonathan Swift: English satirist of the sixteenth and seventeenth centuries, the author of *Gulliver's Travels*, which is set in the fictional land of Lilliput, as well as other imaginary places.

Henry David Thoreau: American essayist who wrote *Walden*.

Leo Tolstoy: Russian novelist who wrote *Anna Karenina* and *War and Peace*.

Anthony Trollope: English novelist of the nineteenth century.

Mark Twain: Pen name of the American author and humorist Samuel Langhorne Clemens, who wrote *Tom Sawyer* and *Huckleberry Finn*.

Vergil (also spelled **Virgil**): Roman epic poet who wrote *The Aeneid*, which features the main character Aeneus.

Francois Voltaire: French author whose novel *Candide* is about a young innocent.

Edith Wharton: American novelist of the late nineteenth and early twentieth centuries.

Walt Whitman: American poet, whose most famous work is *Leaves of Grass*.

Virginia Woolf: English novelist of the late nineteenth and early twentieth centuries, who wrote *The Waves, To the Lighthouse*, and *Mrs. Dalloway*.

William "the bard" Shakespeare

Voltaire

William Butler Yeats: Irish poet of the late nineteenth and early twentieth centuries.

Emile Zola: French novelist of the nineteenth century.

VISUAL ARTISTS

Hieronymus Bosch: Dutch painter of the late fifteenth and early sixteenth centuries. He painted many scenes of strange distorted monsters in his most famous work, *The Garden of Earthly Delights*.

Sandro Botticelli: Italian painter of the fifteenth century. One of his most well-known works is *The Birth of Venus*, which depicts Venus coming from the waves of the ocean on a half-shell.

Peter Breughel: Sixteenth-century Flemish painter.

Alexander Calder: American sculptor of the twentieth century who was widely known for his mobiles. (A mobile is a hanging sculpture.)

Michelangelo de Caravaggio: Not to be confused with *the* Michelangelo, Caravaggio was a sixteenth-century Italian painter known for his dramatic lighting effects.

Mary Cassatt: American late-nineteenth- and early-twentieth-century painter.

Paul Cezanne: A French painter of the late nineteenth and early twentieth centuries.

Marc Chagall: A Russian painter of the twentieth century, famous for his stained glass and his Jewish themes.

John Constable: English landscape painter from the late eighteenth and early nineteenth centuries.

Leonardo da Vinci: Italian painter, sculptor, scientist, and inventor of the fifteenth and early sixteenth centuries who painted the *Mona Lisa* and *The Last Supper*, among other famous works.

Edgar Degas: French nineteenth-century artist, known for his paintings of the ballet.

Andrea del Sarto: Italian painter of the sixteenth century.

Donatello: Italian sculptor of the fifteenth century.

Albrecht Durer: German engraver and painter of the late fifteenth and early sixteenth centuries.

Fra Angelico: Late-fourteenth- and early-fifteenth-century Italian painter.

Thomas Gainsborough: English eighteenth-century painter.

Paul Gaugin: Nineteenth-century French painter famed for his paintings of women in Tahiti.

Giotto: Italian painter and sculptor of the thirteenth and fourteenth centuries.

Francisco Goya: Spanish painter of the eighteenth and nineteenth centuries.

Walt Whitman

The Mona Lisa by Leonardo da Vinci

El Greco: Greek-born Spanish painter of the late sixteenth and early seventeenth centuries, known for his long distorted paintings of Spain, most notably *View of Toledo*. (That's Toledo, Spain, not Toledo, Ohio.)

Edouard Manet: Not to be confused with Monet, Manet was a nineteenth-century French painter.

Henri Matisse: French painter of the late nineteenth and early twentieth centuries.

Michelangelo: His full name, Michelangelo Buonarroti, is almost never used. He was an Italian sculptor and painter of the late fifteenth and early sixteenth centuries; his important works are the sculpture *David*, and the fresco on the ceiling of the Sistine Chapel in the Vatican in Rome, Italy.

Claude Monet: French painter of the late nineteenth and early twentieth centuries who painted in the Impressionist style; he produced many famous paintings of water lilies.

I. M. Pei

I. M. Pei: Architect of the twentieth century who rebuilt the entrance to the Louvre.

Pablo Picasso: Spanish painter and sculptor of the twentieth century who helped introduce cubism.

Camille Pissaro: French painter who worked in the pointillist style (lots of little dots).

Jackson Pollock: Twentieth-century American artist who specialized in the splatter technique for his abstract art.

Rembrandt: Dutch painter of the seventeenth century who produced mostly portraits.

Pierre Renoir: Nineteenth to twentieth-century French painter

Auguste Rodin: French sculptor of the nineteenth and early twentieth centuries.

Sir Christopher Wren

Peter Paul Rubens: A Flemish painter of the sixteenth and seventeenth centuries, noted for painting full-figured women and men.

George Seurat: Nineteenth-century French painter who introduced and popularized the pointillist style.

Titian: Italian painter who used a certain red so much the color became called "Titian."

Vincent van Gogh: Dutch painter who painted many scenes in Arles, a town in the south of France.

Diego Velazquez (or **Velasquez**): Spanish painter of the seventeenth century.

Sir Christopher Wren: English architect of the seventeenth and eighteenth centuries.

Frank Lloyd Wright

Frank Lloyd Wright: American architect of the late nineteenth and early twentieth centuries.

PLACES OF ART

Where can you find specific pieces of art? The MAT writers want you to know, possibly with the hopes that you will take them there. It seems likely that they don't get out much. In any case, the following information regarding location may be helpful to you.

Rembrandt

British Museum: Art museum in London, England.

Frick Collection: Art museum in New York City.

Guggenheim: Modern art museum in New York City.

La Scala: Opera house in Milan, Italy.

Louvre: Art museum in Paris, France.

The Met: The Metropolitan Museum of Art, located in New York City.

MOMA: The Museum of Modern Art—an art museum in New York City.

National Gallery: Art museum in London, England.

National Gallery of Art: Art museum in Washington, D.C.

Prado: Art museum in Madrid, Spain.

Tate Gallery: Art museum in London, England.

Victoria and Albert Museum: Art museum in London, England.

The Whitney: Another art museum in New York City.

THE PLACES OF PIECES OF ART

Sometimes the MAT people want to know the names of particular works of art, as well as where that art can be found. So, forewarned, forearmed!

David: Famous sculpture by Michelangelo, in Florence, Italy.

Creation of Adam: Part of a famous fresco (painting on a plaster wall or ceiling) by Michelangelo, on the ceiling of the Sistine Chapel in the Vatican in Rome, Italy.

Birth of Venus: A painting by Botticelli depicting—guess what?—the birth of the goddess Venus.

Mona Lisa: Portrait of woman of the same name, by Leonardo da Vinci, in the Louvre, in Paris.

The Kiss and *The Thinker:* Both sculptures by Rodin, located in Paris.

Venus de Milo: An armless statue of Venus at the Louvre in Paris.

Winged Victory: A headless statue of Victory, a woman, at the Louvre in Paris.

The Last Supper: Painting of Christ's last supper by Leonardo da Vinci, a fresco in Milan, Italy.

Assorted Other Cultural Figures

Aristotle: A Greek philosopher of the fourth century B.C.

René Descartes: French philosopher most famous for his argument, "Cogito ergo sum," which is Latin for "I think, therefore I am."

Vaslav Nijinsky: Russian ballet dancer of the early twentieth century.

Anna Pavlova: Russian ballerina of the early twentieth century.

Plato: Greek philosopher of the fourth century B.C.

Anna Pavlova

MUSIC

The writers of the MAT are also interested in music, but it is almost always (surprise, surprise) music that is unfamiliar to many people, such as opera and classical. Musical terms are also worked into the mix.

MUSICIANS

Enrico Caruso: An Italian opera singer, and one of the most famous tenors of the late nineteenth and early twentieth centuries.

Frederic Chopin: Polish composer of classical music during the late nineteenth century.

Claude Debussy: French composer of classical music of the late nineteenth and early twentieth centuries.

Wolfgang Amadeus Mozart: Eighteenth-century Austrian composer who wrote *The Marriage of Figaro* and other well-known operas, as well as various symphonies.

Stravinsky

Sergei Prokofiev: Russian composer of the twentieth century.

Giacomo Puccini: Italian composer, particularly of operas such as *Madame Butterfly*.

Igor Stravinsky: Russian-born composer of the twentieth century, who wrote the scores of many ballets.

Peter Tchaikovsky: Nineteenth-century Russian composer who wrote the scores for several ballets, most notably *Swan Lake* and *The Nutcracker*.

Ludwig van Beethoven: A German composer of the late eighteenth and early nineteenth centuries.

Antonio Vivaldi: Eighteenth-century Italian composer.

Richard Wagner: Nineteenth-century German composer.

THE TERMS

Two to know before the others will make sense:

Tempo: Pace or speed at which music is played.

Tone: The quality of a sound.

Tchaikovsky

Adagio: A slow or leisurely tempo.

Allegretto: Somewhat fast tempo.

Allegro: Fast tempo.

Andante: Somewhat slow tempo.

Aria: A long song for a solo voice within an opera.

Chromatic Scale: A consecutive arrangement of all twelve pitches (all the notes full, sharp, and flat) within an octave.

Consonance: The feeling of stability produced by certain chords or tones.

Crescendo: A tone becoming gradually louder.

Diminuendo (also **Decrescendo**): A tone becoming gradually softer.

Dissonance: The feeling of instability produced by certain chords or tones.

Forte: Loud tone.

Forte-piano: Loud followed by soft tone.

Fortissimo: Very loud tone.

Grave: Extremely slow and solemn tempo.

Largo: Extremely slow and broad tempo.

Lento: Slow tempo.

Libretto: The written text or words of an opera.

Mezzo-forte: Moderately loud tone.

Mezzo-piano: Moderately soft tone.

Moderato: Moderate tempo.

Octave: A scale interval that encompasses eight pitches or full notes.

Period: A musical form made up of two smaller parts termed the "question" and "answer."

Pianissimo: Very soft tone.

Piano: Soft tone.

Prestissimo: Extremely fast tempo.

Presto: Very fast tempo.

Sforzano (also **Sforzato**): Sudden accent on a single tone or chord.

Timbre: The quality of a musical tone that enables a person to distinguish one tone from another.

Vivace: Brisk and lively tempo.

Vivaldi

Tempi (that's the plural of tempo): moderato, prestissimo, presto, vivace, largo, lento, grace, andante, allegretto, adagio

Do the people who write the MAT care about the subtle analyses of the various trends that have brought us to where we are today as a society? Of course not.

CHAPTER 10 QUIZ

Try the following analogies. and test your grasp of this superficial review!

1. RODIN : (*a.* sculptor, *b.* architect, *c.* portraitist, *d.* novelist) ::
   MATISSE : PAINTER

2. (*a.* Candide, *b.* Jane, *c.* Emile, *d.* Charlotte) : EMMA ::
   VOLTAIRE : AUSTEN

3. (*a.* Hester, *b.* Ahab, *c.* Melville, *d.* Scarlet) : HAWTHORNE ::
   RASKALNIKOV : DOSTOEVSKY

4. TCHAIKOVSKY : PUCCINI :: (*a.* opera, *b.* aria, *c.* fugue, *d.* ballet)
   : OPERA

5. (*a.* Moby-Dick, *b.* Hawthorne, *c.* Melville, *d.* Ishmael) :
   AHAB :: FLAUBERT : EMMA

6. WONDERLAND : (*a.* Mann, *b.* Spenser, *c.* Carroll, *d.* Lewis) ::
   NOTRE DAME : HUGO

7. TEMPO : (*a.* tone, *b.* tempo, *c.* loudness, *d.* pitch) ::
   PRESTISSIMO : VIVACE

8. THE LAST SUPPER : (*a.* David, *b.* Sistine chapel, *c.* Pieta,
   d. Mona Lisa) :: DA VINCI : MICHELANGELO

9. TATE : FRICK :: (*a.* London, *b.* Dublin, *c.* Marseilles,
   d. Madrid) : NEW YORK

10. ITALY : VIVALDI :: (*a.* Austria, *b.* Germany, *c.* Poland,
    d. Russia) : WAGNER

11. PROKOFIEV : STRAVINSKY :: SERGEI : (*a.* Otto, *b.* Ivan, *c.* Igor,
    d. Peter)

12. LILLIPUT : (*a.* Swift, *b.* Dickens, *c.* Donne, *d.* Shakespeare) ::
    YOKNAPATAWPHA : FAULKNER

13. MATISSE : PAINTER :: (*a.* Michelangelo, *b.* da Vinci, *c.* Rodin,
    d. Moore) : SCULPTOR

14. EL GRECO : BOSCH :: (*a.* Greek, *b.* French, *c.* Spanish,
    d. German) : DUTCH

15. VAN GOGH : REMBRANDT :: (*a.* Picasso, *b.* Renoir, *c.* Vincent,
    d. Jans) : VELASQUEZ

16. FIREBIRD : STRAVINSKY :: (*a*. Swan Lake, *b*. the Nutcracker, *c*. the Red Shoes, *d*. the Spirit of the Rose) : TCHAIKOVSKY

17. MELVILLE : (*a*. Poe, *b*. Whitman, *c*. Hawthorne, *d*. Dickinson) :: WORDSWORTH : COLERIDGE

18. DICKINSON : (*a*. Don Juan, *b*. Eliot, *c*. Emerson, *d*. Sade) :: CASANOVA : SAND

19. WATER LILIES : SUNFLOWERS :: (*a*. Manet, *b*. Monet, *c*. flowers, *d*. van Eyck) : VAN GOGH

20. (*a*. Keats, *b*. Yeats, *c*. Vergil, *d*. Dickinson) : WHITMAN :: WOOLF : WHARTON

CHAPTER 10 QUIZ ANSWERS

1. (*a*) Matisse was a painter, and Rodin was a sculptor.

2. (*a*) Jane Austen wrote the novel *Emma*, and Voltaire wrote the novel *Candide*.

3. (*a*) Raskalnikov is the main character in one of Dostoevsky's novels, and Hester is the main character in one of Hawthorne's novels.

4. (*d*) Puccini is known for his scores for the opera, and Tchaikovsky is known for his scores for the ballet.

5. (*c*) Emma is the first name of a character in a book by Flaubert (*Madame Bovary*), and Ahab is the first name of a character in a book by Melville (*Moby-Dick*).

6. (*c*) Notre Dame is the setting of one of Hugo's famous novels (*The Hunchback of Notre Dame*) and Wonderland is the setting of Carroll's famous novels (*Alice in Wonderland* and *Through the Looking Glass*).

7. (*b*) Prestissimo is an example of a tempo, and so is vivace.

8. (*b*) *The Last Supper* is one of da Vinci's famous frescoes, and the Sistine Chapel is one of Michelangelo's famous frescoes.

9. (*a*) The Frick is a museum in New York, and the Tate is a museum in London.

10. (*b*) Vivaldi was a composer from Italy, and Wagner was a composer from Germany.

11. (*c*) Sergei is the composer Prokofiev's first name, and Igor is Stravinsky's first name.

12. (*a*) Yoknapatawpha is a fictional area created by Faulkner for his fiction, and Lilliput serves the same purpose in Swift's fiction (*Gulliver's Travels*).

13. (*c*) Matisse was a French painter, and Rodin was a French sculptor. The others were often sculptors as well; they just weren't French.

14. (*c*) Bosch was a Dutch painter, and El Greco was a Spanish one.

15. (*a*) Rembrandt and Van Gogh were both Dutch painters, and Velasquez and Picasso were both Spanish painters.

16 (*a*) Careful, this is tricky. Stravinsky wrote the score for the ballet about birds, *The Firebird*, and Tchaikovsky wrote the score for *Swan Lake*, another ballet about birds. Tchaikovsky also wrote the score for the Nutcracker, but there are no birds in its title.

17. (*c*) Wordsworth and Coleridge were both English poets, Melville and Hawthorne were both American novelists. Poe was also an American fiction writer, but not a novelist.

18. (*b*) Casanova and Sand are both memoirists, and Dickinson and Eliot (T.S.) are both poets.

19. (*b*) Van Gogh is noted for his paintings of sunflowers, and Monet is noted for his paintings of water lilies.

20. (*a*) Wharton and Whitman were both American writers, and Woolf and Keats were both English writers (Yeats was Irish).

11

History, Religion, Mythology, and Geography

The writers of the MAT want you to have exactly that grasp on history, religion and geography that is most useless: a superficial memorization of names. It's unfortunate, but again, we can say this a million times and it still won't be enough: Confine your study to what you need to make a specific sentence in an MAT pair, and you will improve your score.

GENERALS, POLITICIANS, AND OTHER HISTORICAL PERSONAGES

Do the people who write the MAT care about subtle analyses of the various trends that have brought us to where we are today as a society? Of course not. All they want is for you to recognize names of, mostly, dead people and the various events they are associated with.

Spiro Agnew: Vice President under President Nixon from 1969 to 1973, when Agnew resigned; he was Vice President during the Vietnam War.

Alexander the Great: King of Macedonia, conqueror of Greece and Persia, 356-323 B.C.

Ethan Allen: A soldier of the American Revolution.

Allies: The nations that came together to fight the Germans and other Axis countries in World War II; the term mainly refers to France, England, and the U.S., though later the Soviet Union joined in.

Idi Amin: Dictator of Uganda, deposed in 1979.

Benedict Arnold: The famous traitor of the American Revolutionary war—he betrayed George Washington and the American side.

Axis: The nations opposed to the allies (see above) in World War II, a group comprised mainly of Germany, Italy and Japan.

Napoleon Bonaparte: No, not the pastry this time—the famous French general and emperor who was ignominiously defeated in the battle of Waterloo, and who was subsequently exiled.

John Wilkes Booth: Assassin of President Abraham Lincoln.

Brutus: Roman military leader who betrayed Julius Caesar.

Julius Caesar: Roman statesman and general.

Caligula: Roman emperor, famous for his depravity.

Charlemagne: King of the Franks (that's the old-time French to you) in the eighth and ninth centuries.

Chiang Kai-shek: Chinese political and military leader.

Winston Churchill: Prime Minister of Britain during World War II.

El Cid: Spanish military leader and hero of the eleventh century.

Claudius: Long-ago Roman emperor.

Benedict Arnold

Cleopatra: Long-ago Queen of Egypt.

Cochise: Apache Indian leader.

Hernando Cortés: Spanish explorer who conquered the Aztecs.

Crazy Horse: Sioux Indian leader.

Croesus: Famously rich King of Lydia.

George Armstrong Custer: General of the Union Army during the American Civil War, known for his ignominious defeat at the hands of Sitting Bull's forces at the Battle of Little Bighorn.

Jefferson Davis: President of the Confederacy during the American Civil War.

Charles de Gaulle: French general and statesman, after whom a French national airport is named.

Hernando de Soto: Spanish explorer.

Alexis de Tocqueville: French author and statesman who wrote *Democracy in America*.

Frederick Douglass: American abolitionist.

Amelia Earhart: American female aviator.

Dwight D. Eisenhower: American president and general, known as "Ike."

Francis Ferdinand: The archduke of Austria whose assassination helped precipitate the beginning of World War I.

Francisco Franco: Spanish dictator and general from the Spanish civil war, in the 1930s, until his death in 1975.

Mohandas Gandhi (also called "**Mahatma**"): Political and spiritual leader of India who helped India separate from British rule through nonviolent means.

Giuseppe Garibaldi: Italian general and patriot.

Genghis Khan: Mongol warrior.

Geronimo: Apache Indian leader.

Ulysses S. Grant: U.S. president and general of the Union army in the U.S. Civil War.

Haile Selassie: Deposed emperor of Ethiopia.

Nathan Hale: American soldier, hung by the British for spying.

Alexander Hamilton: First head of the U.S. Treasury, his face is on the twenty dollar bill.

Adolph Hitler: Leader of Germany before and during World War II, head of the Nazi party.

Hirohito: Royal family of Japan, also emperor of Japan during World War II.

Ho Chi Minh: Vietnamese communist leader during the Vietnam war.

Amelia Earhart

Gandhi

Ulysses S. Grant

Andrew Jackson: American president known as (no kidding) "Old Hickory."

Thomas Jackson: A general of the confederate army, also known as "Stonewall."

John Fitzgerald Kennedy: American President assassinated by Lee Harvey Oswald.

Robert E. Lee: Confederate general in the U.S. Civil War; he surrendered to Union general Ulysses S. Grant at Appomattox.

Liliuokalani: Queen of Hawaii deposed by the U.S. government.

Abraham Lincoln: American president during the Civil War, assassinated by John Wilkes Booth.

Mao Tse-tung: Chinese communist leader.

William McKinley: Yet another American president who was assassinated.

Montezuma: Last Aztec emperor of Mexico.

Benito Mussolini: Fascist dictator of Italy before and during World War II, also known as "Il Duce."

Nebuchadnezzar: King of Babylon.

Richard Milhous Nixon: Former U.S. president who resigned during his second term as president due to the Watergate scandal. He was responsible for pulling U.S. troops out of the Vietnam War.

Ponce de Leon: Spanish explorer who searched for the fountain of youth.

Pontiac: A chief of the Ottawa Indians.

William Sherman: Union general in the U.S. Civil War.

Sitting Bull: A leader of the Dakota Indians.

Joseph Stalin: Communist leader of the Soviet Union, known for party purges and violent acts.

Leon Trotsky: Russian communist revolutionary, who was assassinated.

Otto von Bismarck: The German empire's first chancellor.

Xerxes: King of Persia.

DOCUMENTS

Bill of Rights: The ten amendments added to the Constitution in 1791.

Constitution: The basic law of the United States, drafted in 1787 in Philadelphia, and ratified in 1789.

Declaration of Independence: A document proclaiming the thirteen American colonies' independence from Great Britain, written by Thomas Jefferson in 1776.

Emancipation Proclamation: An amendment to the Constitution drafted by then-President Abraham Lincoln during the Civil War. It is amendment thirteen of the Constitution.

Mao Tse-tung

Sitting Bull

Gettysburg Address: A speech written and delivered by President Abraham Lincoln in honor of the war dead at the Battle of Gettysburg.

Magna Carta: The document specifying English political and civil liberties in 1215, written in Runnymede, England.

Eighteenth Amendment: The amendment to the Constitution that enforced prohibition of liquor.

Nineteenth Amendment: The amendment to the Constitution approved in 1919 granting women the right to vote.

PLACES/BATTLE SITES

Alamo: Site of a huge defeat of the rebelling Texan settlers by the Mexicans.

Appomattox: Town in Virginia where Confederate general Robert E. Lee surrendered to Union general Ulysses S. Grant, bringing the Civil War to an end.

Bull Run: The first battle of the American Civil war.

Bunker Hill: Important battle in the American Revolutionary War; the Americans lost.

Concord: Where the American revolutionaries fired "the shot heard round the world" that precipitated the Revolutionary war.

Waterloo: The site of Napoleon's greatest defeat.

Civil War battles:
Appomattox, Bull Run

Revolutionary War battles:
Bunker Hill, Concord

RELIGION AND MYTHOLOGY

Much as with other important subjects, religions and their histories are given short and shallow shrift on the MAT. Again we have to beg your pardon for writing the following embarrassingly superficial outline of major religions and their important personages, and again we implore you to avoid getting caught up in trying to learn more than you need to know for the MAT. Of course, you should always learn more than you need to know in life as a whole, but here and now, as you prepare for your test, is neither the correct time nor place to do so.

THE BOOKS

Bhagavad Gita: Sacred book of Hinduism.

Bible: The holy book of Judeo-Christian religions, though these vary depending on what sections of the Bible are mentioned.

Koran: The holy book of Islam.

Tao te Ching: A book containing the sacred teachings of Taoism (sometimes called Daoism), a Chinese religious philosophy.

Torah: The sacred books of Judaism, contained within the Bible.

The Gods and the People

Abel: Son of Adam and Eve (the first people, according to the Bible), killed by his brother Cain.

Abraham: Patriarch of the Jews.

Allah: God of Islam.

Aquinas: Italian saint and philosopher.

Buddha: Indian philosopher and founder of Buddhism.

Confucious: Chinese philosopher and teacher, founder of Confucianism.

Jesus: Son of God in Christian religion.

Judas: Betrayer of Jesus.

Mohammed: Muslim prophet and founder of Islam.

Shiva: Hindu god of destruction.

Vishnu: Hindu god of order.

Buddha

Mythology—Greek and Roman

You may remember back in about ninth grade or so learning about all the different Greek and Roman gods and the strange stories of their births and reigns. And you probably thought, "This stuff is pretty cool, too bad I'll have no earthly use for it ever again." Well, here's your chance to test your memory and refresh it, if need be.

The following covers Greek mythology, and the Roman names for the same basic gods. One helpful point to remember is that generally, names of the Roman gods are also the names of planets.

The Roman Gods are the ones with the names of the planets.

Titans: These are the elder gods, the big, major, important gods, the most important of whom was **Cronus**, who was the father of Zeus, Hera, and Poseidon. Other Titans were **Ocean**, the god of guess what (that's right, the oceans), and **Hyperion**, the father of the Sun, the Moon, and Dawn.

Olympians: These were the next generation of gods after the Titans. They lived on Mount Olympus (hence the term Olympians) and were more or less headed by Zeus.

Zeus: Roman name Jupiter. He was the head of the Olympians and had sex with just about everything in the world. He used thunderbolts to get the world's and the gods' attention when necessary.

Poseidon: Roman name Neptune. Zeus's brother, he ruled the oceans and carried a three-pronged, pitchfork-type instrument called a trident.

Hades: Roman name Pluto. He ruled the underworld and married Persephone (also known as Proserpine), who represented Spring.

Hestia: Roman name Vesta. She was pretty much of a big zero as far as gods go, and wasn't known for anything in particular.

Neptune

Hera: Roman name Juno. She was Zeus's wife and sister (charming, right?) and she was viewed as a protector.

Ares: Roman name Mars. He was the god of war, and the son of Zeus and Hera.

Athena or **Pallas Athena:** Roman name Minerva. She is famous for having sprung fully formed from Zeus's head rather than having been born the old-fashioned way. Athena was the goddess of wisdom, reason, and purity.

Apollo: He didn't have a Roman name. Another son of Zeus, his name meant brilliance and it is this he was known for, as well as for beauty.

Aphrodite: Roman name Venus. She was also the child of Zeus, and was the goddess of beauty and romantic love.

Hermes: Roman name Mercury. The child of Zeus (who wasn't?) and the god of speed, he was associated with a winged helmet. The FTD florists' trademark was modeled after him, though that probably won't be on the MAT.

Artemis: Roman name Diana. Another one of Zeus' many offspring, she was the goddess of wild things and the hunt. She was often depicted with a quiver full of arrows.

Hephaestus: Roman name Vulcan. He was Hera's child only, and was the only one of the gods who was noted for being ugly and lame. He controlled fire and was often depicted working a forge.

Separate from the Olympians were the earth gods.

Demeter: Mother of Persephone (from above, the one who married Hades) and the goddess of the earth.

Dionysus: Roman name Bacchus. God of the vine and all things debauched.

Nike: Goddess of victory.

Pan: Roman name Faunus. God of shepherds, above the waist he was a man and below the waist he was a goat. He was also known to play a flute-like instrument called a pipe.

Pan

MYTHICAL CREATURES

Centaurs: Half man, half horse.

Druids or **Dryads:** Tree nymphs.

Gorgons: Three monsters, one of whom was Medusa, who had snakes for hair. Her victims turned to stone when they looked at her face.

Griffin: A violent beast with the body of a lion and the face and wings of an eagle.

Harpies: With women's faces and the bodies of birds, they were creatures known for being unpleasant.

Minotaur: A fierce monster with the body of a man and the head of a bull.

Naiads: Water nymphs.

Phoenix: A mythical bird that could recreate itself out of its own ashes.

Satyrs: Like Pan, these beings were goats below the waist and men above it.

Unicorn: A beautiful mythical beast shown as a horse or goat with a single spiraling horn growing from the center of its forehead.

unicorn

GEOGRAPHY

For reasons that they choose to keep undisclosed, the people who write the MAT are interested in geography only as far as it extends to places that have changed their names. This is probably related to naming issues buried deep among their childhood traumas, but whatever the cause, the following name changes are ones you should be aware of. We have organized the section so the current names are in bold, and the former or alternate names are with the explanations to the right, in plain text.

Biafra: Former republic located in Nigeria, West Africa.

Botswana: Formerly Bechuanaland.

Cambodia: OK, this one is tricky. First the country was called Cambodia, then it changed its name to the Khmer Republic, then to People's Republic of Kampuchea, and then back to Cambodia.

Cape Canaveral: Present and previous name of the cape that was once also called Cape Kennedy for ten years following the assassination of President John F. Kennedy.

Formosa: Alternative name for Taiwan.

Friendly Islands: Alternative name for Tonga.

Germany: Formerly (or formerly made up of the principle state of) Prussia.

Ghana: Formerly the Gold Coast.

Hawaii: Formerly the Sandwich Islands.

Ho Chi Minh City: Formerly Saigon.

Iran: Formerly Persia.

Israel: Formerly Canaan or Palestine.

Kinshasa: Formerly Leopoldville, in Zaire.

Malawi: Formerly Nyasaland.

Romania: Formerly Dacia.

Sri Lanka: Formerly Ceylon.

St. Petersburg: OK, here's another tricky one. First this Russian city was called St. Petersburg, then it was called Petrograd, then it changed its name to Leningrad, and for the present it is back to St. Petersburg.

Tanzania: Formerly Tanganyika.

Thailand: Formerly Siam.

Tokyo: Formerly Edo.

Ulster: Alternative name for Northern Ireland.

Vanuata: Formerly New Hebrides.

Zimbabwe: Formerly Rhodesia.

CHAPTER 11 QUIZ

Want to see how you do on a few questions of this type?

1. WATERLOO : APPOMATTOX :: NAPOLEON : (*a.* Eisenhower, *b.* Lee, *c.* Grant, *d.* Lincoln)

2. TIMOTHY : (*a.* Hebrews, *b.* Tim, *c.* Mark, *d.* Kings) :: NEW TESTAMENT : OLD TESTAMENT

3. OLD HICKORY : (*a.* Lincoln, *b.* Tyler, *c.* Jackson, *d.* Washington) :: MAHATMA : GANDHI

4. SIAM : THAILAND :: (*a.* Palestine, *b.* Arab, *c.* Semite, *d.* Lebanon) : ISRAEL

5. ABRAHAM : NOAH :: GENESIS : (*a.* Genesis, *b.* Exodus, *c.* Leviticus, *d.* Deuteronomy)

6. LINDBERGH : EARHART :: XERXES : (*a.* Attila, *b.* Liliuokalani, *c.* Charlemagne, *d.* Nebuchadnezzar)

7. LAOTSZE : TAOISM :: KORAN : (*a.* Judaism, *b.* Hinduism, *c.* Buddhism, *d.* Islam)

8. DWIGHT : (*a.* Mahatma, *b.* Mohandas, *c.* raji, *d.* Ike) :: EISENHOWER : GANDHI

9. CEYLON : DACIA :: SRI LANKA : (*a.* Romania, *b.* Yugoslavia, *c.* Czechoslovakia, *d.* Bulgaria)

10. COCHISE : (*a.* Michigan, *b.* Dakota, *c.* Apache, *d.* Sioux) :: PONTIAC : OTTOWA

11. (*a.* Ferdinand, *b.* Franco, *c.* Guevera, *d.* Garibaldi) : DE LEON :: EL CID : DE SOTO

12. CONFEDERACY : (*a.* Grant, *b.* Sherman, *c.* Lee, *d.* Davis) :: UNION : LINCOLN

13. PLUTO : (*a.* Jupiter, *b.* Hades, *c.* Vesta, *d.* Diana) :: JUNO : HERA

14. BRUTUS : CAESAR :: ARNOLD : (*a.* Nero, *b.* Lincoln, *c.* Washington, *d.* Franklin)

15. SANTIAGO : SIENA :: CHILE : (*a.* Spain, *b.* France, *c.* Italy, *d.* Portugal)

16. (a. Ruby, b. Oswald, c. Kesey, d. Ness) : KENNEDY :: BOOTH : LINCOLN

17. WORLD WAR I : TREATY OF VERSAILLES :: REVOLUTIONARY WAR : (a. Bunker Hill, b. Constitution, c. Treaty of Delaware, d. Treaty of Paris)

18. (a. Japan, b. Moscow, c. Osaka, d. Edo) : TOKYO :: PETROGRAD : SAINT PETERSBURG

19. SAIGON : PETROGRAD :: (a. Ho Chi Minh city, b. Moscow, c. Vietnam, d. Southeast Asia) : ST. PETERSBURG

20. AZTEC : MONTEZUMA :: (a. Apache, b. Sioux, c. Maya, d. Mexico) : COCHISE

CHAPTER 11 QUIZ ANSWERS

1. (b) Napoleon's defining loss in battle was at Waterloo, and Lee's was at Appomattox (he lost to Grant).

2. (d) Timothy is a book in the New Testament, and Kings is a book in the Old Testament.

3. (c) Mahatma was Gandhi's nickname, and Old Hickory was Jackson's nickname.

4. (a) The land that is now called Thailand was once known as Siam, and the land that is now called Israel was once called Palestine.

5. (a) The story of Abraham is in the Bible in the book of Genesis, and so is the story of Noah.

6. (b) Lindbergh and Earhart were male and female pilots respectively; Xerxes and Liliuokalani were male and female rulers respectively.

7. (d) The Laotsze is the sacred book of Taoism, and the Koran is the sacred book of Islam

8. (b) Eisenhower's first name was Dwight and Gandhi's first name was Mohandas. (Mahatma was his nickname.)

9. (a) Ceylon is the former name of Sri Lanka, and Dacia is the former name of Romania.

10. (c) Pontiac was an Ottowa chief, and Cochise was an Apache chief.

11. (b) De Soto and de Leon were both Spanish explorers, and El Cid and Franco were both Spanish warriors.

12. (d) Abraham Lincoln was President of the Union during the Civil War, and Jefferson Davis was President of the Confederacy during the Civil War.

13. (*b*) Juno is the Roman name for the goddess Hera, and Pluto is the Roman name for the god of the underworld, Hades.

14. (*c*) Brutus betrayed Caesar, and Benedict Arnold betrayed Washington.

15. (*c*) Santiago is a city in Chile, and Siena is a city in Italy.

16. (*b*) Booth assassinated Lincoln, and Oswald assassinated Kennedy.

17. (*d*) The Treaty of Versailles ended World War I, and the Treaty of Paris ended the Revolutionary War.

18. (*d*) St. Petersburg was formerly called Petrograd, and Tokyo was formerly called Edo.

19. (*a*) What was once Petrograd is now St. Petersburg, and what was once Saigon is now Ho Chi Minh City.

20. (*a*) Montezuma was an Aztec ruler, and Cochise was an Apache ruler.

12

Sciences

THE SCIENCES

First of all DON'T PANIC! You do not actually have to know or understand any science to do well on this test, which is actually rather unfortunate, as it is not as daunting or difficult as many people seem to feel. But, whether you are comfortable with science or not, all you have to know to do well on the MAT are some basic terms and definitions.

CLASSIFICATION SYSTEMS

Biology generally classifies living matter; this process of classification is called **taxonomy**. The following classification system goes from the largest groups, the Kingdoms, to the smallest subgroups of those, called the Species.

Kingdom
Phylum
Subphylum
Class
Order
Family
Genus
Species

For instance, for us humans (which we assume includes most of you reading this book), we belong to the animal kingdom also known as Animalia, the phylum Chordata (that means we have hollow nerves and such), the subphylum Vertebrata, the class Mammalia, the order of Primates, the family Hominadae, the genus Homo and the species Homo sapiens. This particular information about humans isn't necessary, but it can help you understand what classification, or taxonomy, is.

Smaller groups of classification you may need to know are those divisions among the mammals. There are three major subgroups among the class of mammals:

Protheria or **Monotremes:** These are alternate names for the same things, strange mammals that reproduce by laying eggs, for example the duckbilled platypus or the anteater.

Metatheria or **Marsupials:** Again, these are alternate names for the same things, and you are probably already familiar with the subclass, most of whose members live in Australia (kangaroos, koala bears et al). What you might not know (nor want to know, but oh well) is that what makes them marsupials is that the young aren't born with placenta, thus the adults have pouches in which to nourish their young.

Some Marsupials: the kangaroo, koala bear, opossum

Eutheria or **Placental Mammals:** This subclass includes the animals you are used to thinking of as mammals, meaning they bear their young live and with placenta. This subclass includes dogs, bats (really!), and people.

BLOOD AND GUTS

Yes, you do need to know a little of the gross stuff, but only the barest bones (sorry) of how they function.

Aorta: The main section responsible for transporting oxygenated blood to most of the body's organs.

Arteries: The tubes that carry blood away from the heart; the carotid arteries are major arteries for example, and they carry blood to the head from the neck.

Atria: The chambers of the heart that receive blood, made up of the two auricles.

Auricle or **Atrium:** One of the two chambers that make up the atria.

Veins: The tubes that carry blood to the heart, the most major of which is the jugular vein, in your neck.

Ventricles: The chambers of the heart that pump blood out to the rest of the body.

BONES

Mandible: The jaw bone.

Cranium: The skull.

Ulna: An arm bone (forearm).

Radius: An arm bone (forearm).

Tibia: A leg bone (calf).

Fibula: A leg bone (calf).

Femur: A leg bone (thigh).

Scapula: Shoulder blade.

Clavicle: Collar bone.

Humerus: An arm bone (upper).

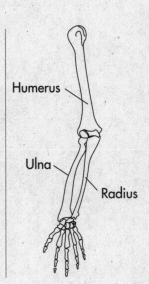

MUSCLES

Striated muscle: These muscles are the ones used for voluntary movements, like lifting; some striated muscles are the biceps, triceps, abs of steel, etc.

Smooth muscle: These are used for involuntary action such as digestion, reproduction, etc.

Cardiac muscle: Special muscle that only exists in the heart.

NERVOUS SYSTEM

Cerebrum: The major part of the brain, thought to be the source of intelligence.

Cerebellum: The big bulb of nerve tissue that forms the base of the brain.

Medulla: The part of the brain that connects it to the spinal cord.

PLANTS

If you know anything about gardening you're ahead of the game, because that seems to be the kind of thing they want to know—what kind of plants grow forever without replanting, what kind need to be resown year after year, and so on. But if you've never really gardened before, just read on and get the information here.

Annuals: Plants that live or grow for only one season such as zinnias and impatiens.

Bryophyta: Basically, this group includes all mosses.

Some Coniferous trees: Douglas Fir, Spruce, Cedar

Coniferous: Cone-bearing trees such as pine, that do not lose their leaves in winter, and usually have needles instead of leaves.

Deciduous: Trees that lose their leaves in winter, such as the oak and the maple.

Some Perennials: daisies, baby's breath, roses, daffodils

Perennials: Plants that keep blooming and do not have to be replanted, such as tulips and baby's breath.

Pistil: The female reproductive organs of plants.

Stamen: The male reproductive organs of plants.

Traceophyta or **Vascular Plants:** Plants with water-carrying systems that can live on land solo, unlike mosses. They include most flowering plants you are familiar with.

CHEMISTRY

The easiest way to deal with the following information is to look at it in groups. Remember, you will have to make workable sentences out of these words, nothing more, so if Argon and Xenon are listed, for instance, all you need to know is that they are both noble gases. Anything else is extraneous and will just end up making you more stressed out than you need to be.

ELEMENTS

Elements are the most basic building blocks of matter. The only ones you might need to know about are a few of the more common ones, as well as the letters that symbolize them.

Arsenic: As

Copper: Cu

Gold: Au

Hydrogen: H

Iron: Fe

Lead: Pb

Mercury: Hg

Potassium: K

Radium: Ra

Silver: Ag

Sodium: Na

Tin: Sn

Californium: Cf, which is a man-made element, as opposed to the others listed here that occur naturally.

COMPOUNDS

Common mixtures of elements, called compounds, that may help you are the following.

CO_2: Carbon dioxide

H_2O: Water

NaCl: Sodium chloride, better known as table salt.

ALLOTROPES

Allotropes are forms of elements in which one element combines with itself to form a compound.

O_3: Ozone

C_6: Diamond

> Allotropes are forms of elements in which one element combines with itself to form a compound. Study that vocabulary!

NOBLE GASES

A few of the elements are noble gases: that is, they can't mix with other elements so they are termed *inert*.

Argon: Ar

Helium: He

Krypton: Kr

Neon: Ne

Radon: Rn

Xenon: Xe

METALS

Most metals you are familiar with, such as silver and gold. But, chemically, there are some distinctions to be made. Silver and gold, as you saw from the elements and symbols section, are elements. That means they are among the building blocks of other matter. Many of the other substances you think of when you think of metals are **alloys**. Alloys are mixtures composed of metal elements.

Brass: An alloy of mostly copper, combined with zinc.

Bronze: An alloy of mostly copper and tin, combined with zinc.

Pewter: An alloy of mostly tin.

Steel: An alloy of mostly iron, nickel, and titanium.

THE SCIENTIST'S TOOLS

You can already guess how useful this next section is going to be if you've been studying and practicing your techniques from the earlier section of the book. Remember one of those common relationships mentioned in chapter 3? "A hoe is used for weeding," or "A farmer uses a hoe"? Well, here are a bunch more of them you didn't even know you wanted to know.

Amber: The clear yellow substance that preserved many of the earliest fossils.

Catalyst: A substance that spurs or changes the speed of a reaction without being changed itself.

Centrifuge: A machine that spins using centrifugal force to separate liquids into their parts.

Desiccant: A substance that absorbs moisture in order to dry things out.

Distillate: The liquid obtained after distilling.

Filtrate: The substance obtained after filtering.

Geiger Counter: A device to measure radioactivity.

Mole: A measure of chemical weight, related to a substance's molecular weight.

Prism: A triangular glass bar that separates light into its colored wavelengths.

CHAPTER 12 QUIZ

Why don't you flex your scientific (and voluntary) muscles on the following analogies?

1. MEDULLA : (*a.* vascular, *b.* skin, *c.* brain, *d.* muscle) :: CLAVICLE : SKELETON

2. ARM : ULNA : (*a.* wrist, *b.* spine, *c.* leg, *d.* foot) : TIBIA

3. CARAT : CALORIE :: (*a.* weight, *b.* burn, *c.* precious, *d.* diet) : HEAT

4. (*a.* reproduction, *b.* striated, *c.* quadriceps, *d.* forceps) : LIFTING :: SMOOTH : DIGESTION

5. METATHERIA : (*a.* placenta, *b.* yolk, *c.* mammals, *d.* pouches) :: PROTHERIA : EGGS

6. WATER : COMPOUND :: NEON : (*a.* element, *b.* pool, *c.* light, *d.* mixture)

7. AMBER : (*a.* wait, *b.* caution, *c.* preserve, *d.* jewel) :: CENTRIFUGE : SEPARATE

8. (*a.* panda, *b.* kangaroo, *c.* squirrel, *d.* grizzly) : KOALA :: RACCOON : BEAR

9. SKELETON : (*a.* skeletons, *b.* bones, *c.* structure, *d.* support) ::
   ATRIA : AURICLE

10. (*a.* nothing, *b.* spray, *c.* gel, *d.* explosion) : SOLID :: NEBULIZE
    : CONGEAL

11. (*a.* skull, *b.* scalp, *c.* shoulder blade, *d.* sternum) : SCAPULA ::
    COLLAR BONE : CLAVICLE

12. TIN : (*a.* lead, *b.* brass, *c.* silver, *d.* pewter) :: HYDROGEN :
    WATER

13. (*a.* keep, *b.* dry, *c.* filter, *d.* titrate) : DESICCANT :: PRESERVE :
    AMBER

14. HELIUM : WATER :: (*a.* neon, *b.* sodium, *c.* hydrogen, *d.* ozone)
    : CARBON DIOXIDE

15. BONE : FEMUR :: (*a.* vein, *b.* atria, *c.* aorta, *d.* artery) : CAROTID

16. TIN : (*a.* krypton, *b.* radioactive, *c.* steel, *d.* lead) :: RADON :
    XENON

17. RADIOACTIVITY : (*a.* radiation, *b.* toxicity, *c.* isotopes, *d.*
    pressure) :: GEIGER COUNTER : BAROMETER

18. (*a.* spider, *b.* cricket, *c.* worm, *d.* snail) : WHALE :: ANT : BAT

19. BRASS : (*a.* nickle, *b.* bronze, *c.* lead, *d.* copper) :: PEWTER :
    TIN

20. (*a.* arteries, *b.* atria, *c.* aorta, *d.* blood) : SPINAL CORD :: VEINS
    : MEDULLA

CHAPTER 12 QUIZ ANSWERS

1. (*c*) The clavicle is part of the skeleton, and the medulla is part of
   the brain.

2. (*c*) The ulna is a bone in the arm, and the tibia is a bone in the leg.

3. (*a*) A calorie is a unit of heat and a carat is a unit of weight.

4. (*b*) Digestion is accomplished by smooth muscle, and lifting is
   accomplished by striated muscle.

5. (*d*) Protheria mammals watch over their young in eggs,
   metatheria mammals, or marsupials, watch over their young
   in pouches.

6. (*a*) Water is a type of compound, and neon is a type of element.
   Light doesn't work because neon here must be a noun, like
   water, instead of an adjective as in neon light.

7. (*c*) A centrifuge acts to separate, amber acts to preserve.

8. (b) Both a bear and a raccoon are placental mammals, and both a koala and a kangaroo are marsupials.

9. (b) The atria make up the auricle, and the bones make up the skeleton.

10. (b) Congeal means to form a solid, and nebulize means to form a spray.

11. (c) The clavicle is the technical name for the collar bone, and the scapula is the technical name for the shoulder blade.

12. (d) Hydrogen is an element in water, and tin is an element in pewter.

13. (b) Amber acts to preserve, and desiccant acts to dry.

14. (a) Water and carbon dioxide are both compounds; helium and neon are both noble gases, even though helium and hydrogen and neon are all elements.

15. (d) The femur is a particular bone, the carotid is a particular artery.

16. (d) Radon and xenon are both noble gases, tin and lead are both metallic elements.

17. (d) A Geiger counter measures radioactivity, and a barometer measures pressure (the atmospheric kind).

18. (b) Bats and whales are both mammals, and ants and crickets are both insects. Beware! A spider is not an insect but an arachnid.

19. (d) Pewter is an alloy made primarily of tin, and brass is an alloy made primarily of copper.

20. (b) The medulla connects to the spinal cord, and veins connect to the atria (when they deliver blood).

13

Numbers: Math, Currencies, and Other Numerical Trivia

MATH

Who ever knew math vocabulary could be so important? The good news is, you learned all these terms when you were in elementary school and your mind was still soft and impressionable, so their imprint will suffice once you refresh yourself with a quick glance at the following. Among the other ways in which math shows up on the MAT is the various currencies of the world. All you have to do is memorize these and they're yours, plus you will instantly become a hit at those international sorts of parties. Another way the MAT uses math is to present relationships between numbers. None of the numerical relationships are that difficult, but if math really makes you anxious, feel free to skip these problems. If you're not afraid of math, by all means take the time to look at these; they're generally simple ratios, and an easy way to pick up one or two extra points. There will be a section on these after this brief glossary.

Acute angle: An angle that measures less than 90°.

Area: The space covered within the outline of a figure.

Cartesian grid: A graph made up of a vertical (y) and a horizontal (x) axis.

Circle words: radius, circumference, diameter

Circumference: The perimeter of a circle.

Complementary angles: Angles whose measures together add up to 90°.

Cube: A three-dimensional box in which all edges and faces are equal.

Cubed: Looks like this: 4^3. Four cubed. A number raised to the third power is being "cubed."

Cube root: A factor of a number that, when cubed, equals the number in question.

Denominator: The bottom part of a fraction.

Difference: The result of subtraction.

Dividend: The number being divided *into* in a division problem.

Divisor: The number being divided *by* in a division problem.

Equilateral triangle: A triangle in which all sides and all angles are equal.

Even: Divisible by 2.

Face: The side of a three dimensional shape.

Factors: The factors of a particular number are the numbers that multiplied together, form the product in question.

Some integers: -5, 0, 1, 7, 1,250,603

Hypotenuse: The side of a right triangle that is opposite the right angle.

Integers: All real numbers other than decimals or fractions.

Isosceles Triangle: A triangle in which two sides are equal, and their corresponding opposite angles are also equal.

Legs: Two sides of a right triangle that are not opposite the right angle.

Length: The longer side of a quadrilateral.

Numerator: The top part of a fraction.

Obtuse: An angle that measures less than 180° and more than 90°.

Odd: Not divisible by 2.

Origin: The point where the x and y axes of a Cartesian grid meet, at 0,0.

Parallelogram: A quadrilateral with two pairs of parallel sides.

Perimeter: The outline measurement of a figure.

π or pi: The ratio of the circumference to the diameter of a circle.

Product: The result of multiplication.

Proportion: A relationship between two ratios.

Quadrant: A section of a Cartesian grid.

Quadrilateral: A figure with four sides.

Quotient: The result of division.

Ratio: A relationship between two quantities.

Reciprocal: The inverse of a number.

Rectangle: A parallelogram with four right angles.

Rhombus: A parallelogram with four equal sides.

Right Angle: An angle measuring exactly 90°.

Scalene triangle: A triangle in which no sides and no angles are equal.

Square: A rectangle with four equal sides.

Squared: Looks like this: 4^2 (which is four squared). A number raised to the second power is being *squared*.

Sum: The result of addition.

Supplementary angles: Angles that together add up to 180°.

Trapezoid: A quadrilateral with two parallel sides and two nonparallel sides.

Volume: The amount of three-dimensional space a three-dimensional shape takes up.

Width: The shorter side of a quadrilateral.

Units of Measurement

Bolt: A unit measure of cloth.

Caliber: The measure of the diameter of a bullet or shell.

Carat: A jeweler's measure of weight.

Cord: A pile of 200 logs, or a measure of logs.

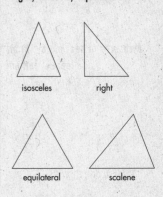

Types of triangles: isosceles, right, scalene, equilateral

isosceles   right

equilateral   scalene

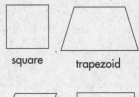

Some quadrilaterals: square, rectangle, parallelogram, rhombus, trapezoid

square   trapezoid

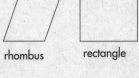

rhombus   rectangle

parallelogram

Elite: A unit of type measurement.

Fathom: A measure of water depth.

Hectares: Measures of land's surface area.

Measures at sea, matey: knot, league, fathom

Knot: A measure of speed on the sea.

League: A unit of distance, often used to measure water for distance or depth.

Level: An architectural term meaning exactly horizontal.

Pica: A unit of type measurement.

Plumb: An architectural term meaning exactly vertical.

Volts: Units of electrical measurement.

SCALES

pH scale: A scale that indicates whether a substance is an acid or a base. It goes from 0 to 14; 0 is an acid, 14 is a base, and 7 is neutral.

Beaufort scale: A scale that measures hurricanes.

Richter scale: A logarithmic scale, from 0 to 8, that measures the magnitude of tremors, earthquakes and other seismic (of the earth) activity.

Freezing: Brr. The freezing temperature of water is 0° Celsius, 32° Fahrenheit, and 273° Kelvin.

Fahrenheit scale: A scale of temperature. According to the Fahrenheit scale, the freezing temperature of water is 32° and the boiling point is 212°.

Celsius scale: A scale of temperature; it is also known as the centigrade scale. According to the Celsius scale, the freezing point of water is 0° and the boiling point is 100°.

Kelvin scale: Yet another temperature scale. It attempts to measure the absolute freezing point of all matter at 0° Kelvin, which is equal to –273° Celsius (–459.67° Fahrenheit).

Troy: A weight scale in which a pound contains 12 ounces, in contrast to the ...

Avoirdupois weight scale you are probably more familiar with, in which a pound contains 16 ounces. Both these systems use the **grain** as their smallest unit of measure.

CALENDARS

There are three types of calendars: The **Gregorian**, which you're probably familiar with, is the January to December calendar in use in the United States and Europe; the **Hebrew** calender, which has twelve months generally, but thirteen in leap years, and the **Moslem** calender, which has twelve months, and moves back through the star year of the Gregorian calender.

Geologic Time Scales

Cenozoic Era: 70,000,000 years ago. Post-dinosaur.

Mesozoic Era: 160,000,000 years ago. Dinosaurs.

Paleozoic Era: 390,000,000 years ago. Pre-dinosaur.

CURRENCIES

Countries that use the **franc**: Algeria, Belgium, Burundi, Cameroon, Central African Republic, Chad, Congo (Republic of), Dahomey, France, Gabon, Guinea, Ivory Coast, Luxembourg, Malagasy Republic, Mali, Niger, Rwanda, Senegal, Switzerland, Togo, Upper Volta.

Countries that use the **pound**: Cyprus, Egypt, Gambia, Ireland, Jamaica, Lebanon, Libya, Malawi, Malta, Nigeria, Sudan, Syria, Turkey, United Kingdom.

Countries that use the **peso**: Argentina, Bolivia, Colombia, Cuba, Dominican Republic, Mexico, Uruguay.

Countries that use the **dollar**: Australia, Barbados, Canada, Ethiopia, Guyana, Liberia, Malaysia, Nauru, New Zealand, Singapore, Trinidad and Tobago, United States.

Countries that use the **dinar**: Iraq, Jordan, Kuwait, Southern Yemen, Yugoslavia.

Countries that use the **schilling**: Austria, Somali Republic.

Countries that use the **rupee**: Sri Lanka, India, Maldive Islands, Mauritius, Nepal, Pakistan.

Other countries use their own particular currencies, such as the yen for Japan or the lira for Italy. Most of these you will be familiar with, or at least familiar enough to identify the type of relationship you are dealing with and to act accordingly.

> Countries that use the peso: Argentina, Bolivia, Columbia, Cuba, Dominican Republic, Mexico, Uruguay

MORE ANCIENT MATH

Haven't you always wanted to know what all the Ms and Ls and Xs stand for on the porticoes of buildings or on the top lines of newspapers? Well, here's your chance. The number system you are probably familiar with is called the Arabic numeral system; this uses the digits 1, 2, 3, and so on. The Roman numeral system uses different "numbers" as follows.

> Portico: Walkway or porch with a roof supported by columns. Study that vocabulary!

I = 1

V = 5

X = 10

L = 50

C = 100

D = 500

M = 1,000

That's it: All the numbers not explicitly represented above are made by different combinations of the numerals. Combinations can include the same numerals in a row, or a smaller number to the *right* of a larger one. In both these cases you should add the numbers. For instance:

III = 1 + 1 + 1 = 3

VI = 5 + 1 = 6

VIII = 5 + 1 + 1 + 1 = 8

Other combinations can include smaller numbers to the *left* of larger ones, like IV, for example. When a numeral smaller is to the left of a larger one, for instance the I in this case, it means you should subtract it. So:

IV = 5 – 1 = 4

IX = 10 – 1 = 9

XLIX = 50 – 10 = 40 + (10 – 1) = 40 + 9 = 49

Roman numerals are often used for giving dates. Try this one:

MCMXCVI

Just go left to right; the first "number" is 1,000, or M, so write that down.

1,000

The Declaration of Independence was signed in MDCCLXXVI. Can you tell when that was?

Then, there is a 100 followed by the larger 1,000—CM—this means you must subtract the number to the left (the 100) from the larger number following it (the 1,000). That gives you 900, which you should write down as well.

900

Next, you again have a smaller number followed by larger—XC—so again you will subtract, in this case 10 from 100.

90

Followed by a plain old VI or 5 + 1, better known as 6. Add them all together, 1,000 + 900 + 90 + 6 = 1996.

Not too bad, right? Plus, now you can always tell what Superbowl we're on.

EXERCISE FIVE

Try translating the next few Roman numerals into Arabic numbers, just to get comfortable.

1. XXXIV

2. XII

3. MDLIII

4. MCMXLI

5. MCDXCII

6. MMI

7. MDCCLXXVI

8. MCMLXXV

9. MDCCCLXI

10. MDCLIV

Answer Key

1. 34

2. 12

3. 1,553

4. 1941

5. 1492

6. 2001

7. 1776

8. 1975

9. 1861

10. 1654

Chapter 13 Quiz

Oh, you lucky thing, here happen to be a few mathematical analogies to hone your skills.

1. 3 : 2 :: (*a.* 10, *b.* 15, *c.* 11, *d.* 27) : 8

2. (*a.* -763 , *b.* -273, *c.* 0, *d.* 32) : 0 :: CELSIUS : KELVIN

3. AUSTRIA : (*a.* New Zealand, *b.* Ivory Coast, *c.* Kuwait, *d.* Syria) :: SCHILLING : POUND

4. PARALLELOGRAM : (*a.* quadrant, *b.* triangle, *c.* line, *d.* rhombus) :: RECTANGLE : SQUARE

5. X : XX :: V : (*a.* I, *b.* V, *c.* X, *d.* XXV)

6. 0 : 32 :: 100 : (*a.* 112, *b.* 124, *c.* 200, *d.* 212)

7. I : (*a.* V, *b.* X, *c.* C, *d.* XX) :: C : M

8. 7 : 5 :: 17 : (*a.* 16, *b.* 15, *c.* 14, *d.* 13)

9. NEGATIVE : ACUTE :: POSITIVE : (*a.* right, *b.* complementary, *c.* obtuse, *d.* supplementary)

10. DIFFERENCE : (*a.* similarity, *b.* divisor, *c.* subtraction, *d.* multiplication) :: QUOTIENT : DIVISION

11. (*a.* rhombus, *b.* trapezoid, *c.* cube, *d.* prism) : PARALLELO-GRAM :: SQUARE : RECTANGLE

12. BEAUFORT : (*a.* base, *b.* metric, *c.* pH, *d.* k) :: HURRICANES : ACIDITY

13. $3^3 : 3^2 :: (a.\ 2,\ b.\ 3,\ c.\ 4,\ d.\ 9) : 1$

14. SYRIA : (*a.* America, *b.* France, *c.* Japan, *d.* Ireland) :: REPUB-LIC OF CONGO : ALGERIA

15. HORIZONTAL : (*a.* level, *b.* diagonal, *c.* vertical, *d.* right) :: X : Y

16. 4 : IV :: 54 : (*a.* IX, *b.* DIV, *c.* CIV, *d.* LIV)

17. WIDTH : (*a.* leg, *b.* angle, *c.* side, *d.* right) :: LENGTH : HYPOT-ENUSE

18. 1.25 : (*a.* 1/2, *b.* 4/5, *c.* 4/3, *d.* 5/4) :: 0.75 : 3/4

19. CUBE : (*a.* edge, *b.* area, *c.* volume, *d.* square) :: RECTANGLE : SIDE

20. POUND : GAMBIA :: (*a.* yen, *b.* lira, *c.* rupee, *d.* peso) : NEPAL

CHAPTER 13 QUIZ ANSWERS

1. (*d*) Two cubed is 8, and 3 cubed is 27.

2. (*b*) Zero degrees Kelvin is equal in temperature to -273 degrees Celsius.

3. (*d*) The schilling is the unit of currency in Austria, and the pound is the unit of currency in Syria.

4. (*d*) A square is a type of rectangle with equal sides, and a rhombus is a type of parallelogram with equal sides.

5. (*c*) The relationship of 10 to 20, or X to XX is 1:2, as is the relationship between 5 and 10, or V and X.

6. (*d*) On the Celsius scale, 0 is the freezing point of water and 100 is the boiling point; on the Fahrenheit scale those numbers are 32 and 212.

7. (*b*) The ratio of the Roman numerals is 100 to 1,000, which becomes 1 to 10, or I to X, for the answer.

8. (*b*) Seven plus 10 is 17, and 5 plus 10 is 15.

9. (*c*) Negative is the opposite of positive, and acute is the opposite of obtuse.

10. (*c*) A quotient is the result of division, a difference is the result of subtraction.

11. (*a*) A rhombus is a parallelogram with equal sides, and a square is a rectangle with equal sides.

12. (c) The Beaufort scale measures hurricanes, and the pH scale measures acidity.

13. (b) The relationship between 3 squared and 3 cubed is 9 to 27, or 1 to 3.

14. (d) Both the Republic of the Congo and Algeria use the same type of currency (the franc), as do Syria and Ireland (the pound).

15. (c) On a Cartesian grid, x is the horizontal axis and y is the vertical axis.

16. (d) IV is the roman numeral expression of 4, and LIV is the expression of 54.

17. (a) The length of a geometric shape is always longer than its width (that's part of the definition for length and width), and the hypotenuse of a geometric shape is always longer than its legs (because the hypotenuse is the side of a right triangle opposite the ninety degree angle, which is always the largest angle).

18. (d) The decimal equivalent of 3/4 is 0.75, and of 5/4 is 1.25.

19. (a) The outside line of a rectangle forms its side, and the outside line of a cube forms its edge.

20. (c) Gambia's unit of currency is the pound, and Nepal's unit of currency is the rupee.

14
Word Particulars

The analogies on the MAT test vocabulary of one kind or another. You can usually get around not knowing a word or two by using the techniques we explained in chapter 4, but it's always going to be helpful to know the sorts of tricks these people are up to with words. Much of what looks like vocabulary is actually a game of some kind. With this in mind, we've prepared the following list of tricks, prefixes, suffixes, and roots. Study them as often as you can, and you'll be in a far more comfortable position on test day.

ROOTS AND SUFFIXES

You probably remember being told by one teacher or another that the best way to learn vocabulary was to study Latin, or, barring that, to learn important roots and suffixes. Your teacher was right, and since you probably don't have the time right now to learn Latin, the best move you can make is to commit the following roots, suffixes, and prefixes to memory.

a- or **an-:** Without, such as amoral or anaerobic.

ab-: Away or off, as in abnormal or abstain.

acro-: Top or most, as in acrobat or acropolis.

ad-: Motion or direction towards, as in addition or adverse.

agro-: Field, as in agriculture.

ambi-: Both, as in ambidextrous or ambiguous.

amphi-: On both sides, as in amphibian or amphitheater.

Some ante words: anterior, antecedent, antebellum, antediluvian

ante-: Before or preceding, such as antecedent.

anti-: Against, such as antipathy (hatred).

apo-: Removal, departure, ending, as in apocalypse.

Some apo words: apology, apostle, apocalypse, apogee, apocryphal, apotheosis, apostasy, apoplexy

arch-: Chief, most, or beginning, as in archbishop or archangel.

auto-: Self, or by or of oneself, as in autobiography or autonomy.

bene-: Good, as in benevolent.

bio-: Life, as in biology.

caco-: Bad, as in cacophonous.

calli-: Beautiful, as in calligraphy (beautiful handwriting) or calisthenics (exercises combining beauty and strength).

Some carn words; carnivorous, carnival, carnal, carnage, reincarnation, incarnation

cardio-: Heart, as in cardiology (the study of the heart).

carn-: Flesh, as in carnal or carnivorous.

contra-: Against, as in contradict or contrary.

credo-: Believe, as in incredible or credulous.

dict-: To say or speak, as in dictation or Dictaphone.

dis-: Negative, as in disappear or distress.

dono-: Give, as in donate or donor

e- or **ex-:** Out, as in external or exoskeleton (like a lobster).

fides-: Faith or loyalty, as in Fido (you know, the loyal dog, man's best friend) or fidelity.

garrio-: Talk or chatter, as in garrulous.

gyn-: Woman, as in misogyny or gynecology.

hetero-: Mixed, as in heterogeneous or heterosexual.

homo-: The same, as in homogeneous or homosexual.

im-: Against or not, as in impossible or impotent.

magnus-: Large or big, as in magnificent or magnanimous.

mal-: Bad or harmful, as in malignant or malicious.

manus-: Hand or by hand, as in manipulate or manufacture.

ob-: By way of, as in observe.

omni-: All, as in omniscient or omnipotent.

phone-: Sound, as in phonetics or telephone.

potens-: Power, as in potency.

pre-: Before, as in prehistoric or preface.

proto-: Earliest, as in prototype, or protozoa.

sciens-: Knowledge, as in prescient or science.

ubiqu-: All, as in ubiquitous.

val-: Farewell, as in the valedictory address (farewell address).

verbus-: Having to do with words, as in verbalize or verbose.

volo-: Want or desire, as in volunteer or volition.

voro-: Eating, as in devour or omnivorous.

> Some words from magnus:
> magnify, magnitude, major, maximum, majestic, magnanimous, magnate, maxim, magniloquent

OTHER TYPES OF WORD PLAY

There are some particularities of words that mightily interest the MAT writers. These include variations on plurals, as well as those phrases in Latin, French, and various other languages that some people are so fond of throwing around in daily conversation, n'est-ce pas?

SINGULAR/PLURAL: THE -UM CONTROVERSY

One of the most ubiquitous words in modern life is "the media." Everywhere you look, particularly on television and in newspapers (the media itself), people are saying, "The media has been entirely irresponsible in its treatment of. . . ." What is often overlooked (even here in this paragraph) is the fact that "media" is a plural word. These people should rightly be saying, "The media *have* been entirely irresponsible in *their* treatment of. . . ." Certain words end in "um" in their singular form: medium, and "a" in their plural form: media. With the specific term "media," it has become too much a part of public life as a singular noun to change now, but you should bear in mind that this is a common pluralization and one that they like to test on the MAT.

Some cool plurals (not always used in normal life): data, strata, media, curricula, gymnasia, auditoria

Medium/Media: Substance or field in which to work, such as oil paints, television, or journalism.

Stratum/Strata: Level or layer of people in a social class or material in the ground.

Curriculum/Curricula: Materials and subjects to be covered in a school class.

RELATED PLURALS

Criterion/Criteria: Basis or standard on which a decision or judgment is based.

Appendix/Appendices: Supplementary material at the end of a book.

Index/Indices: A listing of words or topics in a book or paper.

ABBREVIATIONS TO KNOW

The Psychological Corporation also seems to feel that knowing abbreviations and a few, choice, foreign expressions is deeply important.

A.D.: Anno Domini. In the year of our lord.

AKA: Also known as. Used to signify an alias.

a.m.: Ante meridiem. Before the sun hits the meridiem (noon), or in the morning.

B.A.: Bachelor of arts degree, also A.B.

B.C.: Before Christ.

The educational degrees: B.A., D.D., D.D.S., J.D., LL.D., Ph.D.

B.C.E.: Before the Common Era.

B.S.: Bachelor of science degree, also S.B.

D.D.: Doctor of divinity degree.

D.D.S.: Doctor of dental science or dental surgery degree.

e.g.: Exempli Grati. For example.

et al: Et alia. And others.

etc.: Et cetera. And so on.

ibid.: Ibidem. In the same place.

i.e.: Id est. That is.

J.D.: Jurum Doctor. Doctor of Law degree.

lb: Libra. Pound, as in the unit of weight.

LL.D.: Legum Doctor. Doctor of Law degree.

Ph.D: Doctor of Philosophy degree.

p.m.: Post meridiem. After noon.

Q.E.D.: Quod erat demonstrandum. Which was to be demonstrated.

FOREIGN WORDS OR PHRASES

Ad locum: At the place.

Ad interim: In the meantime.

Ad valorem: In proportion to the value.

Decessit sine prole: Died without children.

Ex officio: By virtue of the office.

Ipso facto: By the fact itself.

Mutatis mutandis: With the necessary changes having been made.

Modus operandi: Particular method of doing something.

Nota bene: Note well, pay attention to this.

Persona non grata: Unwelcome personage.

Pro tempore: Temporarily.

Quid pro quo: Something for something, as in: You scratch my back and I'll scratch yours.

Quod vide: Which see.

Sine anno: Without a date (meaning time sort of date).

Sine prole supersite: Without surviving offspring.

Sine qua non: An indispensable condition.

Notice the Latin words that come up frequently: anno (year), sine (without), quod (something). They may appear in different combinations and it can only help you to know them.

> Notice the Latin words that come up frequently; they will reappear in different combinations and it can only help if you know them.

CHAPTER 14 QUIZ

Here are some ultra-strange word-game-type analogies to try. As for the vocabulary—study it!

1. (*a.* shopping, *b.* hand, *c.* go, *d.* fist) : FISH :: CART : CARP

2. COST : POST :: (*a.* cast, *b.* last, *c.* host, *d.* pest) : PAST

3. HEART : BOAST :: (*a.* heat, *b.* ship, *c.* hearth, *d.* love) : BOAT

4. DICTIONARY : THESAURUS :: (*a.* words, *b.* definitions, *c.* dictionaries, *d.* dictionari) : THESAURI

5. (*a.* fell, *b.* fail, *c.* foal, *d.* feel) : PEEL :: FOOL : POOL

6. PLAIT : GREAT :: PLATED : (*a.* grated, *b.* wonderful, *c.* covered, *d.* greatness)

7. NADIR : SLIVER :: DRAIN : (*a.* peaks, *b.* ebbs, *c.* livers, *d.* lungs)

8. TAIL : TRAM :: (*a.* insinuator, *b.* inflation, *c.* infidel, *d.* infamous) : INFORMANT

9. ETC. : N.B. :: AND SO ON : (*a.* with others, *b.* in place of, *c.* not barring, *d.* note well)

10. CITE : (*a.* cited, *b.* sated, *c.* sitting, *d.* sighting) :: BIGHT : BITING

11. STORE : STOREY :: CAN : (*a.* canny, *b.* cant, *c.* ca, *d.* corey)

12. FACE : (*a.* cafe, *b.* thrash, *c.* bruise, *d.* confront) :: ABET : BEAT

13. ELITE : TILE :: (*a.* vault, *b.* expel, *c.* effete, *d.* elope) : POLE

14. (*a.* pans, *b.* plants, *c.* grows, *d.* trats) : START :: POTS : STOP

15. CRASS : LACK :: CROSS : (*a.* gross, *b.* locker, *c.* surfeit, *d.* lock)

16. (*a.* clamber, *b.* weight, *c.* climate, *d.* clime) : WEIGH :: CLIMB : WHEY

17. STOUT : TOUT :: STRAIN : (*a.* train, *b.* rain, *c.* trains, *d.* taint)

18. LOG : ACT :: ANTHOLOGY : (*a.* record, *b.* perform, *c.* contraction, *d.* digest)

19. (*a.* ratio, *b.* bottom, *c.* bias, *d.* partial) : SIDE :: GENERATION : CONSIDERABLE

20. SAG : (*a.* resale, *b.* fund, *c.* sale, *d.* fun) :: USAGE : REFUND

CHAPTER 14 QUIZ ANSWERS

1. (*d*) The word carp changes to the word cart by changing the last letter to a *t*, and the same goes for the words fish and fist. While a carp is a type of fish, this relationship does not work for cart and any of the available words.

2. (*a*) Post becomes past by changing the *o* to an *a*, and the same is true of cost and cast.

3. (*a*) Boast becomes boat—another word entirely—by removing the fourth letter. The same is true of heart and heat.

4. (*c*) The plural of thesaurus is thesauri, the plural of dictionary is dictionaries.

5. (*d*) The word *pool* changes to *peel* when the two *o*s become *e*s; the same for fool and feel.

6. (*a*) Plated adds an "ed" sound to the way the word plait sounds, grated does the same thing with great.

7. (*c*) Drain is an anagram of nadir, and silver is an anagram of livers.

8. (*b*) Train comes from a rearrangement of some of the letters in informant, and tail does the same with inflation.

9. (*d*) Etc. is the abbreviation for et cetera which means "and so on," N.B. is the abbreviation for nota bene which means "note well."

10. (*b*) When only one letter, a *y*, is added to store it forms another English word, *storey* (as in, of a building), and when only one letter is added to can to form a word it becomes *cant* or persuasive speech.

11. (*d*) Biting sounds like the word bight with an *ing* sound added to it; the same sound-alike principle applies to cite and sighting.

12. (*c*) A carat is a unit of weight, and a pica is a unit of type.

13. (*d*) Elite is tile spelled backward with an *e* added to the end, and the same is true of elope and pole.

14. (*d*) Stop is pots reversed, and the same is true of start and trats. Pans are not the opposite of pots if that's the one you chose; think about it—they are the same things, just variations.

15. (*d*) Crass and cross are two different words changed only by the alteration of their vowel, and the same goes for lack and lock.

16. (*d*) Weigh and whey are homophones, and so are climb and clime.

17. (*a*) Stout becomes tout by dropping the first "s," the same way strain becomes train.

18. (*c*) The word log is inside the word anth*olog*y, and the word act is inside the word contr*act*ion.

19. (*a*) The word side is found in the middle of the larger word con*side*rable, and the word ratio can be found in the middle of the larger word gene*ratio*n.

20. (*d*) Sag is a word found inside the word u*sag*e, and fun is a word found inside the word re*fun*d. Fund, however, is not inside refund, but at one end.

PART ◆ V

The Sample Tests

SAMPLE TEST 1

Time: 50 Minutes
100 Questions

Directions: The following analogy pairs contain four choices with which to combine the unpaired word. Choose the answer that best corresponds to the full analogy pair. There is only one right answer.

1. IMBROGLIO : (*a.* ado, *b.* fete, *c.* fight, *d.* feat) :: SITUATION : ACHIEVEMENT

2. LOGS : (*a.* diameter, *b.* sine, *c.* circumference, *d.* cord) :: PAPER : REAM

3. MOZART : (*a.* Austria, *b.* Germany, *c.* France, *d.* Poland) :: BEETHOVEN : GERMANY

4. (*a.* novels, *b.* morals, *c.* rhymes, *d.* poems): KEATS :: FABLES : AESOP

5. DEFINITIONS : DICTIONARY :: (*a.* meaning, *b.* pronunciation, *c.* synonyms, *d.* pseudonyms) : THESAURUS

6. SANGUINE : JAUNDICED :: RUDDY : (*a.* muddy, *b.* callow, *c.* sallow, *d.* yellow)

7. OPINION : (*a.* distaste, *b.* prison, *c.* magnet, *d.* revulsion) :: CONVICTION : REPULSION

8. (*a.* equality, *b.* decision, *c.* equanimity, *d.* sit) : EQUIVOCAL :: STAND : FICKLE

9. SKULL : CRANIUM :: (*a.* mouth, *b.* tooth, *c.* jaw, *d.* chew) : MANDIBLE

10. SLEEP : PEELS :: (*a.* sheets, *b.* decal, *c.* pillows, *d.* bed) : LACED

11. PRAGMATIC : (*a.* utilitarian, *b.* pacifist, *c.* frivolous, *d.* reluctant) :: TRUCULENT : SERENE

12. PRANCE : CAPER :: PICKLE : (*a.* olive, *b.* dance, *c.* mince, *d.* preserve)

13. (*a.* whole number, *b.* odd number, *c.* integer, *d.* variable) : -4 :: DECIMAL : 0.53

14. DE FACTO : APOCRYPHAL :: (*a.* grandiose, *b.* apocalyptic, *c.* hour, *d.* de Soto) : MINUTE

15. i : 7 :: (*a.* fake, *b.* imaginary, *c.* genuine, *d.* irrational) : REAL

16. REVOLT : (*a.* truce, *b.* broker, *c.* recantor, *d.* insurgent) :: TREATY : MEDIATOR

17. SURMOUNT : SURPASS :: (*a.* questionnaire, *b.* answer, *c.* examine, *d.* sanitize) : SURVEY

18. (*a.* Omoo, *b.* Typee, *c.* whale, *d.* Budd) : BILLY :: DICK : MOBY

19. TEMBLORS : RICHTER :: (*a.* fissure, *b.* fault, *c.* tornadoes, *d.* hurricanes) : BEAUFORT

20. (*a.* Persian, *b.* French, *c.* Arabic, *d.* Chinese) : LATIN :: IRAN : ROME

21. (*a.* hurt, *b.* humble, *c.* hush, *d.* hose) : ABASH :: REVERE : HONOR
22. ISSUE : OPT :: (*a.* magazine, *b.* distribute, *c.* opinion, *d.* select) : CHOOSE
23. (*a.* parody, *b.* disappear, *c.* roe, *d.* brat) : SPOOF :: FISH : SPRAT
24. SCRIPT : PLAY :: (*a.* aria, *b.* score, *c.* allegretto, *d.* libretto) : OPERA
25. (*a.* gull, *b.* irritate, *c.* provoke, *d.* embarrass) : ANNOY :: GULLIBLE : IRASCIBLE

26. FRAY : CUFF :: (*a.* sleeve, *b.* fight, *c.* edge, *d.* tatter) : STRIKE
27. QUINTAL : STERE :: WEIGHT : (*a.* length, *b.* weight, *c.* volume, *d.* mass)
28. NIXON : (*a.* Clinton, *b.* Adams, *c.* Burr, *d.* Madison) :: AGNEW : JEFFERSON
29. AWARENESS : (*a.* pity, *b.* nerve, *c.* happiness, *d.* cruel) :: OBLIVIOUS : RUTHLESS
30. EXCORIATE : (*a.* vomit, *b.* demon, *c.* free, *d.* scold) :: HEAVE : TOSS

31. BULLFROG : (*a.* amphibian, *b.* entomologist, *c.* herpetologist, *d.* ornithologist) ::
    BUTTERFLY : ENTOMOLOGIST
32. CANDY : (*a.* joint, *b.* iron, *c.* steel, *d.* torch) :: CONFECTIONER : WELDER
33. FLOCK : (*a.* sheep, *b.* bird, *c.* mimic, *d.* follow) :: CONGREGATE : PARROT
34. ANTHROPOLOGY : HAGIOGRAPHY :: MAN : (*a.* history, *b.* religion, *c.* saints,
    d. art)
35. DOGS : (*a.* cats, *b.* mice, *c.* cows, *d.* birds) :: KENNEL : AVIARY

36. ETCH : EMBROIDER :: (*a.* awl, *b.* scraper, *c.* acid, *d.* needle) : THREAD
37. NIP : SIP :: CARP : (*a.* water, *b.* harp, *c.* drink, *d.* tarp)
38. (*a.* lento, *b.* fortissimo, *c.* andante, *d.* pianissimo) : PIANO :: PRESTO : ADAGIO
39. (*a.* eats, *b.* fights, *c.* talks, *d.* ignores) : FLIRTS :: PUGILIST : COQUETTE
40. WHALE : ANTEATER :: PLACENTAL : (*a.* fish, *b.* marsupial, *c.* protheria,
    d. mammal)

41. BLAZE : RAZE :: (*a.* indicate, *b.* building, *c.* fire, *d.* erect) : DESTROY

42. Q.E.D. : (*a.* aka, *b.* ibi*d.*, *c.* et*c.*, *d.* i.e.) :: WHICH WAS TO BE DEMONSTRATED : IN THE SAME PLACE

43. (*a.* clerestory, *b.* moat, *c.* window, *d.* protector) : WALL :: FAN : COOLANT

44. DISSONANCE : CONSONANCE :: (*a.* innuendo, *b.* diminuendo, *c.* pianissimo, *d.* sforzano) : CRESCENDO

45. GAME : COWED :: PLUCKY : (*a.* bird, *b.* intimidated, *c.* wild, *d.* tame)

46. INVECTIVE : (*a.* adulatory, *b.* denigrating, *c.* auspicious, *d.* laity) :: JARGON : PROFESSIONAL

47. ONE : (*a.* one, *b.* five, *c.* ten, *d.* fifty) :: WASHINGTON : GRANT

48. OROTUND : (*a.* fat, *b.* round, *c.* pompous, *d.* slim) :: OBESE : CORPULENT

49. CALUMNIATE : STATE :: PERJURE : (*a.* testify, *b.* government, *c.* justice, *d.* court)

50. CALDER : (*a.* mobile, *b.* audio, *c.* collage, *d.* prose) :: CHAGALL : STAINED GLASS

51. IMMORAL : (*a.* licentious, *b.* rare, *c.* fine, *d.* course) :: COARSE : COMMON

52. EVIL : STAB :: (*a.* vampire, *b.* die, *c.* jab, *d.* live) : BATS

53. VAPOR : (*a.* gas, *b.* solid, *c.* liquid, *d.* crust) :: EVAPORATE : CONGEAL

54. (*a.* date, *b.* stone, *c.* affection, *d.* adored) : BELOVED :: HUNT : QUARRY

55. CARPENTER : GLAZIER :: WOOD : (*a.* glass, *b.* glue, *c.* glade, *d.* globe)

56. (*a.* lung, *b.* sound, *c.* respiration, *d.* air) : BREATH :: CACOPHONY : HALITOSIS

57. THUG : FARMER :: BRUTAL : (*a.* violent, *b.* occupation, *c.* agrarian, *d.* cultivating)

58. BLOOD : BONE :: HEME : (*a.* osteo, *b.* ortho, *c.* homo, *d.* onco)

59. DECLARATION OF INDEPENDENCE : GETTYSBURG ADDRESS :: (*a.* Jefferson, *b.* Madison, *c.* Washington, *d.* Franklin) : LINCOLN

60. PREVENT : (*a.* catabolism, *b.* catatonic, *c.* filter, *d.* filibuster) :: ENCOURAGE : CATALYST

61. COMESTIBLES : TANGIBLES :: (*a.* culpable, *b.* frangible, *c.* edible, *d.* potable) : PALPABLE

62. FORK : KNIFE :: (*a.* prong, *b.* branch, *c.* tine, *d.* food) : STAB

63. (*a.* pen, *b.* whine, *c.* pooh, *d.* hen) : HOOP :: WHEN : WHOOP

64. V : L :: (*a.* I, *b.* X, *c.* L, *d.* M) : D

65. CLIP : CARTRIDGES :: BOARD : (*a.* typing, *b.* ribbon, *c.* members, *d.* letters)

66. STRUT : (*a.* swagger, *b.* disease, *c.* supercilious, *d.* shame) :: PROSTRATE : HUMBLE

67. CLEANLINESS : SULLY :: (*a.* immorality, *b.* morality, *c.* building, *d.* structure) : EDIFY

68. TOUGH : LOTION :: ROUGH : (*a.* scruff, *b.* sandpaper, *c.* motion, *d.* scab)

69. (*a.* mud, *b.* sludge, *c.* viscous, *d.* apex) : MENISCUS :: NADIR : SEDIMENT

70. (*a.* smirch, *b.* arrest, *c.* try, *d.* knight) : VALORIZE :: EXCULPATE : INDICT

71. THERMOSTAT : RHEOSTAT :: TEMPERATURE : (*a.* thermometer, *b.* current, *c.* magnetism, *d.* gravity)

72. METAL : (*a.* rabbits, *b.* disease, *c.* lumber, *d.* stones) :: METALLURGIST : LAPIDARY

73. ROTE : RIGHT :: EXTEMPORANEOUS : (*a.* unjust, *b.* extirpate, *c.* written, *d.* oral)

74. ANAGOGICAL : UTILITARIAN :: (*a.* analogy, *b.* spiritual, *c.* history, *d.* culture) : PRACTICAL

75. (*a.* and alia, *b.* and others, *c.* et cetera, *d.* with any) : THAT IS :: ET ALIA : ID EST

76. (*a.* cure, *b.* cougar, *c.* cough, *d.* cinch) : SURE :: CIRCLE : SUGAR

77. COERCE : FORCE :: EXACT : (*a.* perfect, *b.* force, *c.* specific, *d.* guile)

78. ARTIFACTS : (*a.* clerics, *b.* plants, *c.* fish, *d.* relics) :: RELIQUARY : TERRARIUM

79. DEBATE : MOOT :: (*a.* dissolution, *b.* understanding, *c.* erasure, *d.* court) : SOLUBLE

80. STARRY NIGHT : VAN GOGH :: VIEW OF TOLEDO : (*a.* Hopper, *b.* el Greco, *c.* Picasso, *d.* Pollock)

81. PICKY : TRICKY :: (*a.* picaresque, *b.* elusive, *c.* sly, *d.* captious) : EVASIVE

82. VINES : (*a.* drones, *b.* brines, *c.* nadirs, *d.* knives) :: VEINS : DRAINS

83. CASANOVA : (*a.* French, *b.* love, *c.* Italian, *d.* romance) :: CERVANTES : SPANISH

84. PLUM : PICKLE :: DESIRABLE : (*a.* repulsive, *b.* brine, *c.* vinegar, *d.* troublesome)

85. LEVER : FULCRUM :: THEORY : (*a.* experiment, *b.* postulate, *c.* thought, *d.* conclusion)

86. (*a.* grassy, *b.* watery, *c.* wooded, *d.* arctic) : BARREN :: LEA : TUNDRA

87. (*a.* shilling, *b.* sharp, *c.* hone, *d.* mob) : CROWD :: HOLE : CROWN

88. JOIST : (*a.* wall, *b.* beam, *c.* omen, *d.* carouse) :: HERALD : HARBINGER

89. REAL : FOURTH :: LAND : (*a.* false, *b.* third, *c.* media, *d.* central)

90. DANTE : MILTON :: DIVINE COMEDY : (*a.* Commedia del Arte, *b.* Inferno, *c.* Lycidas, *d.* Odyssey)

91. SUPPORTS : (*a.* receives, *b.* betrays, *c.* donates, *d.* rebels) :: BENEFACTOR : QUISLING

92. THIRTEENTH : EIGHTEENTH :: (*a.* arms, *b.* assembly, *c.* slavery, *d.* taxation) : LIQUOR

93. (*a.* Titian, *b.* van Gogh, *c.* Velazquez, *d.* Miro) : DA VINCI :: GAUGIN : CEZANNE

94. ROAM : RHYME :: ROME : (*a.* rime, *b.* reign, *c.* rame, *d.* Roma)

95. EQUABLE : EQUIVOCAL :: EVEN : (*a.* fickle, *b.* odd, *c.* even, *d.* fair)

96. PRIMATE : HUMAN :: (*a.* pole, *b.* monkey, *c.* evolution, *d.* standard) : STANCHION

97. (*a.* cancer, *b.* malignant, *c.* prose, *d.* poetry) : TUMORS :: PROSODY : ONCOLOGY

98. LEXICON : WORDS :: NECROLOGY : (*a.* magic, *b.* mortalities, *c.* charms, *d.* runes)

99. MEDIUM : IT :: MEDIA : (*a.* it, *b.* he, *c.* its, *d.* they)

100. PUNISHMENT : (*a.* love, *b.* wealth, *c.* fame, *d.* sadism) :: MASOCHISM : CUPIDITY

ANSWER KEY

1. (*d*) An imbroglio is a difficult situation, a feat is a difficult achievement.

2. (*d*) A ream is a measure of paper, and a cord is a measure of logs.

3. (*a*) Beethoven was from Germany, and Mozart was from Austria.

4. (*d*) Aesop wrote fables, and Keats wrote poems (a rhyme is not a full work).

5. (*c*) A dictionary provides definitions for words, a thesaurus provides synonyms for words.

6. (*d*) A sanguine complexion is ruddy, and jaundiced complexion is yellow.

7. (*a*) A conviction is a strong opinion, a repulsion is a strong distaste (not a strong revulsion, a revulsion is already strong and this is a degree relationship).

8. (*b*) Someone fickle can't take a stand, someone equivocal can't make a decision.

9. (*c*) Cranium is the technical term for the skull, and mandible is the technical term for the jaw.

10. (*b*) Sleep is the reverse of peels, and the same is true of laced and decal.

11. (*c*) Someone pragmatic is not frivolous, and someone truculent is not serene.

12. (*d*) To prance means to caper (dance around), and to pickle means to preserve.

13. (*c*) An example of a decimal is 0.53, and an example of an integer is -4 (integers include negative numbers, unlike whole numbers).

14. (*a*) Something de facto is real, or not apocryphal, where something grandiose, or huge, is not minute.

15. (*b*) The term *i* represents an imaginary number, while 7 represents a real number.

16. (*d*) An insurgent brings about a revolt, but a mediator brings about a treaty.

17. (*c*) To surmount means to surpass or get over and beyond, while to survey means to examine.

18. (*d*) *Moby-Dick* is the title of a novel by Herman Melville, as is *Billy Budd*.

19. (*d*) The Richter scale measures temblors (another name for earthquakes), and the Beaufort scale measures hurricanes.

20. (*a*) Latin was the language spoken in ancient Rome, and Persian was the language spoken in ancient Iran.

21. (*b*) To honor someone is to revere her, while to abash someone is to humble her.

22. (*b*) To opt means to choose or select, and to issue means to distribute as in issuing a proclamation.

23. (*a*) A spoof is a type of parody, and a sprat is a type of fish.

24. (*d*) A script provides the written text of a play, and a libretto provides the written text of an opera.

25. (*a*) Someone irascible is easy to annoy, and someone gullible is easy to gull. (To gull means to trick.)

26. (*d*) To fray means to tatter, and to cuff means to hit or strike.

27. (*c*) A quintal is a measure of weight, and a stere is a measure of volume.

28. (*b*) Agnew was Nixon's vice president, and Jefferson was Adams's vice president.

29. (*a*) Oblivious means lacking awareness, and ruthless means lacking pity.

30. (*d*) To heave is an extreme version of to toss, and to excoriate is an extreme version of to scold.

31. (*c*) A butterfly might be the subject of study for an entomologist (insect specialist), a bullfrog might be the subject of study for a herpetologist (reptiles and amphibians).

32. (*a*) A confectioner makes candy, and a welder makes joints (of buildings).

33. (*c*) To flock means to congregate or gather, and to parrot means to mimic or copy.

34. (*c*) Anthropology is the study of man, and hagiography is the study of saints.

35. (*d*) A kennel is a structure built to house dogs, and an aviary is a structure built to house birds.

36. (*c*) To embroider means to decorate using thread, and to etch means to decorate using acid.

37. (*b*) To nip means to take a sip, or just plain to sip, and to carp means to complain, nag, or in other words, to harp.

38. (*b*) Adagio is a slow tempo, and presto is a fast one; piano is a soft tone and fortissimo is a loud one.

39. (*b*) A coquette flirts, and a pugilist fights.

40. (*c*) A whale is a placental mammal, and an anteater is a protheria mammal.

41. (*a*) To raze means to destroy, and to blaze means to indicate, as in blazing a trail.

42. (*b*) *Which was to be demonstrated* is expressed by the abbreviation Q.E.D., and in *the same place* is expressed by the abbreviation ibid.

43. (*a*) A fan is a type of coolant, and a clerestory is a type of (or part of a) wall.

44. (*b*) Consonance is (this is one of the few times you can effectively use this "opposite" sentence construction) the opposite of dissonance, and crescendo is the opposite of diminuendo.

45. (*b*) To be game means to be plucky or brave, while to be cowed means to be intimidated or frightened.

46. (*b*) Jargon is professional language, and invective is denigrating language.

47. (*d*) Washington's portrait is on the one dollar bill, and Grant's portrait is on the fifty dollar bill.

48. (*c*) Someone obese is corpulent, or fat, while someone orotund is pompous or full of himself.

49. (*a*) To calumniate is to state falsely, or to lie or slander, and to perjure is to testify falsely.

50. (*a*) Chagall is known for his stained glass artworks, and Calder is known for his mobile artworks.

51. (*a*) Licentious means immoral, and common means coarse.

52. (*d*) The word stab is the reverse of bats, and evil is the reverse of live.

53. (*b*) To evaporate means to become a vapor, and to congeal means to become a solid.

54. (*c*) A quarry is the object of the hunt, and a beloved is the object of affection.

55. (*a*) A carpenter works in wood, and a glazier works in glass.

56. (*b*) Halitosis is unpleasant breath, and cacophony is an unpleasant sound.

57. (*c*) A thug is by definition brutal, while a farmer is by definition agrarian.

58. (*a*) The prefix "heme" means blood or blood-related, and the prefix "osteo" means bones or bone-related.

59. (*a*) Lincoln wrote the Gettysburg Address, and Jefferson wrote the Declaration Of Independence.

60. (*d*) A filibuster is used to prevent something, while a catalyst is used to encourage something.

61. (*c*) Comestibles are by definition edible, and tangibles, or things that can be touched, are by definition palpable.

62. (*b*) To knife someone or something means to stab it, and to fork means to branch or divide.

63. (*d*) Whoop becomes hoop by removing the *w*, the same goes for when and hen.

64. (*c*) The ratio of 50 to 5 is 10 to 1, so the Roman numeral equivalent must be 500 to 50, or D to L.

65. (*c*) A clip contains cartridges, as in the clip of a gun, while a board contains members, such as the board of directors.

66. (*c*) To prostrate oneself means to move in a physically humble manner, to strut oneself means to move in a physically supercilious—or arrogant—manner.

67. (*a*) To sully means to rid of cleanliness, to edify means to rid of immorality.

68. (*c*) Tough becomes rough by changing the first letter, the same is true of lotion and motion.

69. (*d*) A meniscus is the top surface of a fluid, while sediment is found at the bottom; the apex is the highest point, while the nadir is the lowest.

70. (*a*) To exculpate is the opposite of indict, while to valorize is the opposite of to smirch.

71. (*b*) A thermostat controls temperature, and a rheostat controls current.

72. (*d*) A metallurgist works with metal, and a lapidary works with stones or gems.

73. (*a*) Rote means known by heart—the opposite of extemporaneous, and right is the opposite of unjust.

74. (b) Utilitarian means having to do with practical aspects, and anagogical means having to do with spiritual aspects.

75. (b) Id est means *that is*, and et alia means *and others*.

76. (d) Sure and sugar both use *su* to sound like *sh*, and circle and cinch both use *ci* to sound like *ess*.

77. (b) To coerce means to convince by force, to exact means to convince by force as well, as in "He exacted a promise from her."

78. (b) A reliquary is a structure that holds artifacts, and a terrarium is a structure that holds plants.

79. (a) Moot means subject to debate, and soluble means subject to dissolution.

80. (b) *Starry Night* is a painting by van Gogh, and *View of Toledo* is a painting by El Greco.

81. (d) Picky means captious or demanding, while tricky means elusive.

82. (a) Vines is an anagram of veins, and nadirs is an anagram of drains.

83. (c) Cervantes wrote in Spanish, and Casanova wrote in Italian.

84. (d) A plum is a desirable situation, often a job, while a pickle is a troublesome situation.

85. (b) A lever rests on a fulcrum, and a theory rests on a postulate.

86. (a) Tundra is, by definition, barren; a lea is, by definition, grassy.

87. (c) Crowd changes to another word, crown, by taking out one letter and adding an *n* in its place. The same is true of hole and hone.

88. (b) A herald serves as a harbinger, and a joist serves as a beam (cross-wise support).

89. (c) Real estate is land, while the fourth estate refers to the media or the press.

90. (c) Dante wrote *The Divine Comedy*, and Milton wrote *Lycidas*.

91. (b) A benefactor supports, and a quisling betrays.

92. (c) The eighteenth amendment of the Constitution outlawed liquor, and the thirteenth amendment outlawed slavery.

93. (a) Cezanne and Gaugin were both French painters, and da Vinci and Titian were both Italian painters.

94. (a) Roam and Rome are homophones, and rhyme and rime are homophones. (Homophones are words that, though spelled differently, sound alike.)

95. (a) Equable means even-tempered or agreeable, while equivocal means fickle or changeable.

96. (a) A human is an upright primate, and a stanchion is an upright pole.

97. (d) Oncology is the study of tumors, and prosody is the study of poetry.

98. (b) A lexicon is a list of words, and a necrology is a list of mortalities.

99. (d) Media is the plural form of medium, and they is the plural form of it.

100. (b) Masochism is the desire for punishment, and cupidity is the desire for wealth.

SAMPLE TEST 2

Time: 50 Minutes
100 Questions

Directions: The following analogy pairs contain four choices with which to combine the unpaired word. Choose the answer that best corresponds to the full analogy pair. There is only one right answer.

1. WEIGHT : DEPTH :: DRAM : (*a.* length, *b.* elasticity, *c.* spool, *d.* fathom)
2. (*a.* casing, *b.* puree, *c.* blade, *d.* motor) : BLENDER :: COG : MACHINE
3. BLIZZARD : FLURRY :: (*a.* irritation, *b.* rage, *c.* patience, *d.* happiness) : ANNOYANCE
4. C.E.O. : EXECUTIVE :: (*a.* enlistee, *b.* sergeant, *c.* general, *d.* captain) : SOLDIER
5. PORCINE : PIG :: BOVINE : (*a.* sheep, *b.* horse, *c.* dog, *d.* cow)

6. CHRISTIANITY : (*a.* Hinduism, *b.* Mecca, *c.* Mohammed, *d.* Islam) :: CHRIST : ALLAH
7. LAMP : (*a.* light, *b.* bulb, *c.* sun, *d.* shade) :: WATCH : TIMEPIECE
8. (*a.* -763 , *b.* 0, *c.* 32, *d.* 216) : 100 :: FREEZING : BOILING
9. QUARREL : BRAWL :: (*a.* surprise, *b.* shock, *c.* breath, *d.* fight) : GASP
10. PITCH : SLANT :: HITCH : (*a.* throw, *b.* knot, *c.* hill, *d.* tilt)

11. SCALPEL : PLANE :: (*a.* pilot, *b.* dentist, *c.* architect, *d.* surgeon) : CARPENTER
12. (*a.* lie, *b.* misrepresent, *c.* testify, *d.* testimony) : PERJURY :: WRITING : FORGERY
13. COPYRIGHT : (*a.* moat, *b.* wave, *c.* plagiarism, *d.* sue) :: RAMPART : ATTACK
14. CRITERION : CRITERIA :: VORTEX : (*a.* angle, *b.* vorte, *c.* vortices, *d.* point)
15. MELEE : VIOLENCE :: FETE : (*a.* celebration, *b.* ballroom, *c.* debauchery, *d.* succulence)

16. EGG : (*a.* yolk, *b.* reproduction, *c.* shell, *d.* scrambled) :: ESCRITOIRE : DESK
17. HORSE : CENTAUR :: (*a.* mule, *b.* bull, *c.* bird, *d.* goat) : SATYR
18. (*a.* height, *b.* profundity, *c.* foreshortening, *d.* truth) : DEPTH :: DECEPTION : HONESTY
19. SIGHT : (*a.* voice, *b.* earshot, *c.* hearing, *d.* amplifier) :: PERISCOPE : MICROPHONE
20. TEACH : LEECH :: (*a.* instruct, *b.* suck, *c.* student, *d.* learn) : BLEED

21. 180° : (*a.* 45°, *b.* 90°, *c.* 100°, *d.* 360°) :: SUPPLEMENTARY : COMPLEMENTARY

22. JOCKEY : GUARD :: (*a.* ride, *b.* horse, *c.* ball, *d.* fight) : PROTECT

23. VERB : NOUN :: EXPRESSES : (*a.* being, *b.* transition, *c.* names, *d.* objects)

24. (*a.* forested, *b.* grassy, *c.* mountainous, *d.* continental) : STEAMY :: STEPPE : JUNGLE

25. OBEDIENT : (*a.* insurgent, *b.* restrained, *c.* officious, *d.* compliant) :: DOUR : STERN

26. FLAG : TAG :: (*a.* patriotism, *b.* mark, *c.* nation, *d.* dark) : MARK

27. (*a.* wet, *b.* hot, *c.* majestic, *d.* summery) : AUGUST :: VAPOROUS : STEAMY

28. (*a.* hex, *b.* axe, *c.* annoy, *d.* select) : PICK :: VEX : PIQUE

29. SPEED : (*a.* acceleration, *b.* cloth, *c.* key, *d.* wood) :: KNOT : BOLT

30. EAGLE : BIRDIE :: DUNK : (*a.* fluid, *b.* foul, *c.* swimming, *d.* donut)

31. HERA : (*a.* Juno, *b.* Aphrodite, *c.* Hephaestus, *d.* Cronus) :: DEMETER : PERSEPHONE

32. BRACE : HEFT :: SUPPORT : (*a.* large, *b.* much, *c.* carry, *d.* lift)

33. DOVE : VULTURE :: PEACE : (*a.* morality, *b.* mortality, *c.* war, *d.* mortuary)

34. PAINTER : (*a.* architect, *b.* sculptor, *c.* collagist, *d.* muralist) :: GAUGIN : WREN

35. BETRAYAL : JUDAS :: (*a.* fidelity, *b.* piety, *c.* chastity, *d.* loyalty) : RUTH

36. PIG : (*a.* bone, *b.* rib, *c.* pork, *d.* tendon) :: CARTILAGE : GRISTLE

37. ARIA : CHROMATIC SCALE :: (*a.* symphony, *b.* opera, *c.* etude, *d.* timbre) : OCTAVE

38. 0 : (*a.* even, *b.* odd, *c.* neutral, *d.* positive) :: 5 : ODD

39. ILIAD : ULYSSES :: HOMER : (*a.* Vergil, *b.* Joyce, *c.* Zeus, *d.* Euripides)

40. DOLLAR : (*a.* rupee, *b.* shekel, *c.* dinar, *d.* pound) :: BARBADOS : JORDAN

41. INDIGO : VIOLET :: ORANGE : (*a.* yellow, *b.* pink, *c.* red, *d.* scarlet)
42. HOLSTER : (*a.* hilt, *b.* haste, *c.* conceal, *d.* carry) :: BRACE : BOLSTER
43. VARNISH : (*a.* paints, *b.* cover, *c.* sully, *d.* fumes) :: TARNISH : TAINT
44. LAW : (*a.* divinity, *b.* doctoral, *c.* dentistry, *d.* justice) :: J.D. : D.D.
45. CAR : CONVERTIBLE :: (*a.* dog, *b.* wolf, *c.* jaw, *d.* tooth) : CANINE

46. MONK : (*a.* gamble, *b.* abstinent, *c.* abbey, *d.* rectory) :: CROUPIER : CASINO
47. (*a.* support, *b.* censure, *c.* contradict, *d.* add to) : DECRY :: DENY : GAINSAY
48. (*a.* evil, *b.* defendant, *c.* plea, *d.* good) : MISCREANT :: CHARGE : COMPLAINANT
49. MARROW : (*a.* shaft, *b.* quiver, *c.* cone, *d.* point) :: ARROW : ONE
50. PHYLUM : KINGDOM :: (*a.* genus, *b.* class, *c.* order, *d.* species) : FAMILY

51. GATHER : (*a.* infer, *b.* sow, *c.* pleat, *d.* crop) :: REAP : HARVEST
52. CHURCH : SYNOD :: (*a.* publishing, *b.* business, *c.* crime, *d.* newspaper) : SYNDICATE
53. SAKE : GOODNESS :: (*a.* purpose, *b.* produce, *c.* type, *d.* Pete's) : QUALITY
54. HACKLE : HOCK :: NECK : (*a.* knock, *b.* spoon, *c.* leg, *d.* arm)
55. CONGRESS : (*a.* congress, *b.* president, *c.* judiciary, *d.* navy) :: LEGISLATION : ARMED FORCES

56. TANZANIA : IRAN :: (*a.* Tanganyika, *b.* Tasmania, *c.* Punjabi, *d.* India) : PERSIA
57. (*A.* CHAPTER, *B.* ARREST, *C.* LIBRARY, *D.* TEXT) : REGIMENT :: BOOK : BATTALION
58. GOD : TAPS :: DOG : (*a.* spot, *b.* reveille, *c.* prayer, *d.* spat)
59. SACRED : STATUS QUO :: (*a.* fighter, *b.* apostle, *c.* apostate, *d.* iconoclast) : REBEL
60. TESTIMONY : (*a.* public, *b.* colon, *c.* grammar, *d.* true) :: APOSTROPHE : IMAGINARY

61. KOALA : (*a.* bear, *b.* kangaroo, *c.* marsupial, *d.* panda) :: MOUSE : RODENT

62. (*a.* calcify, *b.* monstrosity, *c.* scold, *d.* expose) : DEBUNK :: REMONSTRATE : RE-PROVE

63. DESTITUTE : IMPECUNIOUS :: (*a.* improvident, *b.* affluent, *c.* tenacious, *d.* honorable) : INDOMITABLE

64. SHARD : SLIVER :: GLASS : (*a.* mirror, *b.* splinter, *c.* wood, *d.* grass)

65. NIGHT : (*a.* day, *b.* made, *c.* damsel, *d.* created) :: KNIGHT : MAID

66. ENUMERATION : (*a.* poisoning, *b.* counting, *c.* multiplying, *d.* stairs) :: VITUPERA-TION : RAILING

67. COLOR : QUIET :: (*a.* serene, *b.* achromatic, *c.* diaphanous, *d.* blue) : CACOPHO-NOUS

68. FLOWERS : (*a.* bouquet, *b.* wreath, *c.* surprise, *d.* horrify) :: HAIR : SHOCK

69. MANET : MONET :: (*a.* cloud, *b.* Eduard, *c.* water lilies, *d.* clause) : CLAUDE

70. WHISPER : PIANO :: SPEECH : (*a.* instrument, *b.* keyboard, *c.* tone, *d.* tempo)

71. VULTURE : BIRD :: (*a.* orca, *b.* panther, *c.* hyena, *d.* dog) : MAMMAL

72. (*a.* stones, *b.* joints, *c.* dowels, *d.* seal) : MORTAR :: WOOD : BRICKS

73. WALL : (*a.* buttress, *b.* parapet, *c.* promontory, *d.* castle) :: DITCH : MOAT

74. POLE : LOPE :: (*a.* read, *b.* fare, *c.* aedr, *d.* drae) : DEAR

75. BOTTOM : (*a.* top, *b.* sky, *c.* Othello, *d.* Lear) :: PUCK : IAGO

76. ANNO : SINE :: YEAR : (*a.* sin, *b.* without, *c.* sign, *d.* month)

77. COMPEER : COMPONENT :: (*a.* piece, *b.* equal, *c.* larger, *d.* subdivision) : PART

78. SCEPTER : (*a.* royalty, *b.* kingdom, *c.* coat of arms, *d.* authority) :: FLAG : NATION

79. (*a.* insects, *b.* reptiles, *c.* bees, *d.* blisters) : BIRDS :: HERPETOLOGY : ORNITHOL-OGY

80. ENAMEL : EPIDERMIS :: (*a.* mouth, *b.* cavity, *c.* tooth, *d.* dentine) : CORIUM

81. ZEBRA : PLATYPUS :: COW : (*a.* whale, *b.* monkey, *c.* anteater, *d.* snake)

82. PEREGRINATION : (*a.* issue, *b.* sell, *c.* travel, *d.* tilt) :: HAWKING : VEND

83. ATOLL : BEZEL :: LAGOON : (*a.* ring, *b.* island, *c.* water, *d.* gem)

84. ADAGIO : ANDANTE :: ALLEGRO : (*a.* largo, *b.* grave, *c.* vivace, *d.* allegretto)

85. (*a.* Wharton, *b.* Dickinson, *c.* Whitman, *d.* Porter) : SAPPHO :: AMERICAN : GREEK

86. LIGATURE : BUILDING :: (*a.* lawmaking, *b.* structure, *c.* binding, *d.* forming) : FORMING

87. SUCROSE : (*a.* predisposed, *b.* precursor, *c.* predominant, *d.* prednisone) :: CUR : DRIPPED

88. AVARICIOUS : (*a.* cow-like, *b.* satyr, *c.* lustful, *d.* greedy) :: RANDY : GOATISH

89. LANK : DANK :: GAUNT : (*a.* emaciated, *b.* damp, *c.* gauntlet, *d.* limp)

90. GOLD : (*a.* karat, *b.* argot, *c.* ingot, *d.* pure) :: ENERGY : CURRENT

91. FISSURE : (*a.* crack, *b.* spine, *c.* shine, *d.* break) :: CHINK : CHINE

92. PROVISO : (*a.* clause, *b.* amendment, *c.* preamble, *d.* bill) :: DOCUMENT : CONSTI-TUTION

93. (*a.* entomology, *b.* seductive, *c.* prodigious, *d.* prodigal) : GRASSHOPPER :: SEDULOUS : ANT

94. INCENDIARY : RECALCITRANT :: COMBUSTION : (*a.* explosion, *b.* declension, *c.* calcification, *d.* fiery)

95. HEROIN : THOUGH :: HEROINE : (*a.* through, *b.* thought, *c.* trough, *d.* tough)

96. CROESUS : CLEOPATRA :: (*a.* Alexandria, *b.* gold, *c.* Lydia, *d.* Persia) : EGYPT

97. (*a.* prose, *b.* rich, *c.* rodent, *d.* ermine) : MINK :: VOLUME : NOVEL

98. RECALCITRANT : (*a.* conniving, *b.* malicious, *c.* subterfuge, *d.* authority) :: RIGID : MANIPULATION

99. DIMINUENDO : DIM :: (*a.* tempo, *b.* tone, *c.* scale, *d.* decrescendo) : LIGHT

100. OMBUDSMAN : ARCHAEOLOGIST :: (*a.* governments, *b.* complaints, *c.* bureaucrats, *d.* civilizations) : RELICS

ANSWER KEY

1. (d) A fathom is a measure of depth, just as a dram is a measure of weight.

2. (c) A blade is the working tooth of a blender, and a cog is the working tooth of a machine.

3. (b) A blizzard is an extreme form of a flurry; remember degree relationships from chapter 7. Rage is an extreme form of annoyance.

4. (c) A general is the highest rank of soldier, just as a C.E.O. or chief operating officer is the highest rank of executive.

5. (d) Porcine means pig-like, or related to the pig. Bovine means cow-like.

6. (d) Christ is the God or savior in Christianity, and Allah is the God or savior in Islam. Mohammed is the prophet who founded Islam, not the one worshipped. That answer would not necessarily work because Christ did not "found" Christianity exactly; it was based on him.

7. (a) A lamp is a modern light; a watch is a modern timepiece.

8. (b) Since 100 is the boiling point of water in degrees Celsius, the correct answer is 0, the freezing point of water in degrees Celsius.

9. (c) A brawl is a loud quarrel, and a gasp is a loud breath.

10. (b) A pitch is a type of slant, as in "The counter had a slight pitch so the water would drip into the sink." And a hitch is a type of knot.

11. (d) A scalpel is the tool of a surgeon, and a plane is the tool of a carpenter.

12. (d) Forgery is deliberately and illegally misleading writing, perjury is deliberately and illegally misleading testimony.

13. (c) A rampart is designed to prevent attack; remember "O'er the ramparts we watched, were so gallantly streaming"? A copyright is designed to prevent plagiarism.

14. (c) Criteria is the plural of criterion, and vortices is the plural of vortex.

15. (a) A melee is a big fight, or an occasion of violence, and a fete is an occasion of celebration.

16. (b) An egg is one form of reproduction, and an escritoire is one form of a desk. In particular, it is a writing desk.

17. (d) A centaur is part man, part horse, and a satyr is part man, part goat.

18. (c) Foreshortening provides the illusion of depth, and deception provides the illusion of honesty.

19. (a) A periscope amplifies one's sight, and a microphone amplifies one's voice.

20. (a) To teach means to instruct, and to leech means to bleed or suck.

21. (b) Supplementary angles add up to 180°, and complementary angles add up to 90°.

22. (d) To jockey means to fight or jostle to get a better position, and to guard means to protect.

23. (c) A verb expresses something, for instance an action, while a noun names.

24. (b) The steppe is characterized as grassy, and the jungle is characterized as steamy.

25. (d) Dour is another word for stern, and compliant is another word for obedient.

26. (b) A tag is a kind of mark, as in when an animal is tagged for further study, and a flag is a mark as well, as in when a certain page of a book is flagged.

27. (c) August, pronounced differently from the month by the way, means majestic or awe-inspiring, and steamy means vaporous, or like steam.

28. (d) To vex someone means to pique or annoy him, while to pick something means to select it.

29. (b) A knot is a unit of speed, and a bolt is a unit of cloth.

30. (b) Both eagle and birdie are terms for what happens in a golf game, and both dunk and foul are terms for what happens in a basketball game.

31. (c) Demeter is the mother of Persephone, and Hera is the mother of Hephaestus.

32. (d) Careful about part of speech here: To brace means to support, and to heft means to lift.

33. (b) A dove is a sign of peace, and a vulture is a sign of mortality.

34. (a) Gaugin was a painter, and Wren was an architect.

35. (d) Judas is a person associated with betrayal (the Bible, again) and Ruth is a person associated with loyalty (the Book of Ruth in the Bible).

36. (c) Pork is the name for pig when the pig is in food form, and gristle is the name for cartilage when the cartilage is in food form.

37. (b) A chromatic scale is within an octave; an aria is within an opera.

38. (a) Five is an odd number, 0 is an even number. (Really! Try dividing it by 2.)

39. (b) *The Iliad* was written by Homer; *Ulysses* was written by James Joyce.

40. (c) The dollar is the unit of currency in Barbados; in Jordan it is the dinar.

41. (a) In the rainbow spectrum, the colors go Red, Orange, Yellow, Green, Blue, Indigo, Violet (Roy G. Biv makes it easier to remember). So indigo comes before violet, and orange comes before yellow.

42. (d) To holster something means to carry it (a holster when it's a noun is actually a carrying case); to brace something means to support or bolster it.

43. (b) To varnish something is to cover it, usually with varnish, and to tarnish something means to taint it.

44. (a) A J.D. is a Jurum Doctor, or doctor of law degree, and a D.D. is a doctorate of divinity.

45. (d) A convertible is a type of car, and a canine is a type of tooth. A dog, however, isn't a type of canine—it is a canine; there are no others.

46. (c) A monk's place is in an abbey, and a croupier's place is in a casino, where she runs the roulette table.

47. (*c*) To gainsay means to speak badly about something or someone, in other words, to decry it. To deny something means to contradict it.

48. (*a*) A complainant is one who makes a formal charge, and a miscreant is one who makes or creates evil. Remember the *mis* prefix.

49. (*c*) The word arrow becomes an entirely different word—marrow—by adding a letter to the beginning of the word; the same with one and cone.

50. (*a*) The next subdivision after kingdom is phylum, and the one after family is genus.

51. (*a*) Reap means to harvest, and gather means to infer. It's a tricky one; you might have had to take some time to see that it's a 1:2 analogy.

52. (*b*) A synod is a group of church officials, and a syndicate is a group of people within a business.

53. (*a*) Goodness means quality, and sake means purpose, as in, for whose sake are you taking this test?

54. (*c*) A hackle refers to an area on the neck of an animal, and a hock refers to an area on the leg of an animal, usually the ankle.

55. (*b*) According to the Constitution, Congress is in charge of guiding legislation and the President is in charge of the armed forces.

56. (*a*) Iran is on the land that was once called Persia, and Tanzania is on the land that was once called Tanganyika.

57. (*c*) A regiment is made up of battalions, and a library is made up of books.

58. (*d*) Dog is god spelled backwards, and spat is taps spelled backwards.

59. (*d*) A rebel fights or objects to the status quo, and an iconoclast fights objects or fights against the sacred. An apostate is one who abandons his faith, not necessarily one who fights against it.

60. (*a*) Apostrophe is an address to an imaginary person or audience, and testimony is an address to the public, or a public declaration. Use process of elimination!

61. (*c*) A mouse is a type of rodent; a koala is a type of marsupial.

62. (*d*) To debunk is to expose something or disprove it, and to reprove means to scold or remonstrate. Study that vocabulary!

63. (*c*) Impecunious means poor or destitute, and indomitable means tough and immovable, also tenacious.

64. (*c*) A shard is a small, broken piece of glass, and a sliver is a small, broken piece of wood.

65. (*b*) Knight and night are homophones, so are maid and made.

66. (*b*) Enumeration is the process of counting, and railing is the process of complaining, scolding, or vituperation.

67. (*b*) Achromatic means without color or colorless, and cacophonous means loud or without quiet.

68. (*a*) A shock is a tuft or bunch of hair, and a bouquet is a bunch of flowers.

69. (*b*) Claude is the first name of the painter Monet, and Edouard is the first name of the painter Manet.

70. (*c*) A whisper is quiet speech, and piano is a quiet tone.

71. (*c*) A vulture is a scavenging bird, and a hyena is a scavenging mammal.

72. (*c*) Mortar is used to join bricks, dowels are used to join wood.

73. (*b*) A parapet is a protective wall, and a moat is a protective ditch.

74. (*c*) Pole is an anagram for lope with the first and third letters transposed, and the same is true of dear and aedr.

75. (*c*) Puck and Bottom appear in the same Shakespeare play (*A Midsummer Night's Dream*), as do Iago and Othello (*Othello*).

76. (*b*) Anno means year in Latin, and sine means without. Both these words often show up in abbreviations and legal expressions.

77. (*b*) A component is a part of something, and a compeer is an equal.

78. (*d*) A flag is the symbol of a nation, and a scepter is the symbol of authority.

79. (*b*) Ornithology is the study of birds, and herpetology is the study of reptiles.

80. (*d*) The corium is the skin layer directly beneath the epidermis, and the dentine is the tooth layer directly beneath the enamel. Work backwards!

81. (*c*) A zebra and a cow are both placental mammals, and a platypus and an anteater are both protheria—mammals that lay eggs.

82. (*c*) To vend means to engage in hawking or selling, and to travel means to engage in peregrination.

83. (*d*) An atoll encloses a lagoon, and a bezel encloses a gem.

84. (*d*) Adagio means slow tempo, and andante means somewhat slow; allegro means fast, and allegretto means somewhat fast.

85. (*b*) Sappho was a Greek poet who was a woman, and Dickinson was an American poet who was also a woman.

86. (*c*) Building is the act of forming, and ligature is the act of binding.

87. (*a*) The word *cur* is formed out of some of the letters in sucrose, and the word *dripped* is formed out of some of the letters in *predisposed*.

88. (*d*) Randy means goatish or lustful; avaricious means greedy.

89. (*b*) Lank means gaunt or emaciated, and dank means damp.

90. (*c*) An ingot is a mass of metal or gold for transportation, and a current is a mass of energy.

91. (*b*) A fissure is a chink or crack, and a chine is a spine.

92. (*b*) A proviso is an addition to a document, and an amendment is an addition to the Constitution.

93. (*d*) The ant is a symbol of being sedulous or hard-working, the grasshopper stands for being prodigal or wasteful.

94. (*b*) Incendiary means prone to combustion or fire, and recalcitrant means prone to disagreement or declension.

95. (*b*) Heroin is transformed into an entirely different word by the addition of a letter onto the end, as is though.

96. (*c*) Cleopatra ruled Egypt, and Croesus ruled Lydia.

97. (*c*) A novel is a type of volume, a mink is a type of rodent.

98. (*d*) Rigid means resisting manipulation, and recalcitrant means resisting authority,

99. (*b*) Dim means softened light, diminuendo means softened tone.

100. (*b*) An archaeologist works with relics, and an ombudsman works with complaints.

SAMPLE TEST 3

Time: 50 Minutes
100 Questions

Directions: The following analogy pairs contain four choices with which to combine the unpaired word. Choose the answer that best corresponds to the full analogy pair. There is only one right answer.

1. (*a.* intelligence, *b.* wisdom, *c.* education, *d.* stupidity) : DEFINITION :: IGNORANT : HAZY

2. MAPS : (*a.* synonyms, *b.* meaning, *c.* definitions, *d.* lists) :: ATLAS : THESAURUS

3. CARUSO : CALLAS :: (*a.* bass, *b.* tenor, *c.* alto, *d.* aria) : SOPRANO

4. SUM : 3 + 4 :: QUOTIENT : (*a.* 3 - 4, *b.* 3 × 4, *c.* 3 ÷ 4, *d.* 4 - 3)

5. MEDIA : MEDIUM :: (*a.* camera, *b.* news, *c.* depths, *d.* heights) : HEIGHT

6. (*a.* heart, *b.* teeth, *c.* kidneys, *d.* bones) : NOSE :: RENAL : NASAL

7. HYDRANGEA : (*a.* vine, *b.* bulb, *c.* weed, *d.* shrub) :: DOGWOOD : TREE

8. PLIABLE : (*a.* bent, *b.* plied, *c.* abused, *d.* plastic) :: OPERABLE : USED

9. VIOLENT : VEHEMENCE :: (*a.* serious, *b.* drinking, *c.* riot, *d.* sagacity) : SOBRIETY

10. KENNEDY : LINCOLN :: (*a.* Ruby, *b.* Wilkes, *c.* Oswald, *d.* Casey) : BOOTH

11. ARISTOTLE : PLAUTUS :: (*a.* Plato, *b.* philosopher, *c.* poet, *d.* Greek) : PLAYWRIGHT

12. DASH : MORSE :: (*a.* puzzle, *b.* cipher, *c.* dot, *d.* symbol) : CRYPTOGRAM

13. (*a.* hail, *b.* rain, *c.* sleet, *d.* ice) : SNOW :: DROP : FLAKE

14. LETTER : (*a.* mail, *b.* alphabet, *c.* word, *d.* unit) :: DIGIT : NUMBER

15. NEW YORK : CALIFORNIA :: ALBANY : (*a.* Sacramento, *b.* Santa Barbara, *c.* Los Angeles, *d.* San Diego)

16. HAKE : DRAKE :: (*a.* fish, *b.* skate, *c.* chicken, *d.* elk) : DUCK

17. FIDDLE : TOY :: TINKER : (*a.* pans, *b.* violin, *c.* build, *d.* trifle)

18. (*a.* subordinate, *b.* subsume, *c.* suborn, *d.* subsidize) : SUBSERVIENT :: MOLLIFY : CALM

19. (*a.* platypus, *b.* antelope, *c.* bat, *d.* dog) : NARWHAL :: MAMMAL : MAMMAL

20. SAVORY : TASTE :: PULCHRITUDINOUS : (*a.* mien, *b.* flavor, *c.* food, *d.* menu)

21. BOLT : REAM :: (*a.* paste, *b.* page, *c.* sheet, *d.* cloth) : PAPER
22. TALLY : (*a.* list, *b.* mark, *c.* poll, *d.* addition) :: CONSENSUS : UNIFICATION
23. FALLOW : (*a.* chill, *b.* heat, *c.* seed, *d.* yellow) :: TEPID : WARMTH
24. BIAS : PARTISAN :: (*a.* prejudice, *b.* sloth, *c.* greed, *d.* objectivity) : AVARICIOUS
25. CAUTERIZE : (*a.* quarter, *b.* flame, *c.* bandage, *d.* needle) :: SEW : THREAD

26. IPSO FACTO : NOTA BENE :: BY THE FACT ITSELF : (*a.* on a good note, *b.* not good, *c.* note well, *d.* not as good)
27. LOQUACIOUS : TACITURN :: (*a.* objection, *b.* vivacious, *c.* shy, *d.* cantankerous) : WITHDRAWN
28. MACERATE : THIN :: (*a.* silver, *b.* eviscerate, *c.* gild, *d.* precious) : GOLD
29. (*a.* labile, *b.* cowardice, *c.* illness, *d.* daring) : BRAVADO :: FEBRILE : FEVER
30. (*a.* Truman, *b.* Roosevelt, *c.* Lee, *d.* MacArthur) : GRANT :: WORLD WAR II : CIVIL WAR

31. LUCRE : APOGEE :: MONEY : (*a.* apex, *b.* silver, *c.* apology, *d.* offering)
32. (*a.* woe, *b.* tough, *c.* trough, *d.* plough) : ENOUGH :: THOUGH : ROUGH
33. REND : RUN :: RENT : (*a.* runt, *b.* rant, *c.* ran, *d.* running)
34. HECTARE : (*a.* heavy, *b.* density, *c.* area, *d.* amount) :: LAND : MASS
35. AROMA : BOUQUET :: (*a.* sound, *b.* fake, *c.* flowers, *d.* smell) : EUPHONY

36. FAN : (*a.* drip, *b.* faun, *c.* fawn, *d.* drab) :: DAB : DAUB
37. MARS : ARES :: (*a.* Apollo, *b.* Poseidon, *c.* Mercury, *d.* Pluto) : HERMES
38. SEMBLANCE : DECOY :: APPEARANCE : (*a.* false, *b.* hunt, *c.* animal, *d.* prey)
39. TABLE : SHELVE :: TEACH : (*a.* instruct, *b.* blackboard, *c.* library, *d.* books)
40. NOD : SEMAPHORE :: (*a.* symphony, *b.* rest, *c.* nation, *d.* movement) : FLAG

41. ARIA : OPERA :: (*a.* epilogue, *b.* chorus, *c.* denouement, *d.* soliloquy) : PLAY

42. ACTUARY : SMITH :: (*a.* Jones, *b.* risk, *c.* wood, *d.* real) : METAL

43. NERVY : (*a.* brazen, *b.* nervous, *c.* timid, *d.* lie) :: FRAUDULENT : FALSE

44. 12 OUNCES : TROY :: (*a.* 8 ounces, *b.* 10 ounces, *c.* 14 ounces, *d.* 16 ounces) : AVOIRDUPOIS

45. MAGNANIMOUS : (*a.* thin, *b.* greed, *c.* obese, *d.* generous) :: CORPULENT : FAT

46. FINE : MISBEHAVIOR :: RENT : (*a.* occupancy, *b.* law, *c.* prison, *d.* lease)

47. ENERVATE : RELATE :: (*a.* frighten, *b.* sharpen, *c.* weaken, *d.* raise) : TELL

48. AU : HG :: GOLD : (*a.* lead, *b.* silver, *c.* helium, *d.* mercury)

49. PATRIOT : (*a.* quisling, *b.* stripling, *c.* hero, *d.* washington) :: ALLEN : ARNOLD

50. (*a.* user, *b.* smell, *c.* and, *d.* or) : PRACTITIONER :: ENT : LIKE

51. (*a.* rig, *b.* clothes, *c.* style, *d.* accoutrement) : OUTFIT :: ADORN : DECORATE

52. EXPIATE : ATONE :: EXTOL : (*a.* alone, *b.* laud, *c.* confess, *d.* sin)

53. (*a.* river, *b.* lake, *c.* reservoir, *d.* energy) : DAM :: HOLE : PLUG

54. RICKETS : (*a.* young, *b.* dotage, *c.* vitamins, *d.* fragility) :: NUTRITION : AGE

55. V : (*a.* I, *b.* X, *c.* II, *d.* L) :: X : XX

56. TEMPORARILY : FOR EXAMPLE :: (*a.* pro tempore, *b.* ex tempore, *c.* sine anno, *d.* ad interim) : EXAMPLI GRATI

57. TOUPEE : STRUT :: HAIR : (*a.* preen, *b.* buttress, *c.* ceiling, *d.* wall)

58. RIGHT : (*a.* obtuse, *b.* supplementary, *c.* equilateral, *d.* acute) :: ZERO : NEGATIVE

59. PEDESTAL : (*a.* statue, *b.* raised, *c.* plinth, *d.* holy) :: IMAGE : ICON

60. DIAMOND : TRACK :: (*a.* sleuth, *b.* oval, *c.* baseball, *d.* discrimination) : RACE

61. (*a.* deciduous, *b.* annual, *c.* stamen, *d.* conifer) : BRYOPHYTE :: PINE : MOSS

62. JAMB : GIRDER :: (*a.* square, *b.* horizontal, *c.* vertical, *d.* diagonal) : HORIZONTAL

63. MISOGYNY : MISOGAMY :: WOMEN : (*a.* men, *b.* woman, *c.* marriage, *d.* engagement)

64. LIVE : (*a.* good, *b.* sanity, *c.* stun, *d.* insanity) :: EVIL : NUTS

65. DRAGON : GAD :: INSECT : (*a.* bug, *b.* monster, *c.* annoyance, *d.* poison)

66. (*a.* fight, *b.* situation, *c.* shine, *d.* abrade) : SCRAPE :: SCUFFLE : SCUFF

67. DRAUGHT : (*a.* raft, *b.* rough, *c.* graft, *d.* draft) :: DROUGHT : ROUT

68. ETCHING : SCRIMSHAW :: (*a.* acid, *b.* plate, *c.* design, *d.* gilded) : IVORY

69. APARTMENT : FLAT :: TRUCK : (*a.* lorry, *b.* eviction, *c.* lobby, *d.* sublease)

70. PONDER : POOL :: (*a.* group, *b.* flood, *c.* reflect, *d.* water) : GATHER

71. HOSEA : (*a.* Job, *b.* Mark, *c.* Jonah, *d.* Exodus) :: MATTHEW : LUKE

72. MIFF : MUFFLE :: UPSET : (*a.* pique, *b.* win, *c.* enrage, *d.* silence)

73. ANON : (*a.* anonymous, *b.* soon, *c.* alone, *d.* later) :: ERST : FORMERLY

74. (*a.* envy, *b.* evil, *c.* scorn, *d.* shocking) : INVIDIOUS :: OUTCRY : PROVOCATIVE

75. UNSTINTINGLY : LAVISH :: (*a.* iron, *b.* extravagantly, *c.* generously, *d.* forcefully) : PRESS

76. (*a.* energy, *b.* stupidity, *c.* deviance, *d.* prescience) : WISDOM :: ECCENTRIC : ORACLE

77. SPAIN : (*a.* Italy, *b.* Spain, *c.* America, *d.* West Indies) :: DE SOTO : COLUMBUS

78. FINAGLE : (*a.* credit, *b.* try, *c.* cheat, *d.* repute) :: IMPUTE : CHARGE

79. (*a.* dock, *b.* bullring, *c.* mine, *d.* office) : STEVEDORE :: LAB : RESEARCHER

80. DATA : DATUM :: DEER : (*a.* doe, *b.* buck, *c.* deer, *d.* deers)

81. ODOR : (*a.* odor, *b.* sound, *c.* sight, *d.* sense) :: FETID : NOISOME
82. BOND : SALVAGE :: (*a.* sinking, *b.* bail, *c.* rescue, *d.* money) : SHIP
83. HORMONES : BILE :: (*a.* heart, *b.* lungs, *c.* thyroid, *d.* spleen) : LIVER
84. COGITATION : MASTICATION :: (*a.* mouth, *b.* brain, *c.* pulmonary, *d.* jaws) : TEETH
85. (*a.* stripling, *b.* baby, *c.* pup, *d.* quisling) : TOT :: TEENAGER : CHILD

86. PUNCTILIO : FETTLE :: (*a.* appointment, *b.* fine, *c.* observance, *d.* lateness) : CONDITION
87. UNHOLY : (*a.* holy, *b.* sacred, *c.* deserted, *d.* arid) :: DESECRATE : DESICCATE
88. FIBRIL : FIBER :: (*a.* febrile, *b.* impurity, *c.* filter, *d.* mote) : DUST
89. (*a.* fall, *b.* gymnastic, *c.* lock, *d.* cart) : WEIGHT :: TUMBREL : ONUS
90. LATITUDINARIAN : (*a.* pain, *b.* freedom, *c.* logistics, *d.* religion) :: HEDONIST : PLEASURE

91. (*a.* chatter, *b.* scold, *c.* advertise, *d.* insult) : PRATE :: CRITICIZE : ANIMADVERT
92. GRASP : FORCEPS :: SMOOTH : (*a.* plane, *b.* scalpel, *c.* silk, *d.* tongs)
93. HATEFUL LOVE : (*a.* synecdoche, *b.* noun, *c.* oxymoron, *d.* metonymy) :: BUZZ : ONOMATOPOEIA
94. TOUCH : (*a.* look, *b.* throb *c.* palpate, *d.* pulsate) :: VISION : PERUSE
95. (*a.* angered, *b.* broken, *c.* hurt, *d.* amused) : DUPED:: FRANGIBLE : GULLIBLE

96. FEINT : (*a.* fine, *b.* fain, *c.* feen, *d.* feent) :: FAINT : FEIGN
97. VANITY : THACKERAY :: HARD : (*a.* magazine, *b.* vice, *c.* Trollope, *d.* Dickens)
98. (*a.* mark, *b.* pound, *c.* schilling, *d.* dollar) : DOLLAR :: AUSTRIA : LIBERIA
99. ANAGOGIC : HERMENEUTIC :: (*a.* religion, *b.* spirituality, *c.* data, *d.* analogies) : ANALYSIS
100. INTEREST : PRESSURE :: REIN TEST : (*a.* spur seer, *b.* saddle gauge, *c.* stirrup level, *d.* bridle resistance)

ANSWER KEY

1. (c) Hazy means without definition, and ignorant means without education.

2. (a) An atlas contains maps, and a thesaurus contains synonyms.

3. (b) Callas was a soprano opera singer, and Caruso was a tenor opera singer.

4. (c) 3 + 4 will result in a sum, and 3 ÷ 4 will result in a quotient.

5. (d) Media is the plural of medium, and heights is the plural of height.

6. (c) Nasal means related to the nose, and renal means related to the kidneys.

7. (d) A hydrangea is a type of shrub, and a dogwood is a type of tree.

8. (a) Operable means able to be used, and pliable means able to be bent.

9. (a) Vehemence is a violent manner, sobriety is a serious manner.

10. (c) Lincoln was assassinated by Booth, and Kennedy was assassinated by Oswald.

11. (b) Plautus was a playwright, and Aristotle was a philosopher.

12. (b) A dash is part of a Morse code, and a cipher is part of a cryptogram.

13. (b) A flake is a unit of snow, and a drop is a unit of rain.

14. (c) A number is made up of a digit or digits, and a word is made up of a letter or letters. The alphabet is also made up of letters, but a word, as a number, is not the regular ordering of digits, but a conscious reordering of them.

15. (a) Albany is the capital of New York State, and Sacramento is the capital of California.

16. (a) A hake is a type of fish, and a drake is a type of duck (a male duck).

17. (d) To fiddle with something is to tinker with it, and to toy with something (or someone) is to trifle with it.

18. (a) To mollify means to put into a calm state, and to subordinate means to put into a subservient state. Part of speech works well here.

19. (b) A narwhal is a horned mammal, and an antelope is a horned mammal.

20. (a) Savory means with a pleasing taste, and pulchritudinous (or beautiful) means with a pleasing mien (or face).

21. (d) A ream is a measure of paper, and bolt is a measure of cloth.

22. (d) A tally means an addition or a process of additions, and a consensus is a process of unification.

23. (c) Tepid is without warmth, and fallow is without seed.

24. (c) Partisan means having bias, and avaricious means having greed.

25. (b) To sew is to seal or close with thread, and to cauterize is to seal or close with flame.

26. (c) Ipso facto means by "the fact itself," and nota bene means "note well."

27. (b) Loquacious means speaking a lot, or not being taciturn, and vivacious means not being withdrawn.

28. (*c*) To macerate means to make thin, and to gild means to make gold.

29. (*d*) The Torah is the sacred book of Judaism, and the Bhagavad Gita is the sacred book of Hinduism.

30. (*d*) Grant was a general in the Civil War, and MacArthur was a general in World War II.

31. (*a*) Lucre is another word for money or wealth, and apogee is another word for apex or peak.

32. (*a*) Rough rhymes with enough, and though rhymes with woe.

33. (*c*) Rent is the past tense of rend, meaning to rip, and ran is the past tense of run.

34. (*b*) A hectare measures the amount of land, and density measures the amount of mass.

35. (*a*) Bouquet is pleasant aroma, and euphony is pleasant sound.

36. (*b*) Dab is changed to another word, daub, by the insertion of a *u*, the same is true of fan and faun.

37. (*c*) Ares is the Greek name for Mars, the god of war, and Hermes is the Greek name of Mercury, the god of speed.

38. (*c*) Semblance is a false appearance, and a decoy is a false animal.

39. (*a*) To table means to shelve, or to put aside temporarily, to teach means to instruct.

40. (*d*) A nod is a type of movement, and a semaphore is a type of flag.

41. (*d*) An aria is a solo performance during an opera, a soliloquy is a solo performance during a play.

42. (*b*) An actuary works with risk, and a smith works with metal.

43. (*a*) Nervy means brazen or bold, and fraudulent means false.

44. (*d*) A pound in the Troy scale has 12 ounces, and a pound in the Avoirdupois scale has 16 ounces.

45. (*d*) Corpulent means fat, and magnanimous means generous.

46. (*a*) A fine is money paid as a result of misbehavior, and rent is money paid as a result of occupancy.

47. (*c*) To enervate means to weaken, and to relate means to tell.

48. (*d*) Au is the chemical symbol for gold, and Hg is the chemical symbol for mercury.

49. (*a*) Allen was a patriot during the American Revolution, and Arnold was a quisling, or traitor, during the American Revolution.

50. (*d*) The suffix "or" means a practitioner, as in a debtor or a suitor, and the suffix "ent" means like or having a specific quality, as in translucent.

51. (*a*) To adorn means to decorate, and to rig means to outfit or provide with equipment.

52. (*b*) To expiate means to atone, and to extol means to laud or praise.

53. (*a*) A plug stops up a hole, and a dam stops up a river. (It also creates a reservoir or lake, but does not stop it up.)

54. (b) Rickets is a condition due to nutrition, and dotage is a condition due to age.

55. (b) The Roman V or 5 is doubled to add up to 10 or X, just as X or 10 is doubled to become XX or 20.

56. (a) Exampli grati means "for example," and pro tempore means "temporarily."

57. (d) A toupee is a reinforcement of hair, a strut is a reinforcement of a wall.

58. (d) Negative means less than zero, and acute means less than right (as in angle measurements).

59. (c) A plinth is a type of pedestal, and an icon is a type of image.

60. (c) Baseball takes place on a diamond, and a race takes place on a track.

61. (d) A moss is a type of bryophyte, and pine is a type of conifer.

62. (c) A jamb is a vertical support, and a girder is a horizontal support.

63. (c) Misogyny is hatred of women, and misogamy is hatred of marriage.

64. (c) Evil is the reverse of live, and nuts is the reverse of stun.

65. (c) A dragonfly is an insect, and a gadfly is an annoyance.

66. (a) To scrape means to scuff, and to scuffle means to fight.

67. (a) Drought rhymes with rout and they begin with a *d* and an *r*, and draught (pronounced "draft") rhymes with raft and they also begin with a *d* and an *r*.

68. (b) Scrimshaw is done on an ivory, and etching is done on a plate.

69. (a) An apartment is referred to as a flat in England, and a truck is referred to as a lorry in England.

70. (c) To ponder means to think or reflect on something, and to pool means to gather or collect. Use part of speech!

71. (c) Matthew and Luke are both books in the Synoptic Gospels, and Hosea and Jonah are both books in Prophets.

72. (d) To miff means to upset, and to muffle means to silence.

73. (b) Anon is the old-time way of saying soon, and erst is the old-time way of saying formerly.

74. (a) Something (or someone) invidious incites envy, and someone (or something, if you like) provocative incites outcry.

75. (d) To lavish means to give unstintingly, and to press means to give forcefully.

76. (c) An oracle is characterized by wisdom, and an eccentric is characterized by deviance.

77. (a) De Soto was an explorer from Spain, and Columbus was an explorer from Italy.

78. (c) To finagle means to cheat, and to impute means to charge or accuse.

79. (a) A researcher works in a lab, and a stevedore works at a dock (lifting things and so on).

80. (c) Data is the plural of datum, and deer is the plural of deer.

81. (a) Fetid means with a nasty odor, and surprisingly enough, noisome means the exact same thing.

82. (b) Salvage is the money paid for a ship, and bond is the money paid for bail.

83. (c) Bile is produced by the liver, and hormones are produced by the thyroid gland.

84. (b) Mastication is done with the teeth, and cogitation is done with the brain.

85. (a) Tot is another name for child, and stripling is another name for teenager.

86. (c) Fettle means condition, as in "She's in a fine fettle," and punctilio is a manner or observance, really, a fine point of etiquette. On something like this, use process of elimination and guess.

87. (d) Desecrate means to make unholy; desiccate means to make arid, or dry.

88. (d) A fibril is a tiny piece of fiber, and a mote is a tiny piece of dust.

89. (d) Onus is another name for weight, and a tumbrel is another name for a cart.

90. (b) A hedonist desires pleasure, and a latitudinarian desires freedom. (Think of the first part of the word, latitude; looking at how words are constructed can help you.)

91. (a) To prate means to chatter, and to animadvert means to criticize.

92. (a) Forceps are used to grasp, and a plane is used to smooth (a carpenter's plane).

93. (c) Buzz is an example of onomatopoeia, and hateful love is an example of an oxymoron.

94. (d) To peruse is to examine using vision, and to palpate is to examine using touch.

95. (b) Gullible means easily duped, and frangible means easily broken.

96. (b) Faint and feint are homophones, and feign and fain are homophones.

97. (d) *Vanity Fair* is the title of a novel by Thackeray, and *Hard Times* is the title of a novel by Dickens.

98. (c) The dollar is the unit of currency in Liberia, and the schilling is the unit of currency in Austria.

99. (b) Hermeneutic means related to analysis, and anagogic means related to spirituality.

100. (a) Rein test is an anagram of interest, and spur seer is an anagram of pressure.

SAMPLE TEST 4

Time: 50 Minutes
100 Questions

Directions: The following analogy pairs contain four choices with which to combine the unpaired word. Choose the answer that best corresponds to the full analogy pair. There is only one right answer.

1. APPENDICES : (*a.* cornet, *b.* cornex, *c.* cornucopia, *d.* cornices) :: APPENDIX : CORNICE

2. MILL : (*a.* factory, *b.* energy, *c.* paper, *d.* studies) :: UNIVERSITY : SCHOLARS

3. BUSS : CLAP :: (*a.* hands, *b.* kiss, *c.* car, *d.* sound) : NOISE

4. THYME : (*a.* salt, *b.* corn, *c.* daisy, *d.* shrub) :: PEPPER : IRIS

5. CARAT : GEM :: (*a.* weight, *b.* gauge, *c.* density, *d.* metal) : SHEET METAL

6. HARVEST : CROPS :: MUSTER : (*a.* troops, *b.* funds, *c.* pesticide, *d.* gather)

7. (*a.* fungus, *b.* moss, *c.* grain, *d.* fruit) : VEGETABLE :: NUT : TURNIP

8. PLAY : PLAIT :: GREY : (*a.* pale, *b.* wan, *c.* braid, *d.* great)

9. MICE : (*a.* mace, *b.* mouse, *c.* rats, *d.* stratum) :: DATA : DATUM

10. LOUDER : SOFTER :: (*a.* decrescendo, *b.* innuendo, *c.* crescendo, *d.* forte-piano) : DIMINUENDO

11. (*a.* dwelling, *b.* situation, *c.* loss, *d.* win) : DEFEAT :: HOVEL : DEBACLE

12. ZERO : DIVIDE :: (*a.* irrational, *b.* adjust, *c.* join, *d.* collate) : SEPARATE

13. CODICIL : WILL :: ANNEX : (*a.* building, *b.* school, *c.* estate, *d.* testament)

14. CENTRIFUGE : PRISM :: (*a.* space, *b.* liquid, *c.* dark, *d.* filtrate) : LIGHT

15. BRUSQUE : (*a.* brisk, *b.* brash, *c.* violent, *d.* curt) :: PIOUS : RELIGIOUS

16. COMA : FAINT :: MARATHON : (*a.* race, *b.* track, *c.* mile, *d.* sprint)

17. (*a.* foolish, *b.* crazy, *c.* rough, *d.* sharp) : INANE :: HARSH : SCATHING

18. (*a.* 1776, *b.* 1783, *c.* 1789, *d.* 1787) : 1865 :: REVOLUTIONARY : CIVIL

19. PLATO : (*a.* Plautus, *b.* Aristotle, *c.* Austen, *d.* Nabokov) :: NIJINSKY : PAVLOVA

20. HUE : COLOR :: HEW : (*a.* and cry, *b.* shade, *c.* cut, *d.* few)

21. ACUITY : (*a.* sweetness, *b.* smallness, *c.* keenness, *d.* slowness) :: ACERBITY : BITTERNESS

22. BHAGAVAD GITA : (*a.* koran, *b.* tao, *c.* bible, *d.* buddha) :: HINDUISM : ISLAM

23. (*a.* forbidden, *b.* explosion, *c.* deadly, *d.* insidious) : BANE :: BENEFICIAL : BOON

24. ALIAS : POUND :: AKA : (*a.* smash, *b.* m.o., *c.* sine qua non, *d.* lb.)

25. PLUMB : LEVEL :: (*a.* depth, *b.* deep, *c.* vertical, *d.* water) : HORIZONTAL

26. HYPER : (*a.* beyond, *b.* behind, *c.* excitable, *d.* between) :: HYPO : BELOW

27. TAT : MAT :: LACE : (*a.* welcome, *b.* frame, *c.* cloth, *d.* hair)

28. LITANY : MARTINET :: REPETITIVE : (*a.* lonely, *b.* rhythmic, *c.* disciplined, *d.* prayerful)

29. GRADIENT : (*a.* grade, *b.* slope, *c.* quality, *d.* spring) :: RESILIENCE : ELASTICITY

30. CASSOCK : WIMPLE :: PRIEST : (*a.* church, *b.* monk, *c.* nun, *d.* altar)

31. INTRIGUE : WALE :: SCHEME : (*a.* ridge, *b.* plot, *c.* tempt, *d.* moan)

32. HOMELY : COMELY :: AFFABLE : (*a.* friendly, *b.* compliant, *c.* laughable, *d.* aloof)

33. (*a.* side, *b.* triangle, *c.* leg, *d.* angle) : HYPOTENUSE :: QUADRILATERAL : TRAPEZOID

34. (*a.* fall, *b.* prayer, *c.* edge, *d.* stall) : PRECIPITATE :: CALL : INVOKE

35. FETTER : FOSTER :: (*a.* shake, *b.* incarcerate, *c.* restrain, *d.* adopt) : ENCOURAGE

36. OSSIFY : PUTREFY :: (*a.* disintegrate, *b.* crumble, *c.* chalk, *d.* set) : ROT

37. OID : (*a.* resemblance, *b.* emptiness, *c.* rehearsal, *d.* antagonism) :: ICS : PRACTICE

38. FINANCIAL : (*a.* coffers, *b.* markets, *c.* stocks, *d.* funds) :: AQUATIC : RESERVOIRS

39. (*a.* bacteria, *b.* spoor, *c.* mold, *d.* fungi) : CELLS :: MYCOLOGY : CYTOLOGY

40. NAIADS : (*a.* flower, *b.* water, *c.* fire, *d.* earth) :: DRYADS : TREE

41. TONE : PIANO :: (*a.* volume, *b.* chord, *c.* tempo, *d.* instrument) : LENTO
42. (*a.* romantic, *b.* mountebank, *c.* apothecary, *d.* stevedore) : SWINDLER :: HARLE-QUIN : CLOWN
43. AWAY : TOWARD :: ARTERIES : (*a.* veins, *b.* ventricles, *c.* aorta, *d.* heart)
44. BUILDING : (*a.* I-beam, *b.* damper, *c.* girder, *d.* truss) :: BRIDGE : SPAR
45. TON : YARD :: (*a.* horse, *b.* cart, *c.* knot, *d.* not) : DRAY

46. WOMAN : (*a.* food, *b.* fight, *c.* man, *d.* harpy) :: HOYDEN : FRACAS
47. BIRD : (*a.* bull, *b.* dog, *c.* horse, *d.* goat) :: HARPY : MINOTAUR
48. LEWIS : CARROLL :: (*a.* Alice, *b.* Narnia, *c.* Lucy, *d.* paradise) : WONDERLAND
49. ENTENTE : TREATY :: DETENTE : (*a.* relaxation, *b.* war, *c.* parry, *d.* pact)
50. UNRULY : HOARY :: (*a.* sweet, *b.* provocative, *c.* obstreperous, *d.* recondite) : ANCIENT

51. STUPEFY : (*a.* stupid, *b.* amaze, *c.* uneducated, *d.* seam) :: SUTURE : SEW
52. (*a.* V, *b.* VI, *c.* LX, *d.* DV) : DC :: X : C
53. CLEANLINESS : PERSNICKETY :: (*a.* filth, *b.* stubbornness, *c.* pliability, *d.* fastidi-ousness) : OBDURATE
54. URBAN : LITTORAL :: CITY : (*a.* country, *b.* town, *c.* shore, *d.* village)
55. STRIPE : (*a.* spritely, *b.* aches, *c.* fight, *d.* priest) :: SNIPE : PINES

56. MIXTURE : (*a.* presentation, *b.* surf, *c.* flower, *d.* gap) :: OLIO : LACUNA
57. GRANT : (*a.* 15, *b.* 16, *c.* 17, *d.* 18) :: LINCOLN : 16
58. HALO : DIADEM :: SANCTIFICATION : (*a.* angel, *b.* devil, *c.* commonality, *d.* royalty)
59. FACILITY : AVIDITY :: (*a.* corporation, *b.* ease, *c.* diligence, *d.* work) : GREED
60. BLUBBER : (*a.* fat, *b.* obese, *c.* cry, *d.* crush) :: STOMP : WALK

61. (*a.* fluid, *b.* appreciation, *c.* smell, *d.* edge) : SAVOR :: TEXTURE : GRIT

62. UNITED UTATES : CANADA :: (*a.* England, *b.* Tahiti, *c.* Spain, *d.* Antigua) : FRANCE

63. HORSE : GEM :: REIN : (*a.* facet, *b.* diamond, *c.* tincture, *d.* bezel)

64. (*a.* quick, *b.* exotic, *c.* broad, *d.* tropical) : LARGO :: SOLEMN : GRAVE

65. EMEND : COMMEND :: (*a.* edit, *b.* insult, *c.* denigrate, *d.* laud) : PRAISE

66. GRAVITY : (*a.* dearth, *b.* ease, *c.* frivolity, *d.* speed) :: LIGHTNESS : SPATE

67. MANDIBLE : CRANIUM :: ULNA : (*a.* tibia, *b.* clavicle, *c.* radius, *d.* femur)

68. MUSE : INSPIRE :: (*a.* oscillate, *b.* consecrate, *c.* ruminate, *d.* emanate) : STIMULATE

69. MESS : CELLAR :: EAT : (*a.* drink, *b.* preserve, *c.* wreck, *d.* muddle)

70. STABLE : HOARSE :: (*a.* friendly, *b.* wild, *c.* steadfast, *d.* equine) : ROUGH

71. (*a.* prolixity, *b.* asphyxia, *c.* aerobics, *d.* propinquity) : OXYGEN :: BOORISHNESS : MANNERS

72. WASPISH : (*a.* aryan, *b.* white, *c.* annoyed, *d.* mean) :: MALLEABLE : BENT

73. RASP : HEMP :: (*a.* filter, *b.* rope, *c.* file, *d.* tooth) : FIBER

74. (*a.* feral, *b.* scary, *c.* chary, *d.* obnoxious) : TRUCULENT :: RELUCTANT : AGGRESSIVE

75. PUNT : FLACON :: BOAT : (*a.* bird, *b.* kick, *c.* float, *d.* bottle)

76. FLOUT : FLIPPANT :: HARANGUE : (*a.* denigrating, *b.* casual, *c.* mocking, *d.* violent)

77. DRINK : IMBIBE :: (*a.* seize, *b.* shirt, *c.* rim, *d.* circle) : COLLAR

78. AMERICAN : (*a.* French, *b.* Spanish, *c.* Greek, *d.* Italian) :: POLLOCK : PICASSO

79. (*a.* bore, *b.* pit, *c.* fungus, *d.* bottom) : MOLD :: HOLE : SHAPE

80. RADIO : (*a.* ad rio, *b.* media, *c.* sierra, *d.* antennae) :: TELEVISION : VISIT LEONE

81. BIND : WALK :: (*a.* hobble, *b.* cobble, *c.* wobble, *d.* foible) : STAGGER
82. IRISH : BLACK :: IRELAND : (*a.* Germany, *b.* Italy, *c.* Turkey, *d.* Poland)
83. CAGEY : (*a.* penal, *b.* shrewd, *c.* vicious, *d.* recidivist) :: SAVAGE : FERAL
84. STOPS : CLAMPS :: TOP : (*a.* peek, *b.* limit, *c.* land, *d.* lamp)
85. CLOVEN : (*a.* split, *b.* craven, *c.* ruthless, *d.* comment) :: CLEMENT : MERCY

86. SPACIOUS : COMMODIOUS :: (*a.* small, *b.* shrunken, *c.* abhorrent, *d.* capacious) : ODIOUS
87. HABILIMENT : (*a.* manners, *b.* title, *c.* dress, *d.* bearing) :: PROTOCOL : BEHAVIOR
88. TURBID : LUCID :: (*a.* confused, *b.* turbine, *c.* engine, *d.* sedimented) : CLEAR
89. ALBEE : (*a.* Shaw, *b.* Joyce, *c.* Ovid, *d.* Keats) :: WORDSWORTH : COLERIDGE
90. (*a.* Jurassic, *b.* Mesozoic, *c.* Cenezoic, *d.* Paleozoic) : CENEZOIC :: 390,000,000 : 70,000,000

91. AWL : HOLES :: DIBBLE : (*a.* dribble, *b.* pockets, *c.* holes, *d.* slits)
92. UNKEMPT : BLOWZY :: (*a.* kempt, *b.* unkempt, *c.* blossoming, *d.* grim) : FROWZY
93. HELP : (*a.* aid, *b.* induce, *c.* force, *d.* legal) :: ABET : SUBORN
94. CLOTURE : DEBATE :: CEASE-FIRE : (*a.* treaty, *b.* ally, *c.* enemy, *d.* fighting)
95. CAPSULE : SPACE :: (*a.* cloaks, *b.* hoods, *c.* speculum, *d.* specula) : CAPES

96. (*a.* fabricate, *b.* bedizen, *c.* obstruct, *d.* stymie) : IMPEDE :: CLOTHE : HAMPER
97. (*a.* Bulge, *b.* Bunker Hill, *c.* Vietnam, *d.* Marne) : ANTIETAM :: REVOLUTIONARY WAR : CIVIL WAR
98. COEVALS : ERA :: PEERS : (*a.* standing, *b.* stare, *c.* gaze, *d.* jury)
99. BOSKY : (*a.* grass, *b.* woods, *c.* skin, *d.* nails) :: HIRSUTE : HAIR
100. CODA : COLOPHON :: MOVEMENT : (*a.* book, *b.* play, *c.* symphony, *d.* poem)

ANSWER KEY

1. (*d*) Appendices is the plural of appendix, and cornices is the plural of cornice.

2. (*c*) Some paper is produced by a mill, as some scholars are produced by a university.

3. (*b*) A clap is a loud noise, and a buss is a loud kiss.

4. (*c*) Thyme and pepper are both spices, and an iris and a daisy are both flowers.

5. (*b*) A carat is the unit of measurement of gems, and gauge is the unit of measurement of sheet metal.

6. (*a*) To harvest means to gather crops, and to muster means to gather troops.

7. (*d*) A turnip is a type of vegetable, and a nut is a type of fruit.

8. (*d*) Plate adds an *ate* sound to play, and great does the same thing for grey.

9. (*b*) Datum is the singular of data, ditto for mouse and mice.

10. (*c*) Diminuendo means for music to get softer, and crescendo means for it to get louder.

11. (*a*) A hovel is a horrible dwelling, and a debacle is a horrible defeat.

12. (*b*) To divide something means to separate it, and to zero something means to adjust it.

13. (*a*) A codicil is the added-on section of a will, and an annex is the added-on section of a building.

14. (*b*) A prism separates light, and a centrifuge separates liquids.

15. (*d*) Pious means very religious, and brusque means very curt.

16. (*a*) A coma is a long faint, and a marathon is a long race.

17. (*a*) Something inane is foolish, and something scathing is harsh.

18. (*b*) The United States Civil War ended in 1865, and the United States Revolutionary War ended in 1783.

19. (*b*) Nijinsky and Pavlova were both dancers, and Plato and Aristotle were both philosophers.

20. (*c*) A hue is a color, and to hew means to cut.

21. (*c*) Acuity means sharpness or keenness, and acerbity means bitterness.

22. (*a*) The Bhagavad Gita is the sacred book of Hinduism, and the Koran is the sacred book of Islam.

23. (*c*) A boon is something beneficial, a bane is something deadly.

24. (*d*) Aka is an abbreviation for alias, and lb. is an abbreviation for pound.

25. (*c*) Level means exactly horizontal, plumb means exactly vertical.

26. (*a*) Hyper is a prefix meaning beyond, as in hypercritical, and hypo is a prefix meaning below, as in hypodermic (under the skin).

27. (*d*) To tat means to make lace, and to mat means to make a frame.

28. (*c*) A litany is by nature repetitive, and a martinet is by nature disciplined.

29. (*b*) The gradient is the measure of slope, and resilience is the measure or extent of elasticity.

30. (*c*) A cassock is worn by a priest, and a wimple is worn by a nun.

31. (*a*) An intrigue is a scheme, and a wale (as in corduroy) is a ridge.

32. (*d*) Homely means ugly, or not comely (pretty), while affable means friendly, or not aloof (cold). Homely and comely don't rhyme either; homely has an 'oh' sound like comb, where comely sounds like come or rum.

33. (*a*) A trapezoid is a type of quadrilateral, as a hypotenuse is a type of side (of a triangle, remember?).

34. (*a*) To precipitate means to fall, as in rain falling, and to invoke is to call.

35. (*c*) To fetter means to restrain, and to foster something is to encourage it.

36. (*d*) To ossify means to harden or set, and to putrefy means to rot.

37. (*a*) The suffix "ics" indicates the practice of, as in aerobics or hysterics, and the suffix "oid" indicates resemblance, as in humanoid.

38. (*a*) Reservoirs are stores of aquatic reserves, and coffers are stores of financial reserves.

39. (*d*) Cytology is the study of cells, and mycology is the study of fungi.

40. (*b*) Dryads are tree nymphs, and naiads are water nymphs.

41. (*c*) Piano is a type of tone, and lento is a type of tempo.

42. (*b*) A mountebank is a swindler, and a harlequin is a clown.

43. (*a*) Arteries carry blood away from the heart, and veins carry blood to the heart.

44. (*c*) A girder is a horizontal support of a building, and a spar is a horizontal support of a bridge.

45. (*d*) Dray is yard backwards, and not is ton backwards.

46. (*b*) A hoyden is a horrible woman, and a fracas is a horrible fight.

47. (*a*) A harpy is a mythological beast that is part bird, and minotaur is a mythological beast that is part bull (the animal, you skeptics).

48. (*b*) Lewis Carroll wrote about the mythical place Wonderland, and C.S. Lewis wrote about the mythical place Narnia.

49. (*a*) An entente is a treaty or agreement, and a detente is a relaxation or an easing of tensions.

50. (*c*) Hoary means ancient, and obstreperous means cranky or unruly.

51. (*b*) Suture means to sew, and stupefy means to amaze.

52. (*c*) The relationship of the roman numerals C to DC is 100 to 600 or 1:6, and the same relationship exists between 10 and 60.

53. (*b*) Someone persnickety is characterized by cleanliness, and someone obdurate is characterized by stubbornness.

54. (*c*) Urban means related to the city, and littoral means related to the shore. Use process of elimination!

55. (*d*) Snipe is an anagram of pines, and stripe is an anagram of priest.

56. (*d*) An olio is a mixture, and a lacuna is a gap.

57. (*d*) Lincoln was the sixteenth president, and Grant was the eighteenth.

58. (*d*) A halo is a sign of sanctification or holiness, and a diadem is a sign of royalty.

59. (*b*) Facility means ease, and avidity means greed.

60. (*c*) Stomp means to walk noisily, and blubber means to cry noisily.

61. (*c*) Grit is a type of texture, and savor is a type of smell, as in "The savor of that meat."

62. (*c*) Canada borders the United States, and France borders Spain. The common language isn't the issue here, as in Canada both French and English are spoken.

63. (*d*) A rein holds in a horse, and a bezel holds in a gem.

64. (*c*) Grave means musically solemn in tone, and largo means musically broad in tone.

65. (*a*) To commend means to praise, and to emend means to edit.

66. (*a*) Gravity (or seriousness) is the absence of lightness, and a dearth occurs in the absence of a spate (a spate is a sudden flood).

67. (*c*) The mandible (jaw bone) is attached to the cranium (skull), and the ulna (arm bone) is attached to the radius (other arm bone).

68. (*c*) To muse means to ruminate or think over, and to inspire means to stimulate.

69. (*b*) A mess is a place to eat as in an army's mess, and a cellar is a place to preserve things.

70. (*c*) Stable means steadfast or unwavering, and hoarse means rough (usually used with voices).

71. (*b*) Asphyxia is a result of a lack of oxygen, and boorishness is a result of a lack of manners.

72. (*c*) Malleable means easily bent, and waspish means easily annoyed.

73. (*d*) A fiber is a unit of hemp or rope, a tooth is a unit of a rasp or file.

74. (*c*) Truculent means aggressive, and chary means reluctant, or shy.

75. (*d*) A punt is a type of boat, and a flacon is a type of bottle.

76. (*a*) To flout means to act in a flippant manner, and to harangue means to act or speak in a denigrating manner.

77. (*a*) Imbibe means to drink, and collar means to seize.

78. (*b*) Pollock was an American painter, and Picasso was a Spanish painter.

79. (*a*) A mold is used to create a shape, and a bore is used to create a hole.

80. (*a*) Visit Leone is an anagram of television, as is Ad Rio for radio.

81. (*b*) To stagger means to walk awkwardly and unevenly, and cobble means to bind awkwardly and unevenly.

82. (*c*) The Irish Sea is off the coast of Ireland, and the Black Sea is off the coast of Turkey.

83. (*b*) A cagey person is shrewd, and a savage person is feral.

84. (*d*) Top is the word taken from between the end letters of stops, and lamp is the word taken from between the end letters of clamps.

85. (*a*) Clement means having mercy, cloven means having a split.

86. (*c*) Commodious means spacious, and odious (or disgusting) means abhorrent.

87. (*c*) Protocol is the rules of behavior and habiliment is the rules of dress. Both these words are used mostly for people of state.

88. (*d*) Lucid means clear, and turbid means sedimented or cloudy with particles.

89. (*a*) Wordsworth and Coleridge were both primarily poets, and Albee and Shaw are both primarily playwrights.

90. (*d*) The Cenezoic period was 70,000,000 years ago, and the Paleozoic period was 390,000,000 years ago.

91. (*c*) An awl is a tool to make holes, and a dibble is also a tool to make holes.

92. (*b*) Blowzy means unkempt, as does frowzy.

93. (*b*) To abet means to help something illegal, to suborn means to induce something illegal, usually perjury.

94. (*d*) Cloture is a process to end debate, and a cease-fire is a process to end fighting.

95. (*d*) Space is an anagram for capes, and capsule is an anagram for specula.

96. (*b*) To impede means to obstruct or hamper progress, and to bedizen means to clothe.

97. (*b*) Antietam was a battle of the Civil War, and Bunker Hill was a battle of the Revolutionary War.

98. (*a*) Coevals are people of the same era, and peers are people of the same standing.

99. (*b*) Hirsute means with lots of hair, and bosky means with lots of woods.

100. (*a*) A coda is the final passage of a movement, and a colophon is the final passage of a book.

SAMPLE TEST 5

Time: 50 Minutes
100 Questions

Directions: The following analogy pairs contain four choices with which to combine the unpaired word. Choose the answer that best corresponds to the full analogy pair. There is only one right answer.

1. NOVEL : (*a.* essay, *b.* symphony, *c.* epic, *d.* poem) :: CHAPTER : STANZA

2. ENGAGE : MESH :: (*a.* speech, *b.* utter, *c.* aloud, *d.* fiance) : SPEAK

3. (*a.* accident, *b.* sneaking, *c.* plotting, *d.* banging) : SPYING :: COLLUSION : ESPIONAGE

4. (*a.* first, *b.* 3, *c.* integer, *d.* cube) : ORDINAL :: 3 : PRIME

5. SUCCUMB : (*a.* ail, *b.* manufacture, *c.* farm, *d.* fail) :: YIELD : PRODUCE

6. PINPOINT : (*a.* sharp, *b.* meticulous, *c.* more or less, *d.* guess) :: ESTIMATE : APPROXIMATE

7. LOATHING : MISANTHROPE :: (*a.* garrulity, *b.* hatred, *c.* love, *d.* stinginess) : MISER

8. MEN : (*a.* mankind, *b.* mens, *c.* man, *d.* humanity) :: STRATA : STRATUM

9. LODE : ORE :: STATIONER : (*a.* paper, *b.* pulp, *c.* static, *d.* motionless)

10. BEACON : BEAUFORT :: SIGNAL : (*a.* help, *b.* mark, *c.* scale, *d.* alarm)

11. (*a.* oat, *b.* boat, *c.* string, *d.* spool) : BOATS :: LOOP : SLOOPS

12. LOOSE : RIGHT :: (*a.* daring, *b.* licentious, *c.* vituperative, *d.* excessive) : VIRTUOUS

13. BOOK : (*a.* read, *b.* chapter, *c.* reader, *d.* library) :: SCENE : ACT

14. PH.D. : J.D. :: PHILOSOPHY : (*a.* justice, *b.* law, *c.* judaism, *d.* doctorate)

15. TOAST : (*a.* saint, *b.* taint, *c.* saints, *d.* stains) :: STOAT : STAIN

16. COMPASS : (*a.* protractor, *b.* edge, *c.* flagstone, *d.* flute) :: ENGINEER : FLAUTIST

17. (*a.* notes, *b.* timbres, *c.* tempo, *d.* scale) : COLORS :: OCTAVE : RAINBOW

18. FEMALE : (*a.* bulb, *b.* seed, *c.* petal, *d.* pistil) :: MALE : STAMEN

19. SPAIN : EL CID :: (*a.* Hun, *b.* Mongolia, *c.* Prussia, *d.* Saxony) : GENGHIS KHAN

20. BUFFER : SHINE :: RASP : (*a.* rough, *b.* cut, *c.* file, *d.* glow)

21. DAMN : DARN :: CONDEMN : (*a.* prison, *b.* mild, *c.* expletive, *d.* mend)
22. CARAT : (*a.* edit, *b.* print, *c.* pica, *d.* insertion) :: WEIGHT : TYPE
23. HAT : RIP :: (*a.* emphatic, *b.* extreme, *c.* grabbed, *d.* bowler) : GRIPPED
24. DATUM : (*a.* horse, *b.* hoove, *c.* foot, *d.* hoof) :: DATA : HOOVES
25. (*a.* shore, *b.* shim, *c.* shun, *d.* shrug) : AVOID :: ESCALATE : INCREASE

26. PROTO : NEO :: (*a.* false, *b.* earliest, *c.* historical, *d.* similar) : NEW
27. TROLL : (*a.* play, *b.* pretend, *c.* fish, *d.* imagine) :: TOY : TRIFLE
28. WORLD WAR I : WORLD WAR II :: 1914 : (*a.* 1936, *b.* 1939, *c.* 1941, *d.* 1945)
29. (*a.* shave, *b.* confront, *c.* grow, *d.* steal) : BEARD :: DEPRIVE : SHEAR
30. BABY'S BREATH : (*a.* wreath, *b.* perennial, *c.* coniferous, *d.* bryophitic) :: IMPA-TIENS : ANNUAL

31. (*a.* wet, *b.* strengthens, *c.* restrains, *d.* flying) : DAMPER :: SUPPORTS : BUTTRESS
32. SINE ANNO : SINE PROLE :: DATE : (*a.* punishment, *b.* power, *c.* common people, *d.* offspring)
33. RAZE : (*a.* raisin, *b.* craze, *c.* lift, *d.* bold) :: BRAISE : BRAZEN
34. CALIBER : HUMIDITY :: (*a.* worth, *b.* aridity, *c.* fat, *d.* viscosity) : MOISTURE
35. PHYSIOGNOMY : PHRENOLOGY :: FACE : (*a.* hand, *b.* feature, *c.* future, *d.* skull)

36. STRICTURE : (*a.* scripture, *b.* longing, *c.* criticism, *d.* ache) :: PANG : PAIN
37. PERIMETER : RECTANGLE :: (*a.* diameter, *b.* radius, *c.* circumference, *d.* area) : CIRCLE
38. SCALE : (*a.* climb, *b.* ruminate, *c.* ponder, *d.* increase) :: WEIGH : CONSIDER
39. (*a.* cook, *b.* pottage, *c.* vegetable, *d.* crock) : STEW :: ROAST : MEAT
40. SNATCH : (*a.* portion, *b.* fragment, *c.* splinter, *d.* sliver) :: STAKE : SHARE

41. AXIS : ALLY :: ITALY : (a. Germany, b. Japan, c. France, d. Spain)

42. SHRIVE : STRIVE :: (a. consider, b. control, c. confabulate, d. confess) : CONTEND

43. PREROGATIVE : RAPIER :: (a. privilege, b. epee, c. foil, d. testament) : SWORD

44. (a. tone, b. tempo, c. soft, d. fast) : FORTE :: TONE : CRESCENDO

45. WHEN IN THE COURSE OF HUMAN EVENTS : WE THE PEOPLE OF THE UNITED STATES :: DECLARATION OF INDEPENDENCE : (a. Gettysburg Address, b. Constitution, c. Emancipation Proclamation, d. Bill of Rights)

46. CODES : (a. graves, b. carts, c. maps, d. writing) :: CRYPTOGRAPHY : CARTOGRAPHY

47. PURLOIN : STEAL :: (a. fleece, b. sidle, c. babble, d. hide) : SNEAK

48. PSEUDONYM : (a. alias, b. alibi, c. author, d. name) :: FACADE : FRONT

49. AVIATE : RECKON :: FLY : (a. navigate, b. calculate, c. debark, d. recede)

50. PAINTER : ARCHITECT :: (a. Moore, b. Wren, c. del Sarto, d. Pei) : WRIGHT

51. FAST : (a. allegretto, b. allegro, c. lento, d. sforzato) :: LEISURELY : ADAGIO

52. (a. hurry, b. wreck, c. lumber, d. scour) : SHAMBLE :: SCRAMBLE : SCURRY

53. CALUMNY : DEXTERITY :: (a. facility, b. slander, c. adulation, d. serenity) : EFFICACY

54. EAT : (a. drink, b. make, c. diet, d. strength) :: EDIBLE : POTABLE

55. (a. reeds, b. water, c. marsh, d. mud) : SWAMP :: AIR : INFLATE

56. LINES : ANGLE :: (a. axes, b. slope, c. rise, d. run) : ORIGIN

57. HERBACEOUS : HERBS :: CUTANEOUS : (a. nails, b. hair, c. skin, d. spices)

58. EXPIATE : ABROGATE :: ATONE : (a. rue, b. abolish, c. scintillate, d. oscillate)

59. BALLAST : (a. wreck, b. wave, c. dam, d. tide) :: CAPSIZE : FLOW

60. SCREEN : PROVE :: (a. film, b. conceal, c. protect, d. advertise) : AUTHENTICATE

61. BONE : WHITE :: OCHRE : (*a.* red, *b.* yellow, *c.* blue, *d.* flower)

62. (*a.* base, *b.* leisurely, *c.* dug, *d.* serious) : QUICK :: GRAVE : VIVACE

63. RECEIPTS : BEATITUDE :: ACQUISITION : (*a.* recklessness, *b.* slackness, *c.* coolness, *d.* blessedness)

64. PRIDE : PREJUDICE :: CRIME : (*a.* war, *b.* peace, *c.* disgrace, *d.* punishment)

65. A : ALPHA :: (*a.* b, *b.* m, *c.* g, *d.* z) : OMEGA

66. DAGUERREOTYPE : (*a.* photograph, *b.* typewriter, *c.* counter, *d.* numbers) :: ABACUS : CALCULATOR

67. (*a.* salary, *b.* price, *c.* tax, *d.* fortress) : LEVY :: WAR : WAGE

68. BAILIFF : COMPTROLLER :: BAILIWICK : (*a.* exchequer, *b.* county, *c.* realm, *d.* maceration)

69. (*a.* -14, *b.* 0, *c.* 7, *d.* 28) : 14 :: BASE : ACID

70. WAINWRIGHT : (*a.* joint, *b.* bartender, *c.* wheel, *d.* gauntlet) :: WAGON : GIMLET

71. SUBJECT : BROACH :: (*a.* buds, *b.* sturgeon, *c.* burden, *d.* topic) : BURGEON

72. JEST : QUEST :: (*a.* jape, *b.* search, *c.* quarry, *d.* joust) : HUNT

73. DILEMMA : ENIGMA :: (*a.* secret, *b.* plot, *c.* quandary, *d.* anagram) : ARCANUM

74. DISCRIMINATION : JINGOISM :: (*a.* sexism, *b.* patriotism, *c.* taste, *d.* prosperity) : CHAUVINISM

75. OMBUDSMAN : BOATSWAIN :: COMPLAINTS : (*a.* romance, *b.* ship, *c.* steerage, *d.* rigging)

76. GRANT : 2 :: HOOVER : (*a.* 1, *b.* 2, *c.* 3, *d.* 4)

77. DEBAR : DEBAUCH :: (*a.* allow, *b.* select, *c.* vitiate, *d.* proscribe) : CORRUPT

78. EMACIATED : (*a.* thin, *b.* challenge, *c.* feat, *d.* moderate) :: GAUNT : GAUNTLET

79. CACOPHONOUS : SOOTHING :: GENIAL : (*a.* palliative, *b.* mollifying, *c.* obstreperous, *d.* effusive)

80. EGRESS : PROGRESS :: (*a.* exit, *b.* entry, *c.* digression, *d.* regression) : FURTHERANCE

81. (*a.* rethink, *b.* started, *c.* jealousy, *d.* obese) : THIN :: INFATUATE : FAT
82. MD : C :: XV : (*a.* I, *b.* V, *c.* III, *d.* XX)
83. DIVAGATE : PROGNOSTICATE :: (*a.* bore, *b.* wander, *c.* nose, *d.* fortune) : AUGUR
84. CRITERIA : CRITERION :: (*a.* multiple, *b.* singles, *c.* plural, *d.* couple) : SINGLE
85. SWIFT : (*a.* London, *b.* Thomas, *c.* Lilliput, *d.* Davis) :: FAULKNER : JEFFERSON

86. PARIETAL : SARTORIAL :: CAVITY : (*a.* dentist, *b.* tailoring, *c.* hole, *d.* romancing)
87. OZONE : (*a.* element, *b.* atmosphere, *c.* oxygen, *d.* allotrope) :: PEWTER : ALLOY
88. (*a.* dinar, *b.* rupee, *c.* schilling, *d.* franc) : PESO :: MALI : ARGENTINA
89. JEJUNE : VAPID :: (*a.* expurgated, *b.* expeditious, *c.* expansive, *d.* explicable) : RAPID
90. (*a.* dourness, *b.* sanguinity, *c.* vacuity, *d.* oblivion) : OBESITY :: CHEERFUL : CORPULENT

91. ELIOT : (*a.* Eliot, *b.* Whitman, *c.* Dickinson, *d.* Pound) :: MIDDLEMARCH : WASTE-LAND
92. VOCALIC : SEMANTIC :: (*a.* speech, *b.* definition, *c.* letter, *d.* vowel) : MEANING
93. (*a.* friendly, *b.* cowardly, *c.* popular, *d.* fanciful) : RECREANT :: EXCLUDED : PARIAH
94. RUBENS : BREUGHEL :: (*a.* Cezanne, *b.* Picasso, *c.* da Vinci, *d.* Rembrandt) : GAUGIN
95. (*a.* calve, *b.* shy, *c.* force, *d.* stupid) : COW :: AFFECTION : FAWN

96. ESCARPMENT : (*a.* hill, *b.* barracks, *c.* fortress, *d.* moat) :: TOWER : BUILDING
97. SUPPORT : (*a.* help, *b.* shrug, *c.* shrub, *d.* soldier) :: SPAR : ESPALIER
98. CALIPER : MEASURE :: CALIBRATOR : (*a.* measure, *b.* pinch, *c.* adjust, *d.* assess)
99. NABOB : (*a.* republican, *b.* power, *c.* stupidity, *d.* wealth) :: SAGE : WISDOM
100. (*a.* route, *b.* barbarian, *c.* fortification, *d.* littering) : BARBICAN :: ROAD : HIGHWAY

ANSWER KEY

1. (*d*) A chapter is a subsection of a novel, and a stanza is a subsection of a poem.

2. (*b*) To mesh means to engage, and to speak means to utter.

3. (*c*) Engaging in spying is espionage, and engaging in plotting is collusion.

4. (*a*) The number 3 is a prime number, and first is an ordinal number, in other words, a number that gives a position relative to others.

5. (*b*) To succumb means to yield to something, and to produce means to manufacture something.

6. (*b*) To estimate means to identify in an approximate manner, to pinpoint means to identify in a fastidious manner.

7. (*d*) A misanthrope is characterized by loathing, and a miser is characterized by stinginess.

8. (*c*) Stratum is the singular of strata, and man is the singular of men.

9. (*a*) A lode is a source of ore, and a stationer is a source of paper.

10. (*c*) A beacon is a type of signal, and Beaufort is a type of scale.

11. (*a*) Loop is the word formed when the first and last letters are dropped from sloops, and oat is the word formed when the first and last letters are dropped from boats.

12. (*b*) Right means virtuous, and loose means licentious (or immoral).

13. (*d*) A scene is a unit of an act, and a book is a unit of a library.

14. (*b*) A Ph.D is a doctorate of philosophy, and a J.D. is a Jurum doctorate, or a doctorate of the law.

15. (*a*) Stoat is an anagram for toast, and stain is an anagram for saint.

16. (*d*) A compass is the instrument of an engineer, and a flute is the instrument of a flautist.

17. (*a*) A rainbow is comprised of colors, and an octave is comprised of notes.

18. (*d*) The stamen is the male reproductive organ of a flower, and the pistil is its female reproductive organ.

19. (*b*) El Cid was a warrior from Spain, and Genghis Khan was a warrior from Mongolia.

20. (*c*) A buffer is used to shine, and a rasp is used to file.

21. (*d*) To damn means to condemn, and to darn means to mend, as in socks.

22. (*c*) A carat is a unit of weight, and a pica is a unit of type.

23. (*a*) Rip is a word taken whole from the middle of *grip*ped, and hat is a word taken whole from the inside of emp*hat*ic.

24. (*d*) Data is the plural of datum, and hooves is the plural of hoof.

25. (*c*) To shun something or someone means to avoid it, and to escalate means to increase.

26. (*b*) The prefix "neo" means new, as in neologism (a newly coined word), and the prefix "proto" means earliest, as in a prototype.

27. (*c*) To troll means to fish, and to toy with something means to trifle with it. Use part of speech!

28. (*b*) World War I began in 1914, and World War II began in 1939. (Be careful to note that the question is not when did United States involvement in these wars occur, but when did the wars begin.)

29. (*b*) To beard means to confront, as in she bearded the dragon in his lair, and to shear means to deprive. Remember to use part of speech and secondary definitions.

30. (*b*) Impatiens is an annual flower, and baby's breath is a perennial flower.

31. (*c*) A buttress supports, and a damper restrains or muffles.

32. (*d*) Sine anno means without a date or time, and sine prole means without offspring or issue.

33. (*a*) The word brazen sounds like the word braise with an *in* sound added to the end, and the same goes for raze and raisin.

34. (*a*) The caliber of something is its worth, as in, "he was a man of great caliber," and the humidity of something is its degree of moisture.

35. (*d*) Physiognomy is the study of faces, and phrenology is the study of skulls.

36. (*c*) A stricture is a criticism, and a pang is a pain or a feeling of pain.

37. (*c*) The measure of the outer edge of a rectangle is the perimeter, and the measure of the outer edge of a circle is the circumference.

38. (*a*) To scale means to climb, as in scaling a cliff, and to weigh something means to consider it, as in weighing a decision.

39. (*b*) A roast is a type of meat, and a pottage is a type of stew.

40. (*b*) A snatch is a fragment of something, as in a snatch of a song, and a stake is a share of something.

41. (*c*) Italy was one of the main Axis countries in World War II, and France was one of the main Allied countries in that same war.

42. (*d*) To shrive means to confess, and to strive or try means to contend, as in "I coulda been a contender ...."

43. (*a*) A rapier is a type of sword, and a prerogative is a type of privilege.

44. (*a*) Crescendo indicates a type of tone, as does forte.

45. (*b*) "When in the course..." begins the Declaration of Independence, and "We the People..." begins the Constitution, or the preamble of the Constitution, to be more exact.

46. (*c*) Cryptography is the study of codes, and cartography is the study of maps.

47. (*a*) To purloin means to fleece, which is another word for steal or cheat, and to steal means to sneak, as in he steals quietly into the room.

48. (*d*) A facade is a false front, and a pseudonym is a false name.

49. (*b*) To aviate means to fly, and to reckon means to calculate or figure.

50. (*c*) Wright was an architect, and del Sarto was a painter (you should have been using process of elimination on this question, as well as every other one).

51. (*b*) Adagio is a leisurely tempo; allegro is a fast tempo.

52. (*c*) To scramble means to rush or scurry, and to shamble means to walk slowly and awkwardly, which is what to lumber means.

53. (*b*) Calumny means slander, and dexterity or deftness, means efficacy.

54. (*a*) Edible means fit to eat, and potable means fit to drink.

55. (*b*) Inflate means fill with air, and swamp means to fill with water, as in "The wave swamped the small boat."

56. (*a*) An angle is formed by lines, and the origin (as in a grid or graph) is formed by axes (plural of axis).

57. (*c*) Herbaceous means having to do with herbs, and cutaneous means having to do with skin.

58. (*b*) To abrogate means to abolish or get rid of something, and to expiate means to atone.

59. (*c*) Ballast, the weight put in the bottom of boats, prevents capsizing, and a dam prevents the flow, usually of a river.

60. (*c*) To screen something can mean to protect it, and to authenticate something is to prove it.

61. (*b*) Bone is a shade of white, and ochre is a shade of yellow.

62. (*b*) Vivace describes a quick tone, and grave describes a leisurely tone.   Grave also means serious, but not a serious tone.

63. (*d*) Receipts are a sign of acquisition or buying, and beatitude is a sign or demonstration of spirituality or blessedness.

64. (*d*) *Pride and Prejudice* is the title of a novel, *Crime and Punishment* is also the title of a novel.

65. (*d*) Alpha is the first letter of the Greek alphabet, and omega is the last, and A is the first letter of the English alphabet, and Z is the last.

66. (*a*) An abacus is a primitive computer, and a daguerreotype is a primitive photograph.

67. (*c*) To wage is the act of having a war, and to levy is the act of having a tax.

68. (*a*) A bailiff controls a bailiwick, and a comptroller controls an exchequer, which is a treasury.

69. (*b*) Fourteen indicates an acid on the pH scale, and 0 indicates a base.

70. (*b*) A wainwright (or wagon-maker) creates a wagon, and a bartender creates a gimlet (gin, lime juice, and sugar, if you're interested).

71. (*a*) Broach means to bring forth a subject, and burgeon means to bring forth buds.

72. (*a*) A quest is a hunt for something, sometimes a grail, and a jest is a joke, also known as a jape. Use process of elimination on hard questions!

73. (*c*) A dilemma is a quandary (a difficult decision or question), and an enigma is an arcanum, which is a puzzle.

74. (*c*) Jingoism is extreme chauvinism, and discrimination is extreme taste. Remember secondary definitions!

75. (*d*) An ombudsman is in charge of complaints, and a boatswain is in charge of the rigging (of a ship).

76. (*a*) Grant served as president for two terms, and Hoover served as president for one.

77. (*d*) To debar means to prohibit or proscribe, and to debauch means to corrupt.

78. (*b*) Gaunt means emaciated, and a gauntlet means a challenge.

79. (*c*) Something cacophonous (unpleasant sounding) is not at all soothing, someone genial is not at all obstreperous (annoying or irritating).

80. (*a*) An egress is a path out or an exit, and progress is furtherance.

81. (*a*) The word *fat* is found inside the word in*fat*uate, and the word *thin* is found inside the word re*think*.

82. (*a*) The Roman numerals depicted give the relationship of 1,500 to 100, or 15 to 1.

83. (*b*) To divagate means to wander or roam, and to prognosticate means to tell the future, or to augur.

84. (*b*) Criterion is the singular form of criteria, as single is the singular form of singles.

85. (*c*) Faulkner created the fictional town of Jefferson for his work, as did Swift with Lilliput.

86. (*b*) Parietal means relating to a cavity or empty space, and sartorial means related to tailoring or clothes.

87. (*d*) Pewter is a type of alloy, and ozone is a type of allotrope.

88. (*d*) Argentina uses the peso as its unit of currency, and Mali uses the franc.

89. (*b*) Jejune means dull or vapid, and expeditious means speedy or rapid.

90. (*b*) Corpulent means having obesity (better known as fatness) and cheerful means having sanguinity (happiness).

91. (*a*) *Middlemarch* was written by George Eliot, and *The Wasteland* was written by T.S. Eliot.

92. (*d*) Vocalic means related to vowels, and semantic means related to meaning.

93. (*b*) A recreant is by definition cowardly, and a pariah is by definition excluded.

94. (*a*) Breughel and Rubens were both Flemish painters, and Gaugin and Cezanne were both French painters.

95. (*c*) Fawn means to act with a show of affection, cow means to act with a show of force, or to intimidate.

96. (*a*) A tower is a tall building, an escarpment is a tall or steep hill.

97. (*c*) A spar is a horizontal support, and an espalier is a horizontal shrub.

98. (*c*) A caliper is used to measure, and a calibrator is used to adjust.

99. (*d*) A sage is characterized by wisdom, and a nabob is characterized by wealth.

100. (*c*) A highway is a type of road, and a barbican is a type of fortification.

SAMPLE TEST 6

Time: 50 Minutes
100 Questions

Directions: The following analogy pairs contain four choices with which to combine the unpaired word. Choose the answer that best corresponds to the full analogy pair. There is only one right answer.

1. LAND : AGRARIAN :: (*a.* country, *b.* farming, *c.* city, *d.* sophistication) : URBAN
2. DAM : SLOOPS :: (*a.* reservoir, *b.* water, *c.* thwart, *d.* mad) : SPOOLS
3. MARTIAL : WAR :: SALUTARY : (*a.* health, *b.* battle, *c.* greeting, *d.* relationship)
4. (*a.* text, *b.* children, *c.* teacher, *d.* governess) : CONDUCTOR :: CLASS : SYMPHONY
5. AGENDA : (*a.* meeting, *b.* discussion, *c.* planner, *d.* notebook) :: ITINERARY : JOURNEY

6. EMPTY : VACUOUS :: (*a.* marsh, *b.* movable, *c.* still, *d.* full) : STAGNANT
7. 1/10 : (*a.* 10, *b.* 5, *c.* 40, *d.* 100) :: 1/5 : 20
8. SOUSE : (*a.* peddle, *b.* drench, *c.* protect, *d.* hover) :: HOUSE : SHELTER
9. POACHING : SAFARI :: COOK : (*a.* hunt, *b.* roast, *c.* Africa, *d.* boil)
10. (*a.* land, *b.* gas, *c.* energy, *d.* weight) : ELECTRICITY :: HECTARE : VOLT

11. PROFICIENT : (*a.* alike, *b.* able, *c.* dissimilar, *d.* money-making) :: QUASI : SIMILAR
12. NOON : BOB :: (*a.* glam, *b.* sham, *c.* ma'am, *d.* ram) : TOT
13. MASON : (*a.* builder, *b.* carpenter, *c.* bird, *d.* fish) :: MARTEN : MAMMAL
14. GRAVE : (*a.* say, *b.* speak, *c.* complete, *d.* burial) :: SERIOUS : UTTER
15. (*a.* flimsy, *b.* shaggy, *c.* full, *d.* sated) : TENUOUS :: EMPTY : VACUOUS

16. EXPEL : HUNKER :: (*a.* secrete, *b.* thrust, *c.* sink, *d.* defy) : SQUAT
17. ASTRONOMY : GASTRONOMY :: STARS : (*a.* bars, *b.* eating, *c.* fuel, *d.* zodiac)
18. MEDIOCRE : (*a.* meditative, *b.* medium, *c.* supernumerary, *d.* superlative) :: MIDDLING : TRANSCENDENT
19. WASHINGTON : PRESIDENT :: HAMILTON : (*a.* secretary of state, *b.* treasurer, *c.* justice, *d.* speaker of the house)
20. HEDONIST : (*a.* sin, *b.* carelessness, *c.* gratification, *d.* liberation) :: ASCETIC : SELF-DENIAL

21. OOCYTE : OVUM :: (*a.* gamete, *b.* fetus, *c.* egg, *d.* cell) : ZYGOTE

22. MAUVE : PUCE :: REDDISH : (*a.* greenish, *b.* brownish, *c.* bluish, *d.* reddish)

23. (*a.* Switzerland, *b.* Alps, *c.* Mexico, *d.* Ecuador) : ANDES :: NEPAL : HIMALAYAS

24. CRITERIA : STRATA :: CRITERION : (*a.* stratums, *b.* stratum, *c.* striate, *d.* straterion)

25. HELICOPTER : TYPEWRITER :: ROTOR : (*a.* wheel, *b.* key, *c.* platen, *d.* paper)

26. BONE : (*a.* joint, *b.* sucker, *c.* cartilage, *d.* marrow) :: TREE : SAP

27. COMPUTER : DOOR :: (*a.* drawer, *b.* desk, *c.* mouse, *d.* printer) : KNOB

28. (*a.* blood, *b.* hermaphroditism, *c.* genetics, *d.* muscle) : HEMATOLOGY :: AGE : GERIATRICS

29. MUFFLER : (*a.* damper, *b.* propellor, *c.* engine, *d.* flue) :: CARBURETOR : MIXER

30. CENTENNIAL : SESQUICENTENNIAL :: 100 : (*a.* 50, *b.* 75, *c.* 150, *d.* 175)

31. EQUILATERAL : 3 :: ISOSCELES : (*a.* 0, *b.* 1, *c.* 2, *d.* 4)

32. LICORICE : STICK :: (*a.* plant, *b.* leaf, *c.* tree, *d.* shrub) : BRANCH

33. RUSSIAN : (*a.* Roman, *b.* historical, *c.* biblical, *d.* Greek) :: CHEKHOV : EURIPIDES

34. (*a.* pack, *b.* interfere, *c.* quiet, *d.* muddle) : MEDDLE :: TAMP : TAMPER

35. YAW : VEER :: PAW : (*a.* turn, *b.* grasp, *c.* near, *d.* sail)

36. DATA : DATUM :: (*a.* indices, *b.* indicates, *c.* indicated, *d.* inducts) : INDEX

37. QUOD VIDE : (*a.* ipso facto, *b.* id est, *c.* et alii, *d.* ex officio) :: WHICH SEE : SO THAT

38. D.O.A. : (*a.* action, *b.* annotation, *c.* accident, *d.* arrival) :: M.I.A. : ACTION

39. STORM : TEMPEST :: (*a.* cuff, *b.* fight, *c.* storm, *d.* seam) : FRAY

40. (*a.* pall, *b.* halo, *c.* thimble, *d.* sprawl) : NIMBUS :: SHROUD : CLOUD

41. IMBROGLIO : SITUATION :: FEAT : (*a.* hands, *b.* placement, *c.* achievement, *d.* daring)

42. GUTTER : (*a.* melt, *b.* roll, *c.* fall, *d.* rain) :: SPUTTER : SPEAK

43. CONSONANCE : DISSONANCE :: (*a.* chords, *b.* tempos, *c.* arias, *d.* scales) : CHORDS

44. MINUEND : DIVIDEND :: (*a.* profited, *b.* added, *c.* multiplied, *d.* subtracted) : DIVIDED

45. BUCK : (*a.* cob, *b.* horse, *c.* throw, *d.* gander) :: RABBIT : SWAN

46. POSITIVE : NEGATIVE :: ANODE : (*a.* diode, *b.* cathode, *c.* gonad, *d.* ion)

47. (*a.* pure, *b.* choosy, *c.* meticulous, *d.* particular) : PRISTINE :: FINICKY : PRISSY

48. ABRAHAM : (*a.* Joseph, *b.* Isaac, *c.* Jacob, *d.* Esau) :: ADAM : ABEL

49. VOLATILE : VIOLENCE :: IRASCIBLE : (*a.* annoyance, *b.* erasure, *c.* evaporation, *d.* evanescence)

50. FISH : BIRD :: SHARK : (*a.* hunt, *b.* raven, *c.* wing, *d.* kite)

51. TEMPO : (*a.* loud tone, *b.* soft tone, *c.* crescendo, *d.* quick tempo) :: MODERATO : MEZZO-PIANO

52. AT THE PLACE : IN THE SAME PLACE :: (*a.* ibid., *b.* op. cit., *c.* sine locum, *d.* ad locum) : IBIDEM

53. (*a.* store, *b.* age, *c.* gasp, *d.* history) : PART :: STONE : PANT

54. SPEECH : (*a.* water, *b.* current, *c.* bubble, *d.* brook) :: STUTTER : GURGLE

55. FECKLESS : (*a.* purpose, *b.* shape, *c.* irresponsible, *d.* radiance) :: AMORPHOUS : FORM

56. LINK : CHAIN :: (*a.* pale, *b.* gate, *c.* pen, *d.* rod) : FENCE

57. (*a.* tie, *b.* coat, *c.* shoe, *d.* cane) : HAT :: BROGUE : CLOCHE

58. TUITION : (*a.* paying, *b.* becoming, *c.* aging, *d.* instructing) :: FRUITION : RIPENING

59. (*a.* ashen, *b.* ruddy, *c.* warm, *d.* clear) : RUBICUND :: PALE : WAN

60. PROCLIVITY : DECLIVITY : TENDENCY : (*a.* slope, *b.* leaning, *c.* repulsion, *d.* activity)

61. DOLLAR : POUND :: AUSTRALIA : (*a.* Austria, *b.* India, *c.* Uruguay, *d.* Nigeria)

62. MAUDLIN : CANTANKEROUS :: (*a.* mawkish, *b.* malleable, *c.* merry, *d.* mean) : IRRITABLE

63. SUBSTANCE : CATALYST :: (*a.* force, *b.* whimsical, *c.* without reason, *d.* chemical) : IMPETUS

64. (*a.* carousel, *b.* cortege, *c.* horses, *d.* soldier) : TROOPS :: CAVALCADE : CAVALRY

65. ABACUS : (*a.* ledger, *b.* clock, *c.* numbers, *d.* calculator) :: SUNDIAL : CHRONOMETER

66. ALASKA : HAWAII :: 1959 : (*a.* 1941, *b.* 1952, *c.* 1959, *d.* 1960)

67. SOUND : HEFT :: (*a.* noise, *b.* heaviness, *c.* volume, *d.* depth) : WEIGHT

68. TEMPER : (*a.* anger, *b.* postpone, *c.* melt, *d.* bend) :: SOFTEN : TEMPORIZE

69. EVANESCE : COALESCE :: (*a.* fade, *b.* shimmer, *c.* separate, *d.* die) : UNITE

70. (*a.* quotidian, *b.* contumacious, *c.* abrasive, *d.* oceanic) : ANOMALOUS :: PACIFIC : USUAL

71. SENSE : (*a.* and nonsense, *b.* and ability, *c.* and prejudice, *d.* and sensibility) :: WAR : AND PEACE

72. VITIATE : SATIATE :: (*a.* empty, *b.* hungry, *c.* worthless, *d.* alive) : FULL

73. (*a.* salubrious, *b.* magnificent, *c.* thrifty, *d.* delirious) : DELETERIOUS :: MUNIFICENT : STINGY

74. TALE : (*a.* achievement, *b.* story, *c.* use, *d.* hero) :: EPIC : EXPLOIT

75. UNIFORM : (*a.* dovish, *b.* peaceful, *c.* static, *d.* formal) :: WAR-LIKE : HAWKISH

76. STRIATED : SMOOTH :: VOLITIONAL : (*a.* rough, *b.* strung, *c.* muscle, *d.* involuntary)

77. DESSERT : (*a.* appetizer, *b.* preface, *c.* coda, *d.* colophon) :: MEAL : BOOK

78. OBSTREPEROUS : CANTANKEROUS :: (*a.* rebellious, *b.* fawning, *c.* difficult, *d.* humble) : OBSEQUIOUS

79. HOOK : HELL :: (*a.* high water, *b.* heaven, *c.* Samaritan, *d.* well) : CROOK

80. 1776 : (*a.* 1862, *b.* 1863, *c.* 1864, *d.* 1865) :: DECLARATION OF INDEPENDENCE : EMANCIPATION PROCLAMATION

81. FORCE : IMPRESS :: (*a*. culture, *b*. repetition, *c*. show off, *d*. imprint) : INCULCATE

82. CHASUBLE : PHYLACTERY :: PRIEST : (*a*. rabbi, *b*. reverend, *c*. nun, *d*. chaplain)

83. (*a*. cast, *b*. smash, *c*. diet, *d*. yearning) : ANALGESIC :: BREAK : ACHE

84. METATHERIA : (*a*. mammals, *b*. trees, *c*. animals, *d*. molluscs) :: CONIFERS : TRACEOPHYTA

85. PEPPER : FLOWER :: (*a*. spice, *b*. sprinkle, *c*. plant, *d*. nature) : MATURE

86. TACIT : (*a*. spoken, *b*. rubber, *c*. wooden, *d*. hidden) :: RIGID : PLASTIC

87. MIRROR : (*a*. silver, *b*. light, *c*. ape, *d*. fight) :: IMPUGN :: ATTACK

88. THUMB : FINGER :: (*a*. wear, *b*. hand, *c*. toss, *d*. pass) : HANDLE

89. (*a*. Argentina, *b*. Australia, *c*. Arabia, *d*. South America) : AFRICA :: ATACAMA : SAHARA

90. IMMORAL : REPROBATE :: (*a*. prurient, *b*. leer, *c*. amoral, *d*. sexist) : LECHER

91. SHEER : (*a*. swerve, *b*. curve, *c*. stare, *d*. insult) :: LEER : OGLE

92. BROWN : TOAST :: (*a*. cool, *b*. brown, *c*. cheery, *d*. smooth) : WARM

93. ITALY : (*a*. China, *b*. Norway, *c*. Japan, *d*. Iran) :: ADRIATIC : CASPIAN

94. (*a*. sketch, *b*. movement, *c*. arc, *d*. finished) : CHARCOAL :: RAW : DRAWER

95. GIBBET : (*a*. ridicule, *b*. stomach, *c*. harmony, *d*. adventure) :: COMMEND : PRAISE

96. PENITENT : CONTRITE :: PENITENTIARY : (*a*. rueful, *b*. venal, *c*. penal, *d*. carnal)

97. (*a*. blizzard, *b*. fox, *c*. hail, *d*. flummox) : SNOW :: TRICK : FOOL

98. ACIDULOUS : TREMULOUS :: (*a*. bitter, *b*. bacterial, *c*. healthful, *d*. cool) : TIMID

99. ALGERIA : AFRICA :: ARGENTINA : (*a*. Europe, *b*. Central America, *c*. South America, *d*. Spain)

100. PRODUCTION : (*a*. lapse, *b*. labyrinths, *c*. laughter, *d*. labor) :: FERTILE : LABILE

ANSWER KEY

1. (*c*) Agrarian means pertaining to the land, and urban means pertaining to the city.

2. (*d*) Spools is the reverse of sloops, and mad is the reverse of dam.

3. (*a*) Martial means having to do with war, and salutary means having to do with health.

4. (*c*) A conductor leads a symphony, a teacher leads a class.

5. (*a*) An itinerary is the plan for a journey, an agenda is the plan for a meeting.

6. (*c*) Vacuous means empty, and stagnant means still.

7. (*a*) One half of 1/5 is 1/10, and one half of 20 is 10.

8. (*b*) To souse something is to drench it, and to house something is to shelter it.

9. (*a*) Poaching is a type of cooking, safari is a type of hunting.

10. (*a*) A volt is a unit of electricity, and a hectare is a unit of land.

11. (*b*) Quasi means similar, and proficient means able.

12. (*c*) Noon, bob, tot, and ma'am are all palindromes, that is, words that are the same forwards and backwards.

13. (*a*) A mason is a type of builder, and a marten is a type of mammal.

14. (*c*) Serious means grave, and utter means complete; don't get trapped by say or speak, because those are not adjectives, as are serious and grave.

15. (*a*) Flimsy means not firmly settled or tenuous, and vacuous means empty, like a vacuum.

16. (*a*) To expel means to get rid of or secrete (as pores secrete oil), and to hunker means to squat.

17. (*b*) Astronomy is study of the stars, and gastronomy is study of food.

18. (*d*) Mediocre means middling or average, and superlative means wonderful or transcendent.

19. (*b*) In the first United States administration, Washington was president, and Hamilton was treasurer.

20. (*c*) An ascetic practices self-denial, and a hedonist practices gratification.

21. (*a*) An oocyte produces an ovum, and a gamete produces a zygote.

22. (*b*) Mauve is a reddish purple, and puce is a brownish purple.

23. (*d*) The himalayas are a mountain range in Nepal, and the Andes are a mountain range in Ecuador.

24. (*b*) Criteria is the plural of criterion, ditto for strata and stratum.

25. (*c*) A rotor is a turning element of a helicopter, and a platen is a turning element of a typewriter.

26. (*d*) Sap runs through a tree, and marrow runs through a bone.

27. (*c*) A knob is part of a door, and a mouse is part of a computer.

28. (*a*) Geriatrics is the science and study of age, and hematology is the science and study of blood.

29. (*a*) A muffler operates as a damper (of sound, in particular) and a carburetor operates as a mixer (of fuel and air).

30. (*c*) A centennial marks a 100 year anniversary, and a sesquicentennial marks a 150 year anniversary.

31. (*c*) An equilateral triangle has three equal sides, and an isosceles triangle has two equal sides.

32. (*a*) Licorice is a type of plant, and a stick is a type of branch.

33. (*d*) Chekhov was a Russian playwright, and Euripides was a Greek playwright.

34. (*a*) To meddle with something means to tamper or mess with it, and to tamp something is to pack it down, as you do with tobacco in a pipe.

35. (*b*) To yaw is to turn or veer, and to paw is to grasp or grope.

36. (*a*) The plural of datum is data, and the plural of index is indices.

37. (*b*) Quod vide is the Latin expression meaning "which see," and id est is the Latin expression meaning "so that."

38. (*d*) The "A" in D.O.A. represents arrival, in Dead on Arrival, and the "A" in M.I.A. represents action, in Missing in Action.

39. (*b*) A tempest is a storm, and a fray is a fight.

40. (*a*) A nimbus is a type of cloud, and a pall is a type of shroud.

41. (*c*) An imbroglio is a difficult situation, and a feat is a difficult achievement.

42. (*a*) To gutter is to melt quickly or unevenly, and to sputter is to speak quickly or unevenly.

43. (*a*) Consonance is a feeling of stability produced by certain chords, the same is true of dissonance, except that it produces a feeling of instability.

44. (*d*) A minuend is the number subtracted from, and a dividend is the number divided into.

45. (*a*) A male rabbit is a buck, and a male swan is a cob.

46. (*b*) An anode is a positively charged electrode, and a cathode is a negatively charged electrode.

47. (*a*) Someone pure is pristine, and someone finicky (or choosy) is prissy (which also means choosy).

48. (*b*) Adam is Abel's father, and Abraham is Isaac's father.

49. (*a*) Volatile means given to violence, and irascible means given to annoyance.

50. (*d*) A shark is a predatory fish, and a kite is a predatory bird.

51. (b) Moderato is an example of a tempo, mezzo-piano is an example of a soft tone.

52. (d) Ibidem means in the same place, and ad locum means at the place.

53. (a) Pant becomes part by changing the *n* to an *r*, where stone becomes store by the same process.

54. (a) A stutter is an interruption in the flow of speech, a gurgle is an interruption in the flow of water.

55. (a) Amorphous means without shape, and feckless means without purpose.

56. (a) A link is the basic element in a chain, and a pale is the basic element in a fence. Remember, part of speech!

57. (c) A cloche is a type of hat, and a brogue is a type of shoe.

58. (d) Tuition is the act of instructing, and fruition is the act of ripening.

59. (b) Wan means pale, and rubicund means ruddy or red-faced.

60. (a) A proclivity is a tendency towards something, and a declivity is a slope or dip.

61. (d) Australia uses the dollar as its unit of currency, and Nigeria uses the pound.

62. (a) Maudlin means mawkish or sentimental, and cantankerous means irritable.

63. (a) A catalyst is an impelling substance, and an impetus is an impelling force.

64. (b) A cavalry is troops on horseback, and a cavalcade is a cortege or procession on horseback.

65. (d) A sundial is a primitive chronometer (time teller), and an abacus is a primitive calculator.

66. (c) Both Alaska and Hawaii became states in 1959.

67. (d) To heft means to measure or assess weight, to sound is to measure depth.

68. (b) To temper something is to soften it, as in tempering a harsh statement, and to temporize means to postpone.

69. (a) To evanesce means to fade and disappear, and to coalesce means to unite.

70. (b) Something anomalous is apart from the usual, and something contumacious or argumentative is apart from pacific (or peaceful).

71. (d) *War and Peace* is the title of a novel, *Sense and Sensibility* is also the title of a novel.

72. (c) To satiate is to make full, to vitiate is to make worthless.

73. (a) Something salubrious is healthful, and certainly not deleterious or harmful, and something (or someone) munificent or generous is not stingy.

74. (a) An epic is a tale of daring and heroism, and an exploit is an achievement of daring and heroism.

75. (c) Uniform means all the same and unchanging, also known as static, and war-like means hawkish.

76. (*d*) Striated muscle is used for volitional activity, and smooth muscle is used for involuntary activity.

77. (*d*) Dessert comes at the end of a meal, and a colophon comes at the end of a book.

78. (*b*) Cantankerous also means obstreperous (they both mean cranky and irritable), and obsequious also means fawning, (they both mean overly attentive and cloying). Don't be distracted by humble, because obsequious and fawning both have a negative nuance, where humble does not.

79. (*a*) The expressions are "By hook or crook," and "Come hell or high water."

80. (*b*) The Declaration of Independence was signed in 1776, and the Emancipation Proclamation was signed in 1863.

81. (*d*) To impress means to force (usually into service), and to inculcate means to imprint.

82. (*a*) A chasuble is used by a priest in prayer, and a phylactery is used by a rabbi in prayer.

83. (*a*) A cast helps a break (a broken arm, for instance), and an analgesic helps an ache.

84. (*a*) Conifers are types of traceophyta (or vascular plants), and metatheria are types of mammals.

85. (*b*) To pepper means to sprinkle, and to flower means to mature.

86. (*a*) Something tacit is not spoken, and something rigid is not plastic (or bendable).

87. (*c*) To mirror means to imitate, reflect, or ape, and to impugn means to attack.

88. (*a*) To thumb something means to wear it away (as in a much-thumbed text), and to finger something means to handle it.

89. (*d*) The Sahara desert is on the continent of Africa, and the Atacama desert is on the continent of South America.

90. (*a*) A reprobate is an immoral person, and a lecher is a prurient or sexual person.

91. (*a*) To sheer means to swerve, and to leer means to ogle.

92. (*b*) To toast something is to make it become warm, and to brown something is to make it become brown.

93. (*d*) The Adriatic Sea borders Italy, and the Caspian Sea borders Iran.

94. (*c*) The word raw is taken from inside the word d*raw*er, and the word arc is taken from inside the word ch*arc*oal.

95. (*a*) To commend means to praise, and to gibbet means to ridicule.

96. (*c*) A penitent is by definition contrite, and a penitentiary is by definition penal or punitive.

97. (*b*) To fox someone is to trick him, and to snow someone is to fool him.

98. (*d*) Dickens was a Victorian writer, and Keats was a romantic writer.

99. (*c*) Algeria is a country in Africa, and Argentina is a country in South America.

100. (*a*) Fertile means prone to production, and labile means prone to lapse.

SAMPLE TEST 7

Time: 50 Minutes
100 Questions

Directions: The following analogy pairs contain four choices with which to combine the unpaired word. Choose the answer that best corresponds to the full analogy pair. There is only one right answer.

1. BARK : (*a.* speak, *b.* dog, *c.* meow, *d.* tree) :: HACK : CUT
2. (*a.* shopping, *b.* delicate, *c.* wings, *d.* uncontrolled) : FRENETIC :: GOSSAMER : SPREE
3. SILVER : ORE :: (*a.* whey, *b.* butter, *c.* cheese, *d.* cow) : MILK
4. FRIVOLOUS : BANAL :: PRAGMATIC : (*a.* dogmatic, *b.* scintillating, *c.* dull, *d.* silly)
5. FUMBLE : STUMBLE :: TOUCH : (*a.* bumble, *b.* ouch, *c.* walk, *d.* crash)

6. (*a.* hearing, *b.* sound, *c.* senses, *d.* speed) : SONIC :: SIGHT : VISUAL
7. BREAD : CRUMB :: (*a.* pits, *b.* food, *c.* poverty, *d.* money) : PITTANCE
8. MARGIN : (*a.* paper, *b.* error, *c.* fresco, *d.* edge) :: FRIEZE : WALL
9. NOVELS : FABLES :: NOVELIST : (*a.* poet, *b.* essayist, *c.* fabulist, *d.* moralist)
10. (*a.* war, *b.* 3, *c.* 4, *d.* 5) : 8 :: PENTAGON : OCTAGON

11. MILE : (*a.* inch, *b.* reporter, *c.* coops, *d.* coop) :: SMILES : SCOOPS
12. POWERFUL : MAGNATE :: (*a.* weak, *b.* dull, *c.* magnetic, *d.* poor) : DOLT
13. TON : (*a.* reveal, *b.* open, *c.* party, *d.* not) :: LEVER : REVEL
14. USE : ATROPHY :: (*a.* aeration, *b.* asphyxiation, *c.* reproach, *d.* misuse) : SUFFO-CATE
15. SANITIZE : WEAN :: GERMS : (*a.* habit, *b.* milk, *c.* childhood, *d.* sterile)

16. (*a.* impermeable, *b.* smooth, *c.* dry, *d.* sweaty) : PERMEABLE :: ARID : PÓROUS
17. MEDIAN : MEAN :: MIDDLE : (*a.* nasty, *b.* average, *c.* affable, *d.* highway)
18. TYPHOON : TYPHUS :: (*a.* storm, *b.* wave, *c.* monsoon, *d.* infection) : DISEASE
19. WHENCE : FROM WHERE :: WHEREFORE : (*a.* where, *b.* to where, *c.* why, *d.* how)
20. WANGLE : (*a.* herd, *b.* connivance, *c.* rustle, *d.* strength) :: COERCE : FORCE

21. (*a.* twist, *b.* lever, *c.* talk, *d.* wander) : TURN :: DIGRESS : PIVOT
22. ELATED : (*a.* ecstatic, *b.* unrelated, *c.* useless, *d.* morose) :: UTILE : FUTILE
23. POEM : (*a.* elegy, *b.* eulogy, *c.* sonnet, *d.* epic) :: SONG : REQUIEM
24. DOG : WHELP :: WHALE : (*a.* guppy, *b.* cow, *c.* calf, *d.* pup)
25. SEDAN : CAR :: (*a.* water, *b.* yawl, *c.* sail, *d.* dray) : BOAT

26. SPEED : HERMES :: (*a.* strength, *b.* victory, *c.* war, *d.* mercury) : MARS
27. (*a.* tie, *b.* braid, *c.* egg, *d.* separate) : BIND :: YOKE : TIE
28. SIMIAN : (*a.* weak, *b.* bull, *c.* monkey, *d.* snake) :: URSINE : BEAR
29. PAUCITY : OVERAGE :: DEARTH : (*a.* age, *b.* youth, *c.* surfeit, *d.* alacrity)
30. FRENZY : FUROR :: (*a.* indecision, *b.* anger, *c.* tempest, *d.* storm) : DITHER

31. RISKY : (*a.* daring, *b.* brash, *c.* dare devil, *d.* brave) :: CLOWNISH : ZANY
32. (*a.* falsity, *b.* probity, *c.* semblance, *d.* guise) : APPEARANCE :: FACADE : FRONT
33. MASS : (*a.* unspecified, *b.* weighty, *c.* sacrilegious, *d.* many) :: HORDE : NUMEROUS
34. WOLF : NIBBLE :: (*a.* beast, *b.* droplet, *c.* teem, *d.* meal) : DRIZZLE
35. SHAKESPEARE : KEATS :: SONNETS : (*a.* odes, *b.* epics, *c.* plays, *d.* tragedies)

36. HANGAR : (*a.* pasture, *b.* field, *c.* stable, *d.* ring) :: AIRPLANE : HORSE
37. HEIGHTS : ACROPHOBE :: (*a.* rodents, *b.* bats, *c.* gases, *d.* foreigners) : XENOPHOBE
38. (*a.* Andrew, *b.* Tyler, *c.* Old Hickory, *d.* Mohandas) : MAHATMA :: JACKSON : GANDHI
39. CATHOLIC : PROVINCIAL :: (*a.* religious, *b.* pious, *c.* vatican, *d.* universal) : NARROW
40. BASIC : RUDIMENTARY :: (*a.* decadent, *b.* complex, *c.* exhausting, *d.* snobbish) : EFFETE

41. (*a.* doe, *b.* fawn, *c.* hart, *d.* calf) : ROOSTER :: DEER : CHICKEN

42. SCOOP : TRUNCATE :: (*a.* hollow, *b.* round, *c.* swirl, *d.* drop) : LOP

43. HAMPER : FACILITATE :: IMPEDE : (*a.* facility, *b.* ease, *c.* laundry, *d.* stymie)

44. CURRICULA : CURRICULUM :: FISH : (*a.* fish, *b.* fishes, *c.* ichthyology, *d.* fish class)

45. ASTRINGENT : (*a.* tiring, *b.* drying, *c.* clear, *d.* stinging) :: STRINGENT : RIGOROUS

46. FOOL : ALOOF :: (*a.* skew, *b.* skwe, *c.* weks, *d.* cool) : ASKEW

47. (*a.* ad locum, *b.* ad interim, *c.* pro tempore, *d.* ad lib) : IN THE MEANTIME :: AD VALOREM : IN PROPORTION TO THE VALUE

48. WEAL : ZEAL :: (*a.* well-being, *b.* sweetness, *c.* zealotry, *d.* caprice) : ENTHUSIASM

49. SFORZANO : (*a.* tempo, *b.* tone, *c.* octave, *d.* scale) :: YELL : WORD

50. EGG : YOKE :: URGE : (*a.* tie, *b.* compel, *c.* break, *d.* help)

51. PASSIM : BLITHE :: FREQUENTLY : (*a.* often, *b.* careless, *c.* fervent, *d.* easy)

52. BROOK : (*a.* water, *b.* tolerate, *c.* army, *d.* babble) :: STORM : ATTACK

53. (*a.* Edison, *b.* Slater, *c.* Whitney, *d.* Sholes) : CARVER :: COTTON GIN : PEANUT BUTTER

54. (*a.* coil, *b.* jug, *c.* bandana, *d.* splotch) : HANK :: VAT : TANK

55. STABILITY : CONSONANCE :: INSTABILITY : (*a.* decrescendo, *b.* assonance, *c.* euphonious, *d.* dissonance)

56. GLOAMING : (*a.* orb, *b.* dusk, *c.* morning, *d.* world) :: REALM : SPHERE

57. ALASKA : HAWAII :: (*a.* Texas, *b.* Ohio, *c.* Georgia, *d.* Vermont) : DELAWARE

58. PARABOLA : (*a.* conic, *b.* square, *c.* angle, *d.* horn) :: GLOCKENSPIEL : INSTRUMENT

59. SEXTANT : (*a.* altitude, *b.* speed, *c.* depth, *d.* piety) :: ODOMETER : DISTANCE

60. (*a.* sorrow, *b.* shadow, *c.* tint, *d.* choler) : HUE :: DOLOR : COLOR

61. FOUND : FOUNDER :: (*a.* establish, *b.* disable, *c.* sink, *d.* lose) : COLLAPSE
62. 0.2 : (*a.* 25, *b.* 0.5, *c.* 4, *d.* 5) :: 0.125 : 8
63. LURCH : DIFFICULT :: (*a.* sinecure, *b.* perch, *c.* stand, *d.* leap) : EASY
64. VIETNAMESE : (*a.* Pol Pot, *b.* Chiang Kai Shek, *c.* Ho Chi Minh, *d.* Saigon) :: CHINESE : MAO TSE-TUNG
65. PAUCITY : DEARTH :: (*a.* empty, *b.* gloat, *c.* lack, *d.* glut) : SURFEIT

66. CAROL : YULETIDE :: (*a.* jig, *b.* chantey, *c.* hymn, *d.* boat) : ASEA
67. (*a.* femur, *b.* circle, *c.* pelvis, *d.* fibula) : ULNA :: TIBIA : RADIUS
68. TERMAGANT : (*a.* shrew, *b.* ape, *c.* squirrel, *d.* mouse) :: DOLT : ASS
69. WAX : GROW :: (*a.* candle, *b.* bemoan, *c.* shave, *d.* elate) : LAMENT
70. CRY : YELP :: (*a.* weep, *b.* turn, *c.* craw, *d.* torn) : YAW

71. I : III :: L : (*a.* V, *b.* D, *c.* CL, *d.* DL)
72. NOSTRUM : (*a.* chignon, *b.* sprawl, *c.* nose, *d.* remedy) :: FALL : HAIR
73. (*a.* hoax, *b.* show, *c.* coax, *d.* smooth) : BLANDISH :: BRANDISH : FLAUNT
74. BARK : (*a.* vision, *b.* voice, *c.* yelp, *d.* cry) :: LOOK : GLIMPSE
75. CREASED : WRINKLES :: MACULATE : (*a.* hands, *b.* spots, *c.* smooth, *d.* unlined)

76. MOTHS : MOSQUITOS :: CAMPHOR : (*a.* citronella, *b.* vinegar, *c.* resin, *d.* amber)
77. (*a.* acid, *b.* racism, *c.* sentence, *d.* predicate) : PREJUDICE :: BASE : BIAS
78. HAWK : (*a.* serene, *b.* voracious, *c.* truculent, *d.* pandemonium) :: DOVE : PEACE-FUL
79. GERONIMO : GARIBALDI :: (*a.* Sioux, *b.* Apache, *c.* Mongol, *d.* Cochise) : ITALIAN
80. CELERITY : (*a.* smell, *b.* crispness, *c.* speed, *d.* languor) :: REDOLENCE : FRAGRANCE

81. (*a.* realist, *b.* pointillist, *c.* modernist, *d.* abstract) : CUBIST :: SEURAT : PICASSO

82. FENDED : DEFEND :: (*a.* tried, *b.* capsule, *c.* tablet, *d.* attack) : BATTLE

83. SIZE : (*a.* evaluation, *b.* worth, *c.* equal, *d.* period) :: COMMENSURATE : COEVAL

84. QUIBBLE : CONFRONT :: (*a.* halt, *b.* palter, *c.* arm, *d.* face) : BREAST

85. RUNG : RISER :: (*a.* alarm, *b.* rail, *c.* wall, *d.* ladder) : STAIR

86. (*a.* Cervantes, *b.* Goethe, *c.* Voltaire, *d.* Milton) : DANTE :: SPENSER : PIRANDELLO

87. TWEETER : (*a.* dog, *b.* tweezer, *c.* woofer, *d.* bass) :: HIGH : LOW

88. SWAN LAKE : (*a.* the Nutcracker, *b.* Giselle, *c.* the Firebird, *d.* the Birds) :: TCHAIKOVSKY : STRAVINSKY

89. CUNEIFORM : (*a.* writing, *b.* nomad, *c.* mathematics, *d.* language):: ARABIC : NUMBER

90. PENTATEUCH : WISDOM :: FIVE : (*a.* three, *b.* five, *c.* seven, *d.* eight)

91. PI : (*a.* circle, *b.* radius, *c.* ratio, *d.* circumference) :: AREA : MEASUREMENT

92. (*a.* Celia, *b.* liberty, *c.* wars, *d.* peaces) : ESCAPE :: STEFAN : FASTEN

93. HELL : INFERNO :: (*a.* Russia, *b.* United States, *c.* England, *d.* Heaven) : LOLITA

94. SOLAR : SUN :: SIDEREAL : (*a.* stars, *b.* moon, *c.* planets, *d.* countryside)

95. BUTTERFLY : DOWNHILL :: CRAWL : (*a.* grass, *b.* steep, *c.* larval, *d.* slalom)

96. WRIGHT : PEI :: (*a.* Goya, *b.* Donatello, *c.* Rembrandt, *d.* da Vinci) : RODIN

97. IMPROMPTU : EXTEMPORANEOUS :: (*a.* erotic, *b.* false, *c.* whimsical, *d.* correct) : ERRONEOUS

98. DESOLATE : INTERPOLATE :: ODE TALES : (*a.* fairy tales, *b.* tragedies, *c.* scene painter, *d.* lot painter)

99. (*a.* word, *b.* judgment, *c.* meaning, *d.* message) : SENTENCE :: NOTICE : AN-NOUNCEMENT

100. LILIUOKALANI : SELASSIE :: LINCOLN : (*a.* Washington, *b.* McKinley, *c.* Adams, *d.* Jefferson)

ANSWER KEY

1. (*a*) To hack means to cut roughly, and to bark means to speak roughly.

2. (*b*) A spree is something frenetic, and gossamer is something delicate—both are nouns.

3. (*a*) Silver is extracted from ore, and whey is extracted from milk, as opposed to cheese and butter, which are produced from changing milk—not extracted from it.

4. (*b*) Something frivolous or silly is not pragmatic, and something banal or dull is not scintillating.

5. (*c*) To fumble is to touch awkwardly, to stumble is to walk awkwardly.

6. (*a*) Something visual is related to sight, and something sonic is related to hearing.

7. (*d*) A crumb is a tiny amount of bread, and a pittance is a tiny amount of money.

8. (*a*) A frieze is the area at the edge of a wall, and a margin is the area at the edge of paper.

9. (*c*) A novelist creates novels, and a fabulist creates fables.

10. (*d*) An octagon has eight sides, and a pentagon has five sides.

11. (*d*) Smiles becomes mile with the removal of the 's' at either side, and scoops becomes coop when the same operation is performed.

12. (*b*) A magnate is a powerful person, and a dolt is a dull person.

13. (*d*) Lever is the reverse of revel, and not is the reverse of ton.

14. (*a*) Without use something will atrophy, and without aeration something (or someone) will suffocate.

15. (*a*) To sanitize means to get rid of germs, and to wean means to get rid of a habit.

16. (*c*) Something porous is permeable, and something arid is dry.

17. (*b*) A median is the middle number of a set, and a mean is the average number of a set.

18. (*a*) A typhoon is a type of storm, and typhus is a type of disease.

19. (*c*) Whence means from where, and wherefore means why. (Makes you rethink the old "Wherefore art thou Romeo?" line, doesn't it?)

20. (*b*) To coerce means to use force, to wangle means to use connivance.

21. (*d*) To pivot means to turn, and to digress means to wander.

22. (*d*) Futile is the absence of utility, and morose is the absence of elation.

23. (*a*) A requiem is a mournful song, usually for one who is dead, and an elegy is a mournful poem, usually for one who is dead. A eulogy, also often spoken for one who is dead, is a praising speech, not necessarily mournful, and not necessarily a poem.

24. (*c*) A whelp is the young offspring of a dog, and a calf is the young offspring of a whale.

25. (*b*) A sedan is a type of car, and a yawl is a type of boat.

26. (*c*) Hermes was the Roman god of speed, and Mars was the Roman god of war.

27. (*a*) To tie means to bind, and to yoke means to tie.

28. (*c*) Ursine means bear-like, and simian means monkey-like.

29. (*c*) Paucity means a lack or dearth, and an overage is a glut or surfeit.

30. (*a*) A furor is a fit of frenzy, and a dither is a fit of indecision.

31. (*a*) Partaking of clownish behavior is zany; partaking of risky behavior is daring. Brash means without thinking; it doesn't pertain to risk, exactly.

32. (*c*) A facade is a false front, and a semblance is a false appearance.

33. (*a*) A mass is characterized by being unspecified, as in a mass of french fries, and a horde is characterized by being numerous.

34. (*c*) To wolf means to nibble hugely, and to teem means to drizzle hugely.

35. (*a*) Shakespeare is known for his sonnets, and Keats is known for his odes; an epic is not necessarily a poem.

36. (*c*) A hangar is the structure airplanes are kept in, and a stable is the structure horses are kept in.

37. (*d*) An acrophobe is afraid of heights, and a xenophobe is afraid of foreigners.

38. (*c*) Gandhi was known as "Mahatma," and Jackson was known as "Old Hickory."

39. (*d*) Provincial means narrow, and catholic means universal. (This is not Catholicism, the religion, but catholic with a lowercase 'c.')

40. (*a*) Rudimentary means basic, and effete means decadent.

41. (*c*) A rooster is a male chicken, and a hart is a male deer.

42. (*a*) To scoop something out is to hollow it, and to truncate something is to cut it off, or lop it off.

43. (*b*) To hamper means to impede, and to facilitate means to ease.

44. (*a*) Curricula is the plural of curriculum, and fish is the plural of fish.

45. (*b*) Astringent means drying, and stringent means rigorous.

46. (*c*) Fool is created by reversing aloof and dropping the *a*; doing the same to askew yields weks.

47. (*b*) Ad valorem means "in proportion to the value of," and ad interim means "in the meantime."

48. (*a*) Weal means well-being, usually in the case of the public weal, and zeal means enthusiasm.

49. (*b*) Yell is a sudden accent on a word, and sforzano is a sudden accent on a tone.

50. (*a*) To egg means to urge on or to goad, and to yoke means to tie, as in yoked oxen.

51. (*b*) Passim means thoroughly or frequently, and blithe means careless.

52. (*b*) To storm means to attack, and to brook means to tolerate. (Look at those secondary definitions).

53. (*c*) George Washington Carver invented peanut butter, and Eli Whitney invented the cotton gin.

54. (*a*) A coil is a type of hank, and a vat is a type of tank.

55. (*d*) Consonance produces a feeling of musical stability, and dissonance produces a feeling of musical instability.

56. (*b*) Gloaming means dusk, and a realm is a sphere or area of influence.

57. (*c*) Hawaii and Alaska were the last states to be admitted to the Union, and Delaware and Georgia were among the first thirteen states to be admitted to the Union.

58. (*a*) A parabola is a type of conic, and a glockenspiel is a type of instrument.

59. (*a*) A sextant measures altitude, and an odometer measures distance.

60. (*a*) Dolor is sorrow, and color is hue.

61. (*a*) To found means to establish, as in to found a school, and to founder means to collapse, as in the ship foundered in the storm.

62. (*d*) The decimal 0.125 is equivalent to 1/8, and the decimal 0.2 is equivalent to 1/5.

63. (*a*) A lurch is a difficult situation, and a sinecure is an easy situation.

64. (*c*) Mao Tse-tung was a Chinese leader, and Ho Chi Minh was a Vietnamese leader.

65. (*d*) A dearth is a paucity or lack, and a surfeit is a glut or excess.

66. (*b*) A carol is a song for yuletide, and a chantey is a song for asea (out on the ocean).

67. (*d*) The radius and the ulna are both bones in the forearm, and the tibia and fibula are both bones in the calf.

68. (*a*) A termagant is a shrew, or a person who acts like a shrew, and a dolt is an ass or a person who acts like an ass.

69. (*b*) To wax means to grow or increase, and to bemoan means to lament or mourn.

70. (*b*) A yelp is a type of cry, and a yaw is a type of turn.

71. (*c*) The ratio between the Roman numerals is 1 to 3, which is also 50 to 150, or L to CL.

72. (*d*) A nostrum is a false remedy, and a fall is false hair.

73. (*c*) To blandish means to coax or convince, and to brandish means to flaunt or show off.

74. (*c*) A yelp is a short bark, and a glimpse is a short look.

75. (*b*) Creased means having wrinkles, and maculate means having spots (remember immaculate? Study those roots).

76. (*a*) Moths are repelled by camphor, and mosquitos are repelled by citronella.

77. (*d*) To prejudice means to bias, to predicate means to base.

78. (c) A dove is a symbol of peace, a hawk is a symbol of war or truculence.

79. (b) Garibaldi was an Italian leader, and Geronimo was an Apache leader.

80. (c) Redolence means fragrance, and celerity means speed.

81. (b) Picasso was most famous as a cubist painter, and Seurat was most famous as a pointillist painter.

82. (c) Defend is an anagram for fended, and battle is an anagram for tablet.

83. (d) Commensurate means of the same size, and coeval means of the same period or era.

84. (b) To quibble means to bicker or palter, and to confront means to breast.

85. (d) A rung is the part of a ladder to be climbed, and a riser is the part of a stair to be climbed.

86. (d) Pirandello and Dante were both Italian writers, and Spenser and Milton were both English writers.

87. (c) A tweeter produces high sounds from an amplifier, and a woofer produces low sounds from an amplifier.

88. (c) Tchaikovsky wrote the score for the ballet *Swan Lake*, and Stravinsky wrote the score for the ballet *The Firebird*.

89. (a) Cuneiform is a type of writing, and arabic is a type of number.

90. (c) The Pentateuch or Torah contains five biblical books; Wisdom contains seven biblical books.

91. (c) Area is one type of measurement, and pi is one type of ratio.

92. (d) Stefan is an anagram of fasten, and peaces is an anagram of escapes.

93. (b) *The Inferno* is set in hell, and *Lolita* is set in the United States.

94. (a) Solar means having to do with the sun, and sidereal means having to do with the stars.

95. (d) Butterfly and crawl are both types of swimming strokes, and slalom and downhill are both types of ski racing.

96. (b) I.M. Pei and Frank Lloyd Wright are both architects, and Rodin and Donatello are both sculptors.

97. (b) Something impromptu is extemporaneous or without preparation, and something erroneous is false.

98. (d) Ode tales is an anagram for desolate, and lot painter is an anagram for interpolate.

99. (b) A sentence is a type of judgement (from a judge or jury), and a notice is a type of announcement.

100. (b) Liliuokalani and Selassie both ended their terms by being deposed, and Lincoln and McKinley both ended their terms by being assassinated.

ABOUT THE AUTHOR

Marcia Lerner graduated from Brown University in 1986. She is the author of *Writing Smart* and *Math Smart*, and has been teaching and writing for The Princeton Review since 1988.

THE PRINCETON REVIEW WORLDWIDE

Each year, thousands of students from countries throughout the world prepare for the TOEFL and for U.S. college and graduate school admissions exams. Whether you plan to prepare for your exams in your home country or the United States, The Princeton Review is committed to your success.

INTERNATIONAL LOCATIONS: If you are using our books outside of the United States and have questions or comments, or want to know if our courses are being offered in your area, be sure to contact the Princeton Review office nearest you:

- HONG KONG   852-517-3016
- JAPAN (Tokyo)   8133-463-1343
- KOREA (Seoul)   822-508-0081
- MEXICO CITY   525-564-9468
- MONTREAL   514-499-0870
- PAKISTAN (Lahore)   92-42-571-2315
- SAUDI ARABIA   413-584-6849 (a U.S. based number)
- SPAIN (Madrid)   341-323-4212
- TAIWAN (Taipei)   886-27511293

U.S. STUDY ABROAD: *Review USA* offers international students many advantages and opportunities. In addition to helping you gain acceptance to the U.S. college or university of your choice, *Review USA* will help you acquire the knowledge and orientation you need to succeed once you get there.

Review USA is unique. It includes supplements to your test-preparation courses and a special series of *AmeriCulture* workshops to prepare you for the academic rigors and student life in the United States. Our workshops are designed to familiarize you with the different U.S. expressions, real-life vocabulary, and cultural challenges you will encounter as a study-abroad student. While studying with us, you'll make new friends and have the opportunity to personally visit college and university campuses to determine which school is right for you.

Whether you are planning to take the TOEFL, SAT, GRE, GMAT, LSAT, MCAT, or USMLE exam, The Princeton Review's test preparation courses, expert instructors, and dedicated International Student Advisors can help you achieve your goals.

For additional information about *Review USA*, admissions requirements, class schedules, F-1 visas, I-20 documentation, and course locations, write to:

The Princeton Review • Review USA
2315 Broadway, New York NY 10024
Fax: 212/874-0775

The Princeton Review

Completely darken bubbles with a No. 2 pencil. If you make a mistake, be sure to erase mark completely. Erase all stray marks.

1

YOUR NAME: _____
(Print)   Last   First   M.I.

SIGNATURE: _____   DATE: ___ / ___ / ___

HOME ADDRESS: _____
(Print)   Number and Street

_____
City   State   Zip Code

PHONE NO.: _____
(Print)

IMPORTANT: Please fill in these boxes exactly as shown on the back cover of your test book.

2. TEST FORM

_____

6. DATE OF BIRTH

Month	Day	Year
◯ JAN		
◯ FEB		
◯ MAR	◯0◯ ◯0◯	◯0◯ ◯0◯
◯ APR	◯1◯ ◯1◯	◯1◯ ◯1◯
◯ MAY	◯2◯ ◯2◯	◯2◯ ◯2◯
◯ JUN	◯3◯ ◯3◯	◯3◯ ◯3◯
◯ JUL	◯4◯	◯4◯ ◯4◯
◯ AUG	◯5◯ ◯5◯	◯5◯
◯ SEP	◯6◯ ◯6◯	◯6◯
◯ OCT	◯7◯ ◯7◯	◯7◯
◯ NOV	◯8◯ ◯8◯	◯8◯
◯ DEC	◯9◯ ◯9◯	◯9◯

3. TEST CODE   **4. REGISTRATION NUMBER**

0 A 0 0 0 | 0 0 0 0 0 0
1 B 1 1 1 | 1 1 1 1 1 1
2 C 2 2 2 | 2 2 2 2 2 2
3 D 3 3 3 | 3 3 3 3 3 3
4 E 4 4 4 | 4 4 4 4 4 4
5 F 5 5 5 | 5 5 5 5 5 5
6 G 6 6 6 | 6 6 6 6 6 6
7 7 7 7 | 7 7 7 7 7 7
8 8 8 8 | 8 8 8 8 8 8
9 9 9 9 | 9 9 9 9 9 9

7. SEX
◯ MALE
◯ FEMALE

THE PRINCETON REVIEW
© 1996 The Princeton Review

5. YOUR NAME

First 4 letters of last name				FIRST INIT	MID INIT
A A A A				A	A
B B B B				B	B
C C C C				C	C
D D D D				D	D
E E E E				E	E
F F F F				F	F
G G G G				G	G
H H H H				H	H
I I I I				I	I
J J J J				J	J
K K K K				K	K
L L L L				L	L
M M M M				M	M
N N N N				N	N
O O O O				O	O
P P P P				P	P
Q Q Q Q				Q	Q
R R R R				R	R
S S S S				S	S
T T T T				T	T
U U U U				U	U
V V V V				V	V
W W W W				W	W
X X X X				X	X
Y Y Y Y				Y	Y
Z Z Z Z				Z	Z

TEST 1

1 a.◯ b.◯ c.◯ d.◯   21 a.◯ b.◯ c.◯ d.◯   41 a.◯ b.◯ c.◯ d.◯   61 a.◯ b.◯ c.◯ d.◯   81 a.◯ b.◯ c.◯ d.◯
2 a.◯ b.◯ c.◯ d.◯   22 a.◯ b.◯ c.◯ d.◯   42 a.◯ b.◯ c.◯ d.◯   62 a.◯ b.◯ c.◯ d.◯   82 a.◯ b.◯ c.◯ d.◯
3 a.◯ b.◯ c.◯ d.◯   23 a.◯ b.◯ c.◯ d.◯   43 a.◯ b.◯ c.◯ d.◯   63 a.◯ b.◯ c.◯ d.◯   83 a.◯ b.◯ c.◯ d.◯
4 a.◯ b.◯ c.◯ d.◯   24 a.◯ b.◯ c.◯ d.◯   44 a.◯ b.◯ c.◯ d.◯   64 a.◯ b.◯ c.◯ d.◯   84 a.◯ b.◯ c.◯ d.◯
5 a.◯ b.◯ c.◯ d.◯   25 a.◯ b.◯ c.◯ d.◯   45 a.◯ b.◯ c.◯ d.◯   65 a.◯ b.◯ c.◯ d.◯   85 a.◯ b.◯ c.◯ d.◯
6 a.◯ b.◯ c.◯ d.◯   26 a.◯ b.◯ c.◯ d.◯   46 a.◯ b.◯ c.◯ d.◯   66 a.◯ b.◯ c.◯ d.◯   86 a.◯ b.◯ c.◯ d.◯
7 a.◯ b.◯ c.◯ d.◯   27 a.◯ b.◯ c.◯ d.◯   47 a.◯ b.◯ c.◯ d.◯   67 a.◯ b.◯ c.◯ d.◯   87 a.◯ b.◯ c.◯ d.◯
8 a.◯ b.◯ c.◯ d.◯   28 a.◯ b.◯ c.◯ d.◯   48 a.◯ b.◯ c.◯ d.◯   68 a.◯ b.◯ c.◯ d.◯   88 a.◯ b.◯ c.◯ d.◯
9 a.◯ b.◯ c.◯ d.◯   29 a.◯ b.◯ c.◯ d.◯   59 a.◯ b.◯ c.◯ d.◯   69 a.◯ b.◯ c.◯ d.◯   89 a.◯ b.◯ c.◯ d.◯
10 a.◯ b.◯ c.◯ d.◯   30 a.◯ b.◯ c.◯ d.◯   50 a.◯ b.◯ c.◯ d.◯   70 a.◯ b.◯ c.◯ d.◯   90 a.◯ b.◯ c.◯ d.◯
11 a.◯ b.◯ c.◯ d.◯   31 a.◯ b.◯ c.◯ d.◯   51 a.◯ b.◯ c.◯ d.◯   71 a.◯ b.◯ c.◯ d.◯   91 a.◯ b.◯ c.◯ d.◯
12 a.◯ b.◯ c.◯ d.◯   32 a.◯ b.◯ c.◯ d.◯   52 a.◯ b.◯ c.◯ d.◯   72 a.◯ b.◯ c.◯ d.◯   92 a.◯ b.◯ c.◯ d.◯
13 a.◯ b.◯ c.◯ d.◯   33 a.◯ b.◯ c.◯ d.◯   53 a.◯ b.◯ c.◯ d.◯   73 a.◯ b.◯ c.◯ d.◯   93 a.◯ b.◯ c.◯ d.◯
14 a.◯ b.◯ c.◯ d.◯   34 a.◯ b.◯ c.◯ d.◯   54 a.◯ b.◯ c.◯ d.◯   74 a.◯ b.◯ c.◯ d.◯   94 a.◯ b.◯ c.◯ d.◯
15 a.◯ b.◯ c.◯ d.◯   35 a.◯ b.◯ c.◯ d.◯   55 a.◯ b.◯ c.◯ d.◯   75 a.◯ b.◯ c.◯ d.◯   95 a.◯ b.◯ c.◯ d.◯
16 a.◯ b.◯ c.◯ d.◯   36 a.◯ b.◯ c.◯ d.◯   56 a.◯ b.◯ c.◯ d.◯   76 a.◯ b.◯ c.◯ d.◯   96 a.◯ b.◯ c.◯ d.◯
17 a.◯ b.◯ c.◯ d.◯   37 a.◯ b.◯ c.◯ d.◯   57 a.◯ b.◯ c.◯ d.◯   77 a.◯ b.◯ c.◯ d.◯   97 a.◯ b.◯ c.◯ d.◯
18 a.◯ b.◯ c.◯ d.◯   38 a.◯ b.◯ c.◯ d.◯   58 a.◯ b.◯ c.◯ d.◯   78 a.◯ b.◯ c.◯ d.◯   98 a.◯ b.◯ c.◯ d.◯
19 a.◯ b.◯ c.◯ d.◯   39 a.◯ b.◯ c.◯ d.◯   59 a.◯ b.◯ c.◯ d.◯   79 a.◯ b.◯ c.◯ d.◯   99 a.◯ b.◯ c.◯ d.◯
20 a.◯ b.◯ c.◯ d.◯   40 a.◯ b.◯ c.◯ d.◯   60 a.◯ b.◯ c.◯ d.◯   80 a.◯ b.◯ c.◯ d.◯   100 a.◯ b.◯ c.◯ d.◯

TEST 2

1 a.○ b.○ c.○ d.○	21 a.○ b.○ c.○ d.○	41 a.○ b.○ c.○ d.○	61 a.○ b.○ c.○ d.○	81 a.○ b.○ c.○ d.○
2 a.○ b.○ c.○ d.○	22 a.○ b.○ c.○ d.○	42 a.○ b.○ c.○ d.○	62 a.○ b.○ c.○ d.○	82 a.○ b.○ c.○ d.○
3 a.○ b.○ c.○ d.○	23 a.○ b.○ c.○ d.○	43 a.○ b.○ c.○ d.○	63 a.○ b.○ c.○ d.○	83 a.○ b.○ c.○ d.○
4 a.○ b.○ c.○ d.○	24 a.○ b.○ c.○ d.○	44 a.○ b.○ c.○ d.○	64 a.○ b.○ c.○ d.○	84 a.○ b.○ c.○ d.○
5 a.○ b.○ c.○ d.○	25 a.○ b.○ c.○ d.○	45 a.○ b.○ c.○ d.○	65 a.○ b.○ c.○ d.○	85 a.○ b.○ c.○ d.○
6 a.○ b.○ c.○ d.○	26 a.○ b.○ c.○ d.○	46 a.○ b.○ c.○ d.○	66 a.○ b.○ c.○ d.○	86 a.○ b.○ c.○ d.○
7 a.○ b.○ c.○ d.○	27 a.○ b.○ c.○ d.○	47 a.○ b.○ c.○ d.○	67 a.○ b.○ c.○ d.○	87 a.○ b.○ c.○ d.○
8 a.○ b.○ c.○ d.○	28 a.○ b.○ c.○ d.○	48 a.○ b.○ c.○ d.○	68 a.○ b.○ c.○ d.○	88 a.○ b.○ c.○ d.○
9 a.○ b.○ c.○ d.○	29 a.○ b.○ c.○ d.○	59 a.○ b.○ c.○ d.○	69 a.○ b.○ c.○ d.○	89 a.○ b.○ c.○ d.○
10 a.○ b.○ c.○ d.○	30 a.○ b.○ c.○ d.○	50 a.○ b.○ c.○ d.○	70 a.○ b.○ c.○ d.○	90 a.○ b.○ c.○ d.○
11 a.○ b.○ c.○ d.○	31 a.○ b.○ c.○ d.○	51 a.○ b.○ c.○ d.○	71 a.○ b.○ c.○ d.○	91 a.○ b.○ c.○ d.○
12 a.○ b.○ c.○ d.○	32 a.○ b.○ c.○ d.○	52 a.○ b.○ c.○ d.○	72 a.○ b.○ c.○ d.○	92 a.○ b.○ c.○ d.○
13 a.○ b.○ c.○ d.○	33 a.○ b.○ c.○ d.○	53 a.○ b.○ c.○ d.○	73 a.○ b.○ c.○ d.○	93 a.○ b.○ c.○ d.○
14 a.○ b.○ c.○ d.○	34 a.○ b.○ c.○ d.○	54 a.○ b.○ c.○ d.○	74 a.○ b.○ c.○ d.○	94 a.○ b.○ c.○ d.○
15 a.○ b.○ c.○ d.○	35 a.○ b.○ c.○ d.○	55 a.○ b.○ c.○ d.○	75 a.○ b.○ c.○ d.○	95 a.○ b.○ c.○ d.○
16 a.○ b.○ c.○ d.○	36 a.○ b.○ c.○ d.○	56 a.○ b.○ c.○ d.○	76 a.○ b.○ c.○ d.○	96 a.○ b.○ c.○ d.○
17 a.○ b.○ c.○ d.○	37 a.○ b.○ c.○ d.○	57 a.○ b.○ c.○ d.○	77 a.○ b.○ c.○ d.○	97 a.○ b.○ c.○ d.○
18 a.○ b.○ c.○ d.○	38 a.○ b.○ c.○ d.○	58 a.○ b.○ c.○ d.○	78 a.○ b.○ c.○ d.○	98 a.○ b.○ c.○ d.○
19 a.○ b.○ c.○ d.○	39 a.○ b.○ c.○ d.○	59 a.○ b.○ c.○ d.○	79 a.○ b.○ c.○ d.○	99 a.○ b.○ c.○ d.○
20 a.○ b.○ c.○ d.○	40 a.○ b.○ c.○ d.○	60 a.○ b.○ c.○ d.○	80 a.○ b.○ c.○ d.○	100 a.○ b.○ c.○ d.○

TEST 3

1 a.○ b.○ c.○ d.○	21 a.○ b.○ c.○ d.○	41 a.○ b.○ c.○ d.○	61 a.○ b.○ c.○ d.○	81 a.○ b.○ c.○ d.○
2 a.○ b.○ c.○ d.○	22 a.○ b.○ c.○ d.○	42 a.○ b.○ c.○ d.○	62 a.○ b.○ c.○ d.○	82 a.○ b.○ c.○ d.○
3 a.○ b.○ c.○ d.○	23 a.○ b.○ c.○ d.○	43 a.○ b.○ c.○ d.○	63 a.○ b.○ c.○ d.○	83 a.○ b.○ c.○ d.○
4 a.○ b.○ c.○ d.○	24 a.○ b.○ c.○ d.○	44 a.○ b.○ c.○ d.○	64 a.○ b.○ c.○ d.○	84 a.○ b.○ c.○ d.○
5 a.○ b.○ c.○ d.○	25 a.○ b.○ c.○ d.○	45 a.○ b.○ c.○ d.○	65 a.○ b.○ c.○ d.○	85 a.○ b.○ c.○ d.○
6 a.○ b.○ c.○ d.○	26 a.○ b.○ c.○ d.○	46 a.○ b.○ c.○ d.○	66 a.○ b.○ c.○ d.○	86 a.○ b.○ c.○ d.○
7 a.○ b.○ c.○ d.○	27 a.○ b.○ c.○ d.○	47 a.○ b.○ c.○ d.○	67 a.○ b.○ c.○ d.○	87 a.○ b.○ c.○ d.○
8 a.○ b.○ c.○ d.○	28 a.○ b.○ c.○ d.○	48 a.○ b.○ c.○ d.○	68 a.○ b.○ c.○ d.○	88 a.○ b.○ c.○ d.○
9 a.○ b.○ c.○ d.○	29 a.○ b.○ c.○ d.○	59 a.○ b.○ c.○ d.○	69 a.○ b.○ c.○ d.○	89 a.○ b.○ c.○ d.○
10 a.○ b.○ c.○ d.○	30 a.○ b.○ c.○ d.○	50 a.○ b.○ c.○ d.○	70 a.○ b.○ c.○ d.○	90 a.○ b.○ c.○ d.○
11 a.○ b.○ c.○ d.○	31 a.○ b.○ c.○ d.○	51 a.○ b.○ c.○ d.○	71 a.○ b.○ c.○ d.○	91 a.○ b.○ c.○ d.○
12 a.○ b.○ c.○ d.○	32 a.○ b.○ c.○ d.○	52 a.○ b.○ c.○ d.○	72 a.○ b.○ c.○ d.○	92 a.○ b.○ c.○ d.○
13 a.○ b.○ c.○ d.○	33 a.○ b.○ c.○ d.○	53 a.○ b.○ c.○ d.○	73 a.○ b.○ c.○ d.○	93 a.○ b.○ c.○ d.○
14 a.○ b.○ c.○ d.○	34 a.○ b.○ c.○ d.○	54 a.○ b.○ c.○ d.○	74 a.○ b.○ c.○ d.○	94 a.○ b.○ c.○ d.○
15 a.○ b.○ c.○ d.○	35 a.○ b.○ c.○ d.○	55 a.○ b.○ c.○ d.○	75 a.○ b.○ c.○ d.○	95 a.○ b.○ c.○ d.○
16 a.○ b.○ c.○ d.○	36 a.○ b.○ c.○ d.○	56 a.○ b.○ c.○ d.○	76 a.○ b.○ c.○ d.○	96 a.○ b.○ c.○ d.○
17 a.○ b.○ c.○ d.○	37 a.○ b.○ c.○ d.○	57 a.○ b.○ c.○ d.○	77 a.○ b.○ c.○ d.○	97 a.○ b.○ c.○ d.○
18 a.○ b.○ c.○ d.○	38 a.○ b.○ c.○ d.○	58 a.○ b.○ c.○ d.○	78 a.○ b.○ c.○ d.○	98 a.○ b.○ c.○ d.○
19 a.○ b.○ c.○ d.○	39 a.○ b.○ c.○ d.○	59 a.○ b.○ c.○ d.○	79 a.○ b.○ c.○ d.○	99 a.○ b.○ c.○ d.○
20 a.○ b.○ c.○ d.○	40 a.○ b.○ c.○ d.○	60 a.○ b.○ c.○ d.○	80 a.○ b.○ c.○ d.○	100 a.○ b.○ c.○ d.○

TEST 4

1 a.○ b.○ c.○ d.○   21 a.○ b.○ c.○ d.○   41 a.○ b.○ c.○ d.○   61 a.○ b.○ c.○ d.○   81 a.○ b.○ c.○ d.○
2 a.○ b.○ c.○ d.○   22 a.○ b.○ c.○ d.○   42 a.○ b.○ c.○ d.○   62 a.○ b.○ c.○ d.○   82 a.○ b.○ c.○ d.○
3 a.○ b.○ c.○ d.○   23 a.○ b.○ c.○ d.○   43 a.○ b.○ c.○ d.○   63 a.○ b.○ c.○ d.○   83 a.○ b.○ c.○ d.○
4 a.○ b.○ c.○ d.○   24 a.○ b.○ c.○ d.○   44 a.○ b.○ c.○ d.○   64 a.○ b.○ c.○ d.○   84 a.○ b.○ c.○ d.○
5 a.○ b.○ c.○ d.○   25 a.○ b.○ c.○ d.○   45 a.○ b.○ c.○ d.○   65 a.○ b.○ c.○ d.○   85 a.○ b.○ c.○ d.○

6 a.○ b.○ c.○ d.○   26 a.○ b.○ c.○ d.○   46 a.○ b.○ c.○ d.○   66 a.○ b.○ c.○ d.○   86 a.○ b.○ c.○ d.○
7 a.○ b.○ c.○ d.○   27 a.○ b.○ c.○ d.○   47 a.○ b.○ c.○ d.○   67 a.○ b.○ c.○ d.○   87 a.○ b.○ c.○ d.○
8 a.○ b.○ c.○ d.○   28 a.○ b.○ c.○ d.○   48 a.○ b.○ c.○ d.○   68 a.○ b.○ c.○ d.○   88 a.○ b.○ c.○ d.○
9 a.○ b.○ c.○ d.○   29 a.○ b.○ c.○ d.○   59 a.○ b.○ c.○ d.○   69 a.○ b.○ c.○ d.○   89 a.○ b.○ c.○ d.○
10 a.○ b.○ c.○ d.○   30 a.○ b.○ c.○ d.○   50 a.○ b.○ c.○ d.○   70 a.○ b.○ c.○ d.○   90 a.○ b.○ c.○ d.○

11 a.○ b.○ c.○ d.○   31 a.○ b.○ c.○ d.○   51 a.○ b.○ c.○ d.○   71 a.○ b.○ c.○ d.○   91 a.○ b.○ c.○ d.○
12 a.○ b.○ c.○ d.○   32 a.○ b.○ c.○ d.○   52 a.○ b.○ c.○ d.○   72 a.○ b.○ c.○ d.○   92 a.○ b.○ c.○ d.○
13 a.○ b.○ c.○ d.○   33 a.○ b.○ c.○ d.○   53 a.○ b.○ c.○ d.○   73 a.○ b.○ c.○ d.○   93 a.○ b.○ c.○ d.○
14 a.○ b.○ c.○ d.○   34 a.○ b.○ c.○ d.○   54 a.○ b.○ c.○ d.○   74 a.○ b.○ c.○ d.○   94 a.○ b.○ c.○ d.○
15 a.○ b.○ c.○ d.○   35 a.○ b.○ c.○ d.○   55 a.○ b.○ c.○ d.○   75 a.○ b.○ c.○ d.○   95 a.○ b.○ c.○ d.○

16 a.○ b.○ c.○ d.○   36 a.○ b.○ c.○ d.○   56 a.○ b.○ c.○ d.○   76 a.○ b.○ c.○ d.○   96 a.○ b.○ c.○ d.○
17 a.○ b.○ c.○ d.○   37 a.○ b.○ c.○ d.○   57 a.○ b.○ c.○ d.○   77 a.○ b.○ c.○ d.○   97 a.○ b.○ c.○ d.○
18 a.○ b.○ c.○ d.○   38 a.○ b.○ c.○ d.○   58 a.○ b.○ c.○ d.○   78 a.○ b.○ c.○ d.○   98 a.○ b.○ c.○ d.○
19 a.○ b.○ c.○ d.○   39 a.○ b.○ c.○ d.○   59 a.○ b.○ c.○ d.○   79 a.○ b.○ c.○ d.○   99 a.○ b.○ c.○ d.○
20 a.○ b.○ c.○ d.○   40 a.○ b.○ c.○ d.○   60 a.○ b.○ c.○ d.○   80 a.○ b.○ c.○ d.○   100 a.○ b.○ c.○ d.○

TEST 5

1 a.○ b.○ c.○ d.○   21 a.○ b.○ c.○ d.○   41 a.○ b.○ c.○ d.○   61 a.○ b.○ c.○ d.○   81 a.○ b.○ c.○ d.○
2 a.○ b.○ c.○ d.○   22 a.○ b.○ c.○ d.○   42 a.○ b.○ c.○ d.○   62 a.○ b.○ c.○ d.○   82 a.○ b.○ c.○ d.○
3 a.○ b.○ c.○ d.○   23 a.○ b.○ c.○ d.○   43 a.○ b.○ c.○ d.○   63 a.○ b.○ c.○ d.○   83 a.○ b.○ c.○ d.○
4 a.○ b.○ c.○ d.○   24 a.○ b.○ c.○ d.○   44 a.○ b.○ c.○ d.○   64 a.○ b.○ c.○ d.○   84 a.○ b.○ c.○ d.○
5 a.○ b.○ c.○ d.○   25 a.○ b.○ c.○ d.○   45 a.○ b.○ c.○ d.○   65 a.○ b.○ c.○ d.○   85 a.○ b.○ c.○ d.○

6 a.○ b.○ c.○ d.○   26 a.○ b.○ c.○ d.○   46 a.○ b.○ c.○ d.○   66 a.○ b.○ c.○ d.○   86 a.○ b.○ c.○ d.○
7 a.○ b.○ c.○ d.○   27 a.○ b.○ c.○ d.○   47 a.○ b.○ c.○ d.○   67 a.○ b.○ c.○ d.○   87 a.○ b.○ c.○ d.○
8 a.○ b.○ c.○ d.○   28 a.○ b.○ c.○ d.○   48 a.○ b.○ c.○ d.○   68 a.○ b.○ c.○ d.○   88 a.○ b.○ c.○ d.○
9 a.○ b.○ c.○ d.○   29 a.○ b.○ c.○ d.○   59 a.○ b.○ c.○ d.○   69 a.○ b.○ c.○ d.○   89 a.○ b.○ c.○ d.○
10 a.○ b.○ c.○ d.○   30 a.○ b.○ c.○ d.○   50 a.○ b.○ c.○ d.○   70 a.○ b.○ c.○ d.○   90 a.○ b.○ c.○ d.○

11 a.○ b.○ c.○ d.○   31 a.○ b.○ c.○ d.○   51 a.○ b.○ c.○ d.○   71 a.○ b.○ c.○ d.○   91 a.○ b.○ c.○ d.○
12 a.○ b.○ c.○ d.○   32 a.○ b.○ c.○ d.○   52 a.○ b.○ c.○ d.○   72 a.○ b.○ c.○ d.○   92 a.○ b.○ c.○ d.○
13 a.○ b.○ c.○ d.○   33 a.○ b.○ c.○ d.○   53 a.○ b.○ c.○ d.○   73 a.○ b.○ c.○ d.○   93 a.○ b.○ c.○ d.○
14 a.○ b.○ c.○ d.○   34 a.○ b.○ c.○ d.○   54 a.○ b.○ c.○ d.○   74 a.○ b.○ c.○ d.○   94 a.○ b.○ c.○ d.○
15 a.○ b.○ c.○ d.○   35 a.○ b.○ c.○ d.○   55 a.○ b.○ c.○ d.○   75 a.○ b.○ c.○ d.○   95 a.○ b.○ c.○ d.○

16 a.○ b.○ c.○ d.○   36 a.○ b.○ c.○ d.○   56 a.○ b.○ c.○ d.○   76 a.○ b.○ c.○ d.○   96 a.○ b.○ c.○ d.○
17 a.○ b.○ c.○ d.○   37 a.○ b.○ c.○ d.○   57 a.○ b.○ c.○ d.○   77 a.○ b.○ c.○ d.○   97 a.○ b.○ c.○ d.○
18 a.○ b.○ c.○ d.○   38 a.○ b.○ c.○ d.○   58 a.○ b.○ c.○ d.○   78 a.○ b.○ c.○ d.○   98 a.○ b.○ c.○ d.○
19 a.○ b.○ c.○ d.○   39 a.○ b.○ c.○ d.○   59 a.○ b.○ c.○ d.○   79 a.○ b.○ c.○ d.○   99 a.○ b.○ c.○ d.○
20 a.○ b.○ c.○ d.○   40 a.○ b.○ c.○ d.○   60 a.○ b.○ c.○ d.○   80 a.○ b.○ c.○ d.○   100 a.○ b.○ c.○ d.○

TEST 6

1 a.○ b.○ c.○ d.○	21 a.○ b.○ c.○ d.○	41 a.○ b.○ c.○ d.○	61 a.○ b.○ c.○ d.○	81 a.○ b.○ c.○ d.○
2 a.○ b.○ c.○ d.○	22 a.○ b.○ c.○ d.○	42 a.○ b.○ c.○ d.○	62 a.○ b.○ c.○ d.○	82 a.○ b.○ c.○ d.○
3 a.○ b.○ c.○ d.○	23 a.○ b.○ c.○ d.○	43 a.○ b.○ c.○ d.○	63 a.○ b.○ c.○ d.○	83 a.○ b.○ c.○ d.○
4 a.○ b.○ c.○ d.○	24 a.○ b.○ c.○ d.○	44 a.○ b.○ c.○ d.○	64 a.○ b.○ c.○ d.○	84 a.○ b.○ c.○ d.○
5 a.○ b.○ c.○ d.○	25 a.○ b.○ c.○ d.○	45 a.○ b.○ c.○ d.○	65 a.○ b.○ c.○ d.○	85 a.○ b.○ c.○ d.○
6 a.○ b.○ c.○ d.○	26 a.○ b.○ c.○ d.○	46 a.○ b.○ c.○ d.○	66 a.○ b.○ c.○ d.○	86 a.○ b.○ c.○ d.○
7 a.○ b.○ c.○ d.○	27 a.○ b.○ c.○ d.○	47 a.○ b.○ c.○ d.○	67 a.○ b.○ c.○ d.○	87 a.○ b.○ c.○ d.○
8 a.○ b.○ c.○ d.○	28 a.○ b.○ c.○ d.○	48 a.○ b.○ c.○ d.○	68 a.○ b.○ c.○ d.○	88 a.○ b.○ c.○ d.○
9 a.○ b.○ c.○ d.○	29 a.○ b.○ c.○ d.○	59 a.○ b.○ c.○ d.○	69 a.○ b.○ c.○ d.○	89 a.○ b.○ c.○ d.○
10 a.○ b.○ c.○ d.○	30 a.○ b.○ c.○ d.○	50 a.○ b.○ c.○ d.○	70 a.○ b.○ c.○ d.○	90 a.○ b.○ c.○ d.○
11 a.○ b.○ c.○ d.○	31 a.○ b.○ c.○ d.○	51 a.○ b.○ c.○ d.○	71 a.○ b.○ c.○ d.○	91 a.○ b.○ c.○ d.○
12 a.○ b.○ c.○ d.○	32 a.○ b.○ c.○ d.○	52 a.○ b.○ c.○ d.○	72 a.○ b.○ c.○ d.○	92 a.○ b.○ c.○ d.○
13 a.○ b.○ c.○ d.○	33 a.○ b.○ c.○ d.○	53 a.○ b.○ c.○ d.○	73 a.○ b.○ c.○ d.○	93 a.○ b.○ c.○ d.○
14 a.○ b.○ c.○ d.○	34 a.○ b.○ c.○ d.○	54 a.○ b.○ c.○ d.○	74 a.○ b.○ c.○ d.○	94 a.○ b.○ c.○ d.○
15 a.○ b.○ c.○ d.○	35 a.○ b.○ c.○ d.○	55 a.○ b.○ c.○ d.○	75 a.○ b.○ c.○ d.○	95 a.○ b.○ c.○ d.○
16 a.○ b.○ c.○ d.○	36 a.○ b.○ c.○ d.○	56 a.○ b.○ c.○ d.○	76 a.○ b.○ c.○ d.○	96 a.○ b.○ c.○ d.○
17 a.○ b.○ c.○ d.○	37 a.○ b.○ c.○ d.○	57 a.○ b.○ c.○ d.○	77 a.○ b.○ c.○ d.○	97 a.○ b.○ c.○ d.○
18 a.○ b.○ c.○ d.○	38 a.○ b.○ c.○ d.○	58 a.○ b.○ c.○ d.○	78 a.○ b.○ c.○ d.○	98 a.○ b.○ c.○ d.○
19 a.○ b.○ c.○ d.○	39 a.○ b.○ c.○ d.○	59 a.○ b.○ c.○ d.○	79 a.○ b.○ c.○ d.○	99 a.○ b.○ c.○ d.○
20 a.○ b.○ c.○ d.○	40 a.○ b.○ c.○ d.○	60 a.○ b.○ c.○ d.○	80 a.○ b.○ c.○ d.○	100 a.○ b.○ c.○ d.○

TEST 7

1 a.○ b.○ c.○ d.○	21 a.○ b.○ c.○ d.○	41 a.○ b.○ c.○ d.○	61 a.○ b.○ c.○ d.○	81 a.○ b.○ c.○ d.○
2 a.○ b.○ c.○ d.○	22 a.○ b.○ c.○ d.○	42 a.○ b.○ c.○ d.○	62 a.○ b.○ c.○ d.○	82 a.○ b.○ c.○ d.○
3 a.○ b.○ c.○ d.○	23 a.○ b.○ c.○ d.○	43 a.○ b.○ c.○ d.○	63 a.○ b.○ c.○ d.○	83 a.○ b.○ c.○ d.○
4 a.○ b.○ c.○ d.○	24 a.○ b.○ c.○ d.○	44 a.○ b.○ c.○ d.○	64 a.○ b.○ c.○ d.○	84 a.○ b.○ c.○ d.○
5 a.○ b.○ c.○ d.○	25 a.○ b.○ c.○ d.○	45 a.○ b.○ c.○ d.○	65 a.○ b.○ c.○ d.○	85 a.○ b.○ c.○ d.○
6 a.○ b.○ c.○ d.○	26 a.○ b.○ c.○ d.○	46 a.○ b.○ c.○ d.○	66 a.○ b.○ c.○ d.○	86 a.○ b.○ c.○ d.○
7 a.○ b.○ c.○ d.○	27 a.○ b.○ c.○ d.○	47 a.○ b.○ c.○ d.○	67 a.○ b.○ c.○ d.○	87 a.○ b.○ c.○ d.○
8 a.○ b.○ c.○ d.○	28 a.○ b.○ c.○ d.○	48 a.○ b.○ c.○ d.○	68 a.○ b.○ c.○ d.○	88 a.○ b.○ c.○ d.○
9 a.○ b.○ c.○ d.○	29 a.○ b.○ c.○ d.○	59 a.○ b.○ c.○ d.○	69 a.○ b.○ c.○ d.○	89 a.○ b.○ c.○ d.○
10 a.○ b.○ c.○ d.○	30 a.○ b.○ c.○ d.○	50 a.○ b.○ c.○ d.○	70 a.○ b.○ c.○ d.○	90 a.○ b.○ c.○ d.○
11 a.○ b.○ c.○ d.○	31 a.○ b.○ c.○ d.○	51 a.○ b.○ c.○ d.○	71 a.○ b.○ c.○ d.○	91 a.○ b.○ c.○ d.○
12 a.○ b.○ c.○ d.○	32 a.○ b.○ c.○ d.○	52 a.○ b.○ c.○ d.○	72 a.○ b.○ c.○ d.○	92 a.○ b.○ c.○ d.○
13 a.○ b.○ c.○ d.○	33 a.○ b.○ c.○ d.○	53 a.○ b.○ c.○ d.○	73 a.○ b.○ c.○ d.○	93 a.○ b.○ c.○ d.○
14 a.○ b.○ c.○ d.○	34 a.○ b.○ c.○ d.○	54 a.○ b.○ c.○ d.○	74 a.○ b.○ c.○ d.○	94 a.○ b.○ c.○ d.○
15 a.○ b.○ c.○ d.○	35 a.○ b.○ c.○ d.○	55 a.○ b.○ c.○ d.○	75 a.○ b.○ c.○ d.○	95 a.○ b.○ c.○ d.○
16 a.○ b.○ c.○ d.○	36 a.○ b.○ c.○ d.○	56 a.○ b.○ c.○ d.○	76 a.○ b.○ c.○ d.○	96 a.○ b.○ c.○ d.○
17 a.○ b.○ c.○ d.○	37 a.○ b.○ c.○ d.○	57 a.○ b.○ c.○ d.○	77 a.○ b.○ c.○ d.○	97 a.○ b.○ c.○ d.○
18 a.○ b.○ c.○ d.○	38 a.○ b.○ c.○ d.○	58 a.○ b.○ c.○ d.○	78 a.○ b.○ c.○ d.○	98 a.○ b.○ c.○ d.○
19 a.○ b.○ c.○ d.○	39 a.○ b.○ c.○ d.○	59 a.○ b.○ c.○ d.○	79 a.○ b.○ c.○ d.○	99 a.○ b.○ c.○ d.○
20 a.○ b.○ c.○ d.○	40 a.○ b.○ c.○ d.○	60 a.○ b.○ c.○ d.○	80 a.○ b.○ c.○ d.○	100 a.○ b.○ c.○ d.○

WE ALSO HAVE BOOKS TO HELP YOU SCORE HIGH ON

THE SAT II, AP, AND CLEP EXAMS:

CRACKING THE AP BIOLOGY EXAM 1997-98 EDITION
0-679-76927-7 $16.00

CRACKING THE AP CALCULUS EXAM AB & BC 1997-98 EDITION
0-679-76926-9 $16.00

CRACKING THE AP CHEMISTRY EXAM 1997-98 EDITION
0-679-76928-5 $16.00

CRACKING THE AP ENGLISH LITERATURE EXAM 1997-98 EDITION
0-679-76924-2 $16.00

CRACKING THE AP U.S. HISTORY EXAM 1997-98 EDITION
0-679-76925-0 $16.00

CRACKING THE CLEP 1998 EDITION
0-679-77867-5 $20.00

CRACKING THE SAT II: BIOLOGY SUBJECT TEST 1998 EDITION
0-679-77863-2 $17.00

CRACKING THE SAT II: CHEMISTRY SUBJECT TEST 1998 EDITION
0-679-77860-8 $17.00

CRACKING THE SAT II: ENGLISH SUBJECT TEST 1998 EDITION
0-679-77858-6 $17.00

CRACKING THE SAT II: FRENCH SUBJECT TEST 1998 EDITION
0-679-77865-9 $17.00

CRACKING THE SAT II: HISTORY SUBJECT TEST 1998 EDITION
0-679-77861-6 $17.00

CRACKING THE SAT II: MATH SUBJECT TEST 1998 EDITION
0-679-77864-0 $17.00

CRACKING THE SAT II: PHYSICS SUBJECT TEST 1998 EDITION
0-679-77859-4 $17.00

CRACKING THE SAT II: SPANISH SUBJECT TEST 1998 EDITION
0-679-77862-4 $17.00